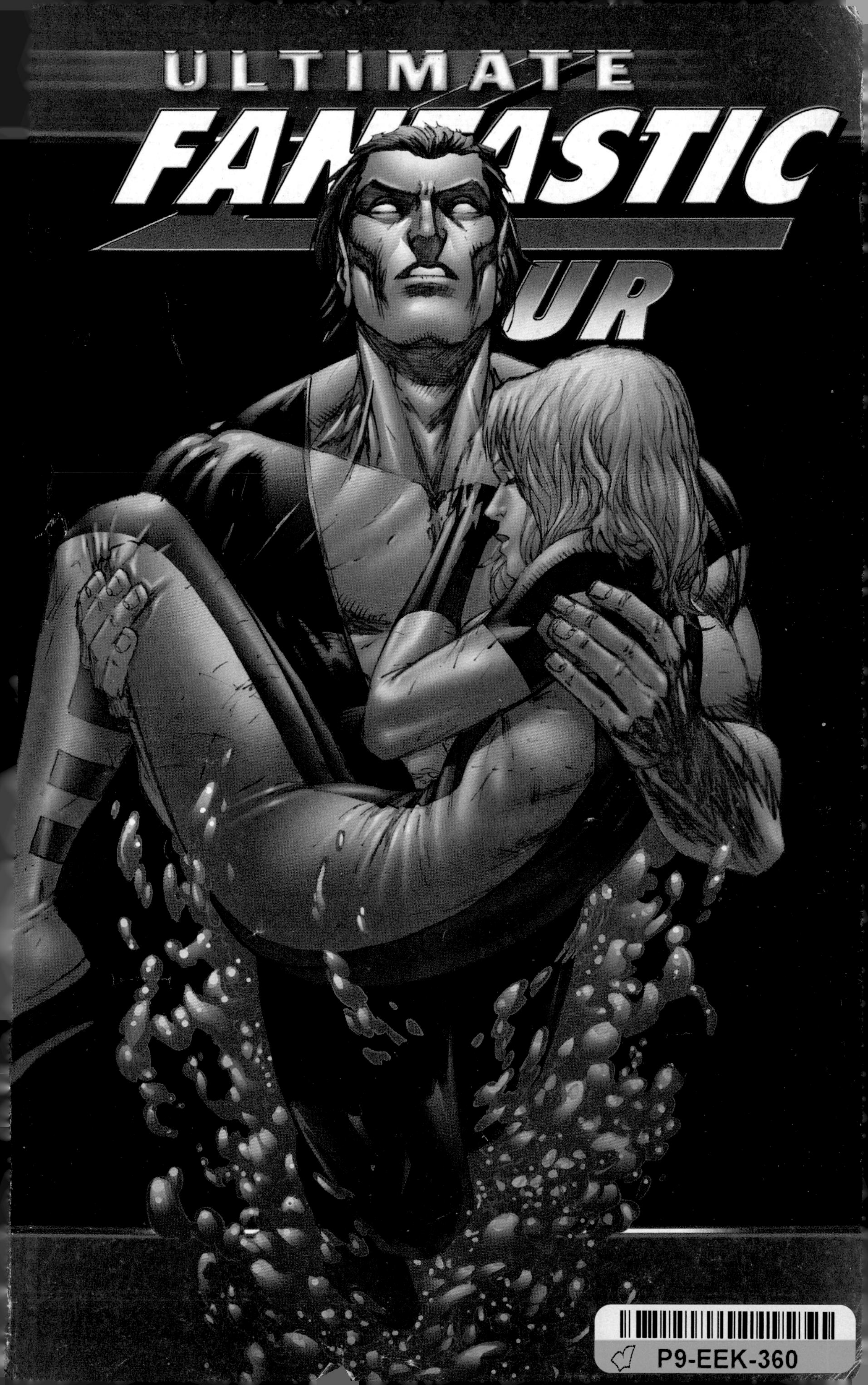
ULTIMATE

ULTIMATE FANTASTIC FOUR
SALEM'S SEVEN

Writer: **MIKE CAREY**
ART BY TOP COW PRODUCTIONS, INC.
Penciler: **TYLER KIRKHAM**
WITH ERIC BASALDUA (ISSUE #56)
Colorist: **BLOND**
Letterer: **VIRTUAL CALLIGRAPHY'S RUS WOOTON**
Cover Artists: **BILLY TAN WITH FRANK D'ARMATA & GURU EFX**
Assistant Editor: **LAUREN SANKOVITCH**
Editor: **BILL ROSEMANN**
Senior Editor: **RALPH MACCHIO**

SPECIAL THANKS TO TOP COW'S ROB LEVIN

Collection Editor: **CORY LEVINE**
Assistant Editor: **JOHN DENNING**
Editors, Special Projects: **JENNIFER GRÜNWALD & MARK D. BEAZLEY**
Senior Editor, Special Projects: **JEFF YOUNGQUIST**
Senior Vice President of Sales: **DAVID GABRIEL**
Production: **RODOLFO MURAGUCHI & JERRY KALINOWSKI**
Editor In Chief: **JOE QUESADA**
Publisher: **DAN BUCKLEY**

Previously:

After an interdimensional accident, young Reed Richards, Sue Storm, her brother Johnny, and Reed's friend Ben Grimm are changed forever. The quartet's genetic structures are scrambled and recombined in a fantastically strange way. Reed's body stretches and flows like water. Ben looks like a thing carved from desert rock. Sue can become invisible. Johnny generates flame. Together, they are the Fantastic Four!

After having been used by the alien tyrant Thanos to create the reality-warping Cosmic Cube, Reed and the rest of the Fantastic Four managed to defeat their foe by unexpectedly using the awesome power of the Cube against him. They were then able to set aright the vast changes that had been wrought on Earth during the evil alien's brief reign.

With the world now back to "normal," the Fantastic Four have returned to the Baxter Building: Johnny and Ben have resumed their routine pranks, with Johnny butting heads with his father, Dr. Franklin Storm, more often than not. And after Reed's destructive behavior while possessed by Thanos, his relationship with Sue may truly be beyond salvaging...

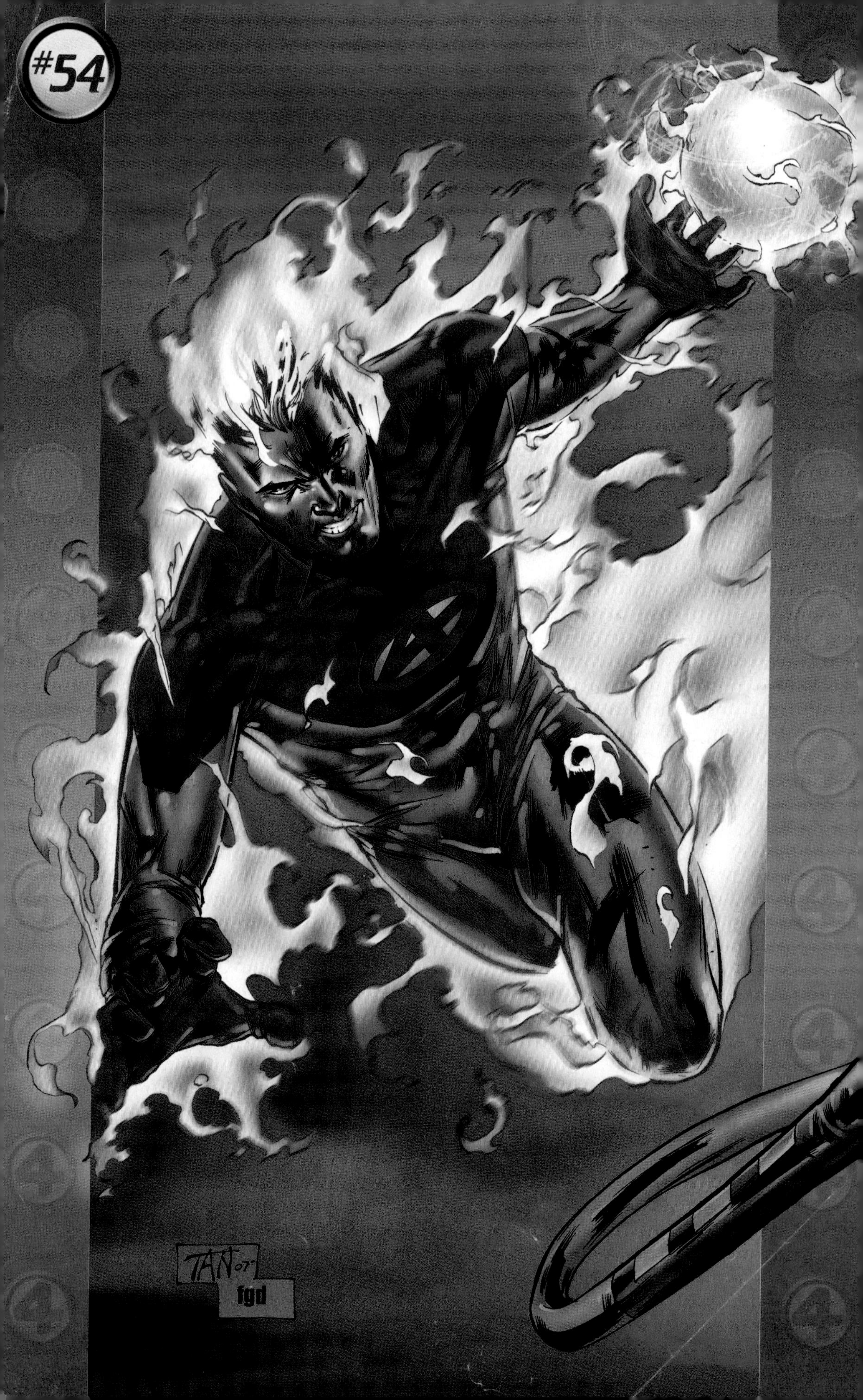
#54
TAN 07
fgd

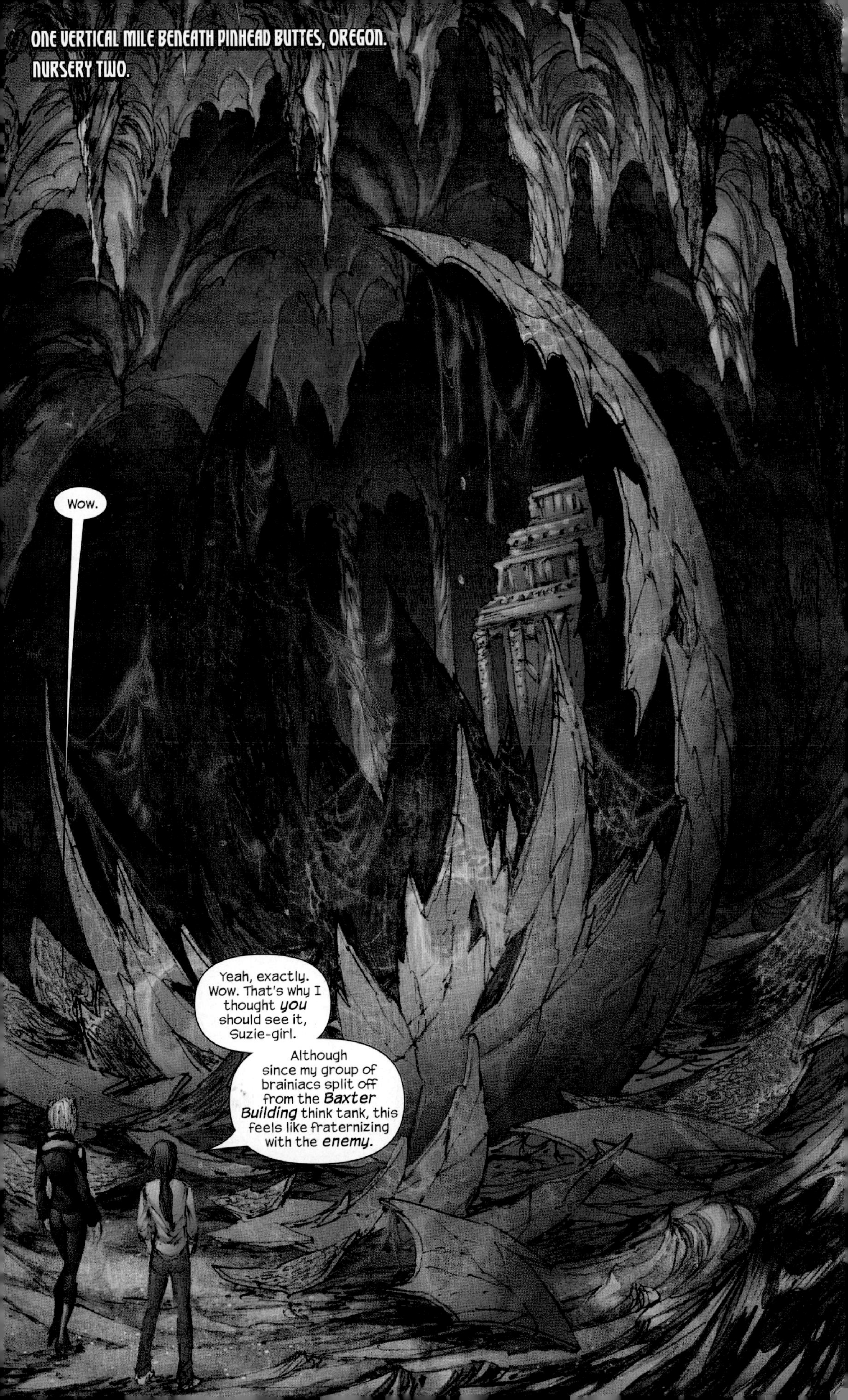
ONE VERTICAL MILE BENEATH PINHEAD BUTTES, OREGON.
NURSERY TWO.
Wow.
Yeah, exactly. Wow. That's why I thought *you* should see it, Suzie-girl.
Although since my group of brainiacs split off from the *Baxter Building* think tank, this feels like fraternizing with the *enemy*.

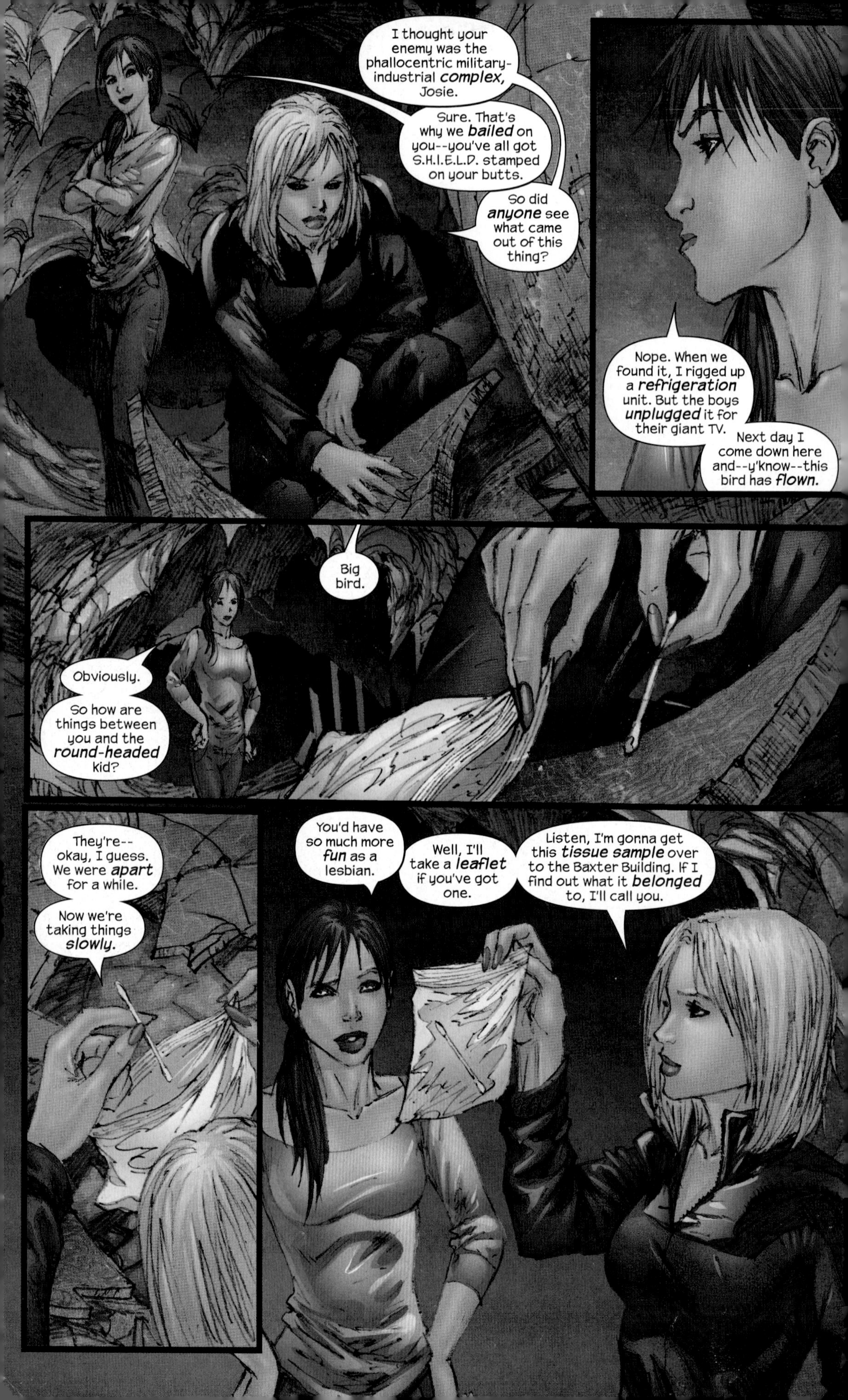

I thought your enemy was the phallocentric military-industrial *complex,* Josie.
Sure. That's why we ***bailed*** on you--you've all got S.H.I.E.L.D. stamped on your butts.
So did ***anyone*** see what came out of this thing?
Nope. When we found it, I rigged up a ***refrigeration*** unit. But the boys ***unplugged*** it for their giant TV.
Next day I come down here and--y'know--this bird has ***flown.***
Big bird.
Obviously.
So how are things between you and the ***round-headed*** kid?
They're--okay, I guess. We were ***apart*** for a while.
Now we're taking things ***slowly.***
You'd have so much more ***fun*** as a lesbian.
Well, I'll take a ***leaflet*** if you've got one.
Listen, I'm gonna get this ***tissue sample*** over to the Baxter Building. If I find out what it ***belonged*** to, I'll call you.

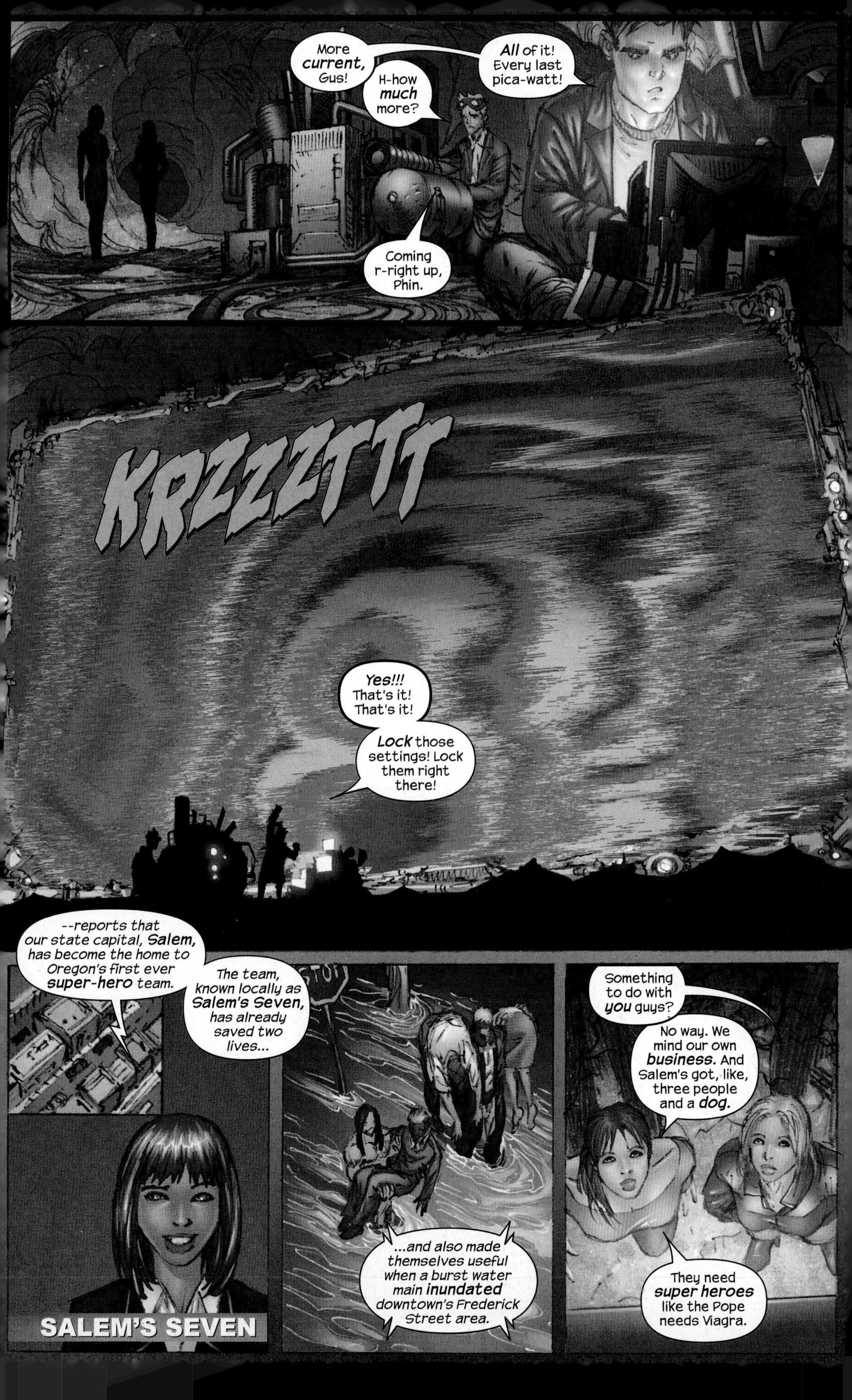
More current, Gus!
H-how much more?
All of it! Every last pica-watt!
Coming r-right up, Phin.
KRZZZTTT
Yes!!! That's it! That's it!
Lock those settings! Lock them right there!
--reports that our state capital, Salem, has become the home to Oregon's first ever super-hero team.
The team, known locally as Salem's Seven, has already saved two lives...
SALEM'S SEVEN
...and also made themselves useful when a burst water main inundated downtown's Frederick Street area.
Something to do with you guys?
No way. We mind our own business. And Salem's got, like, three people and a dog.
They need super heroes like the Pope needs Viagra.

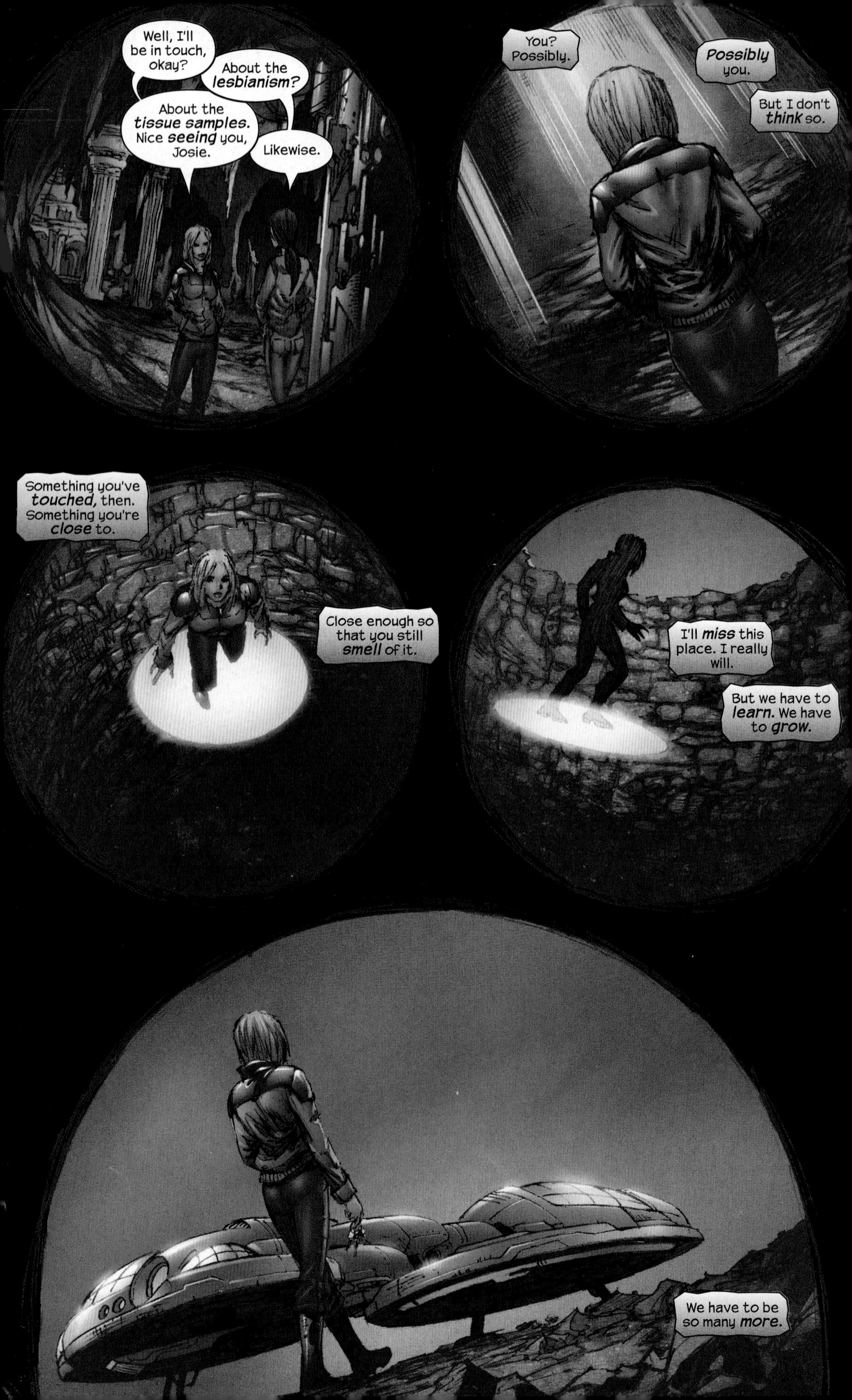
Well, I'll be in touch, okay?
About the lesbianism?
About the tissue samples. Nice seeing you, Josie.
Likewise.
You? Possibly.
Possibly you.
But I don't think so.
Something you've touched, then. Something you're close to.
Close enough so that you still smell of it.
I'll miss this place. I really will.
But we have to learn. We have to grow.
We have to be so many more.

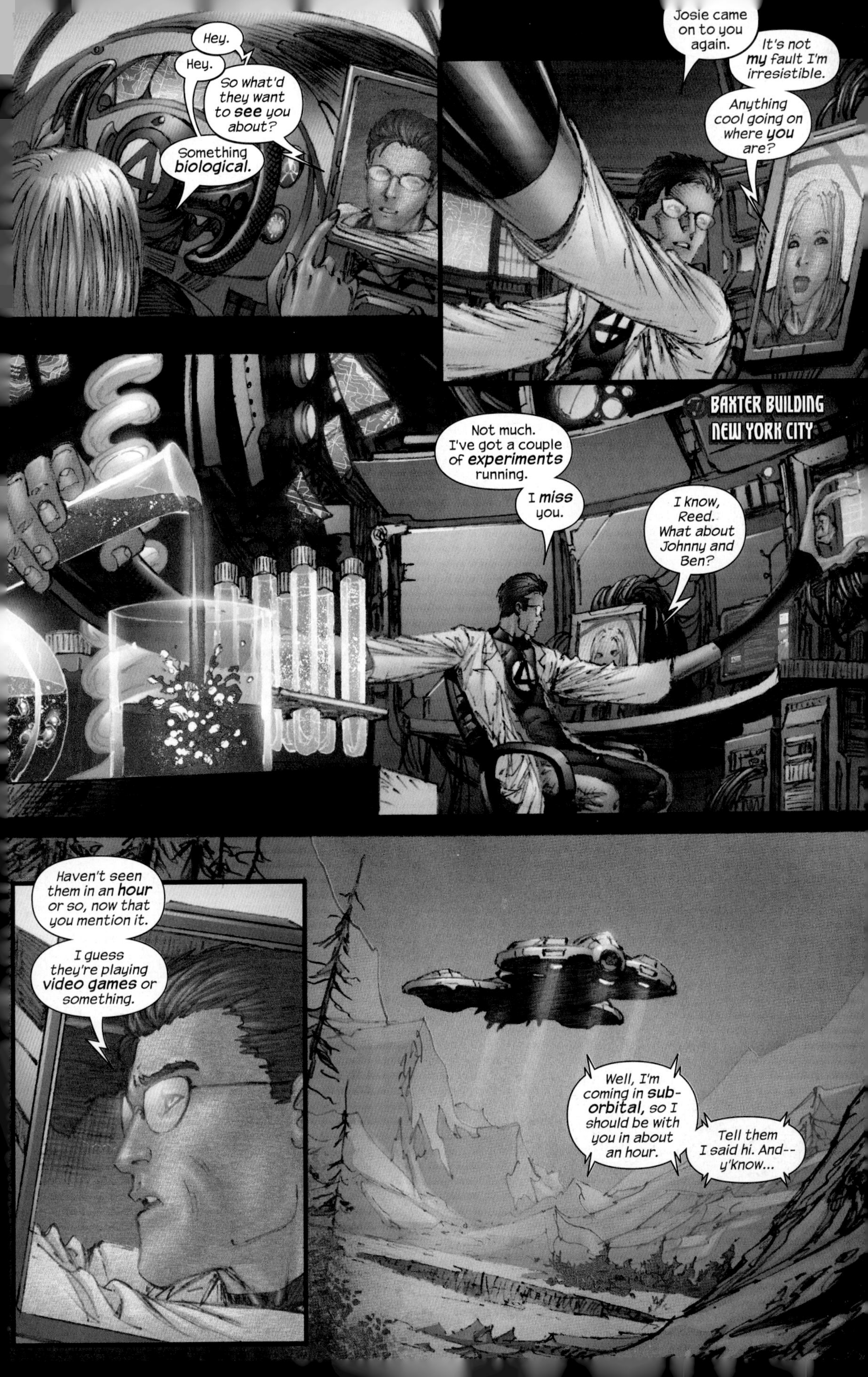
Hey.
Hey.
So what'd they want to see you about?
Something biological.
Josie came on to you again.
It's not my fault I'm irresistible.
Anything cool going on where you are?
BAXTER BUILDING NEW YORK CITY
Not much. I've got a couple of experiments running.
I miss you.
I know, Reed. What about Johnny and Ben?
Haven't seen them in an hour or so, now that you mention it.
I guess they're playing video games or something.
Well, I'm coming in sub-orbital, so I should be with you in about an hour.
Tell them I said hi. And-- y'know...

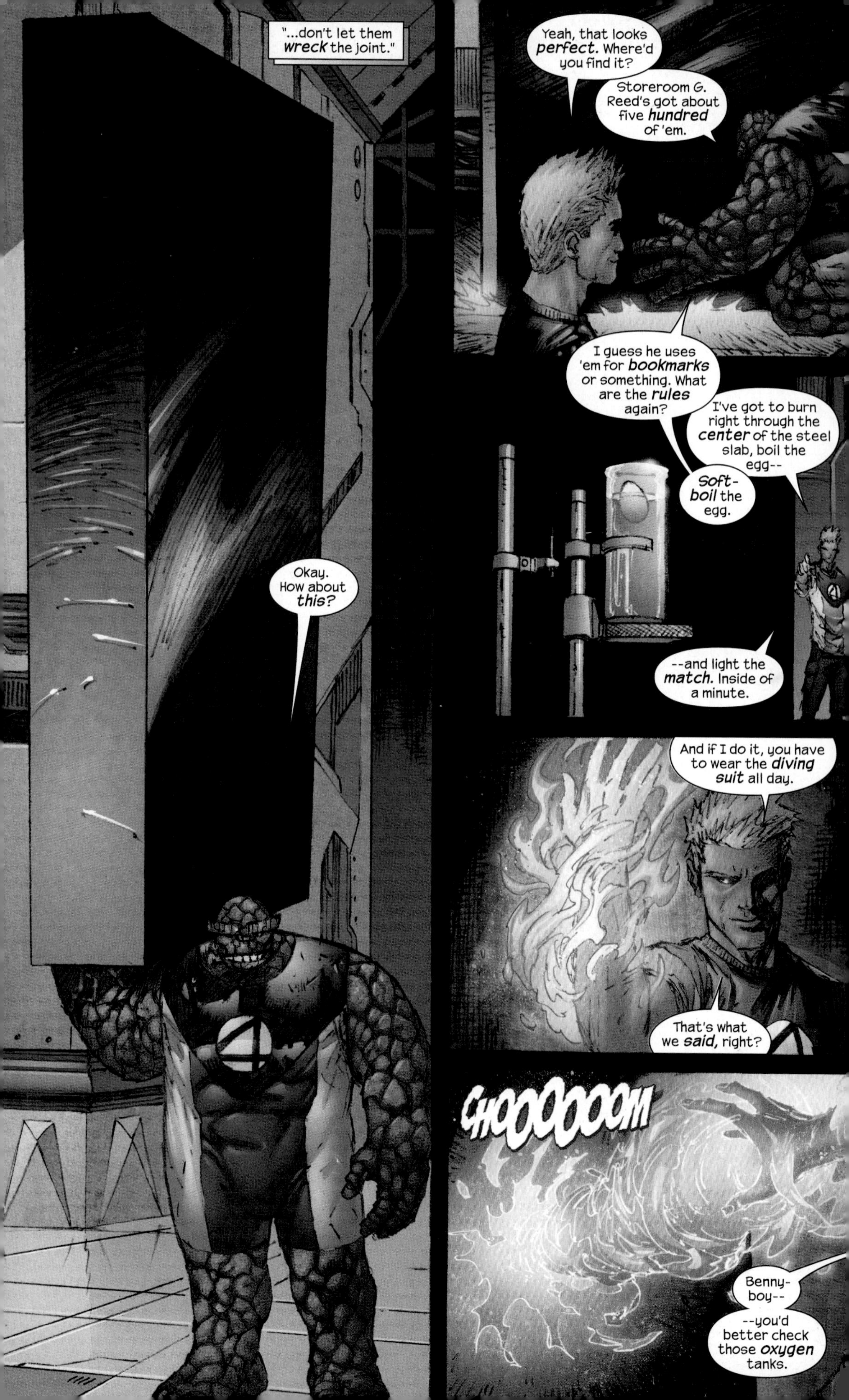
"...don't let them wreck the joint."
Okay. How about this?
Yeah, that looks perfect. Where'd you find it?
Storeroom G. Reed's got about five hundred of 'em.
I guess he uses 'em for bookmarks or something. What are the rules again?
I've got to burn right through the center of the steel slab, boil the egg--
Soft-boil the egg.
--and light the match. Inside of a minute.
And if I do it, you have to wear the diving suit all day.
That's what we said, right?
CHOOOOOOM
Benny-boy--
--you'd better check those oxygen tanks.

SHOWWWWWWWW
BLUG
BLUG
BLUG
BLUG
FRUFFFF
Wha--?!
That couldn't have been us.
Absolutely *not.*
But maybe we should split anyway.
I'm *gone.*

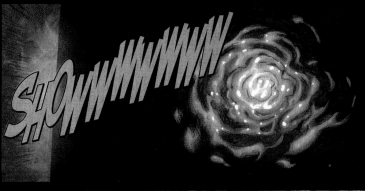

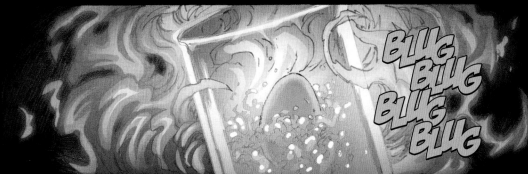

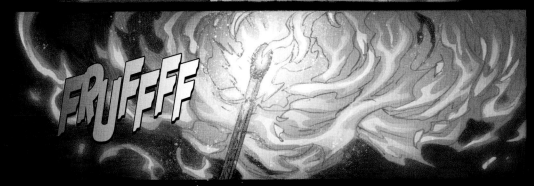

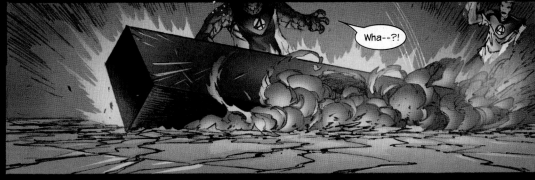

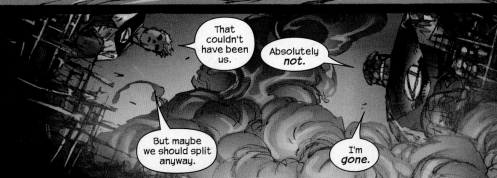

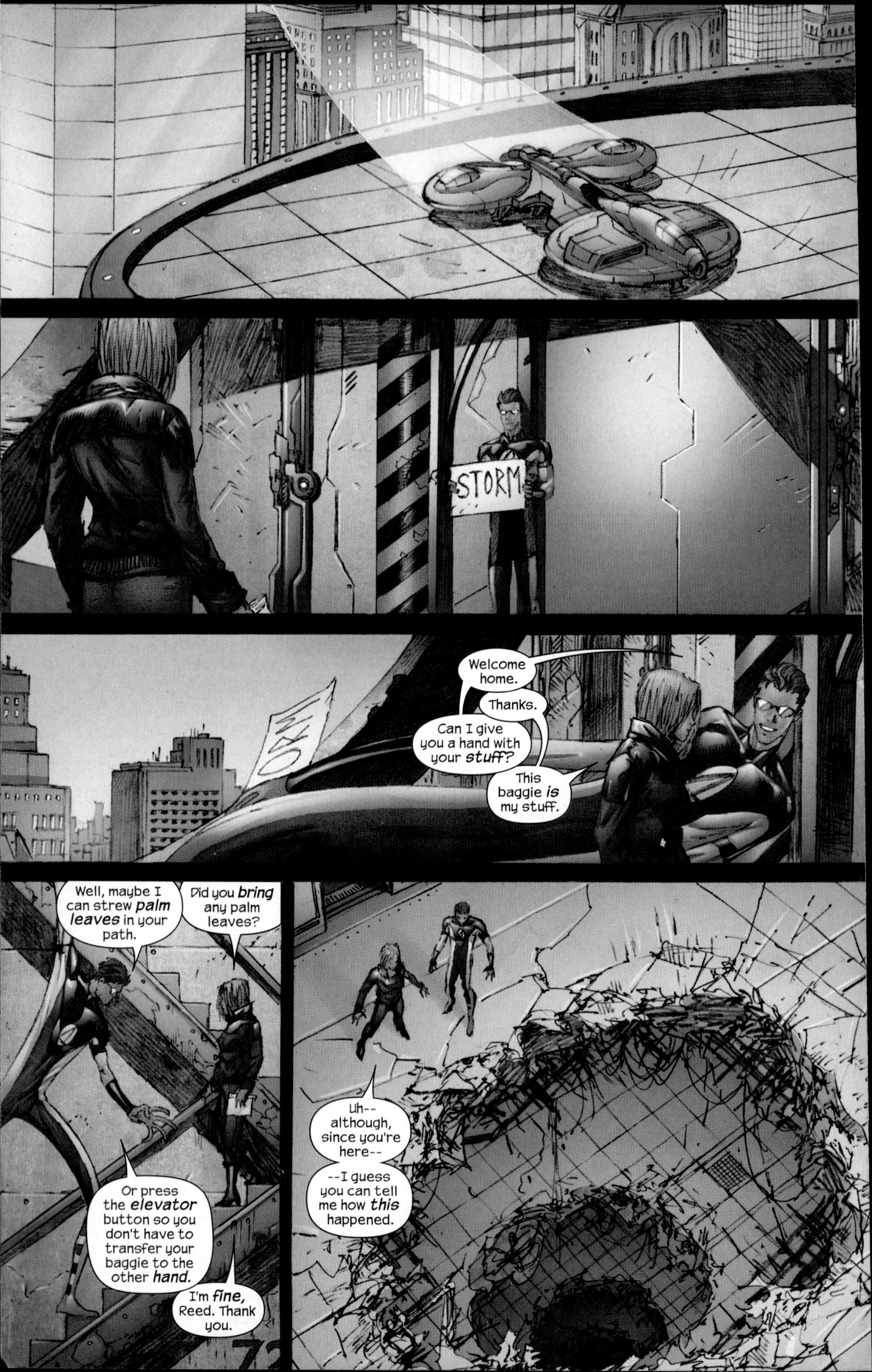
STORM
Welcome home.
Thanks.
Can I give you a hand with your *stuff?*
This baggie *is* my stuff.
Well, maybe I can strew *palm leaves* in your path.
Did you *bring* any palm leaves?
Or press the *elevator* button so you don't have to transfer your baggie to the other *hand.*
I'm *fine,* Reed. Thank you.
Uh-- although, since you're here--
--I guess you can tell me how *this* happened.

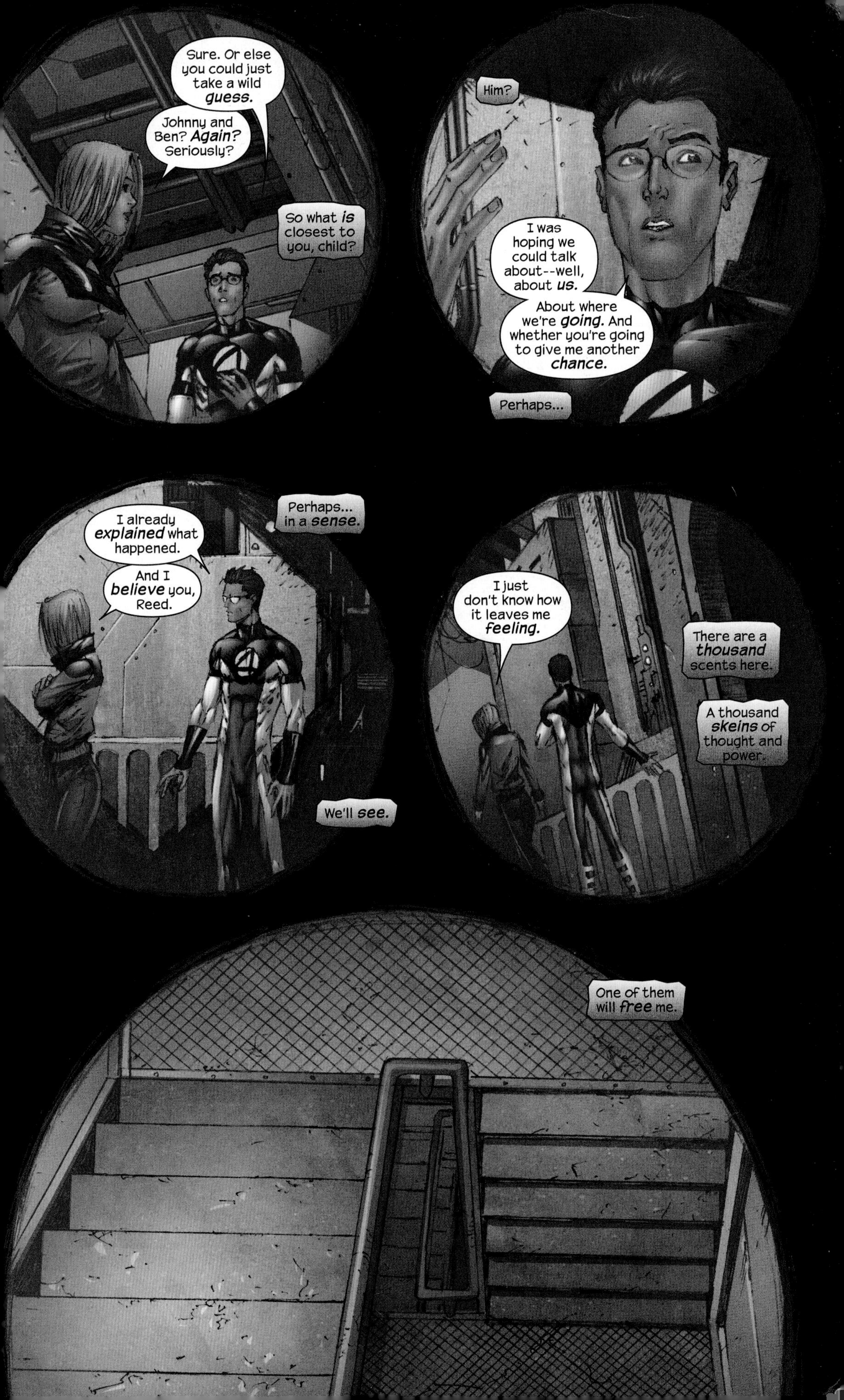

Sure. Or else you could just take a wild *guess.*
Johnny and Ben? *Again?* Seriously?
So what *is* closest to you, child?
Him?
I was hoping we could talk about--well, about *us.*
About where we're *going.* And whether you're going to give me another *chance.*
Perhaps...
I already *explained* what happened.
And I *believe* you, Reed.
Perhaps... in a *sense.*
We'll *see.*
I just don't know how it leaves me *feeling.*
There are a *thousand* scents here.
A thousand *skeins* of thought and power.
One of them will *free* me.

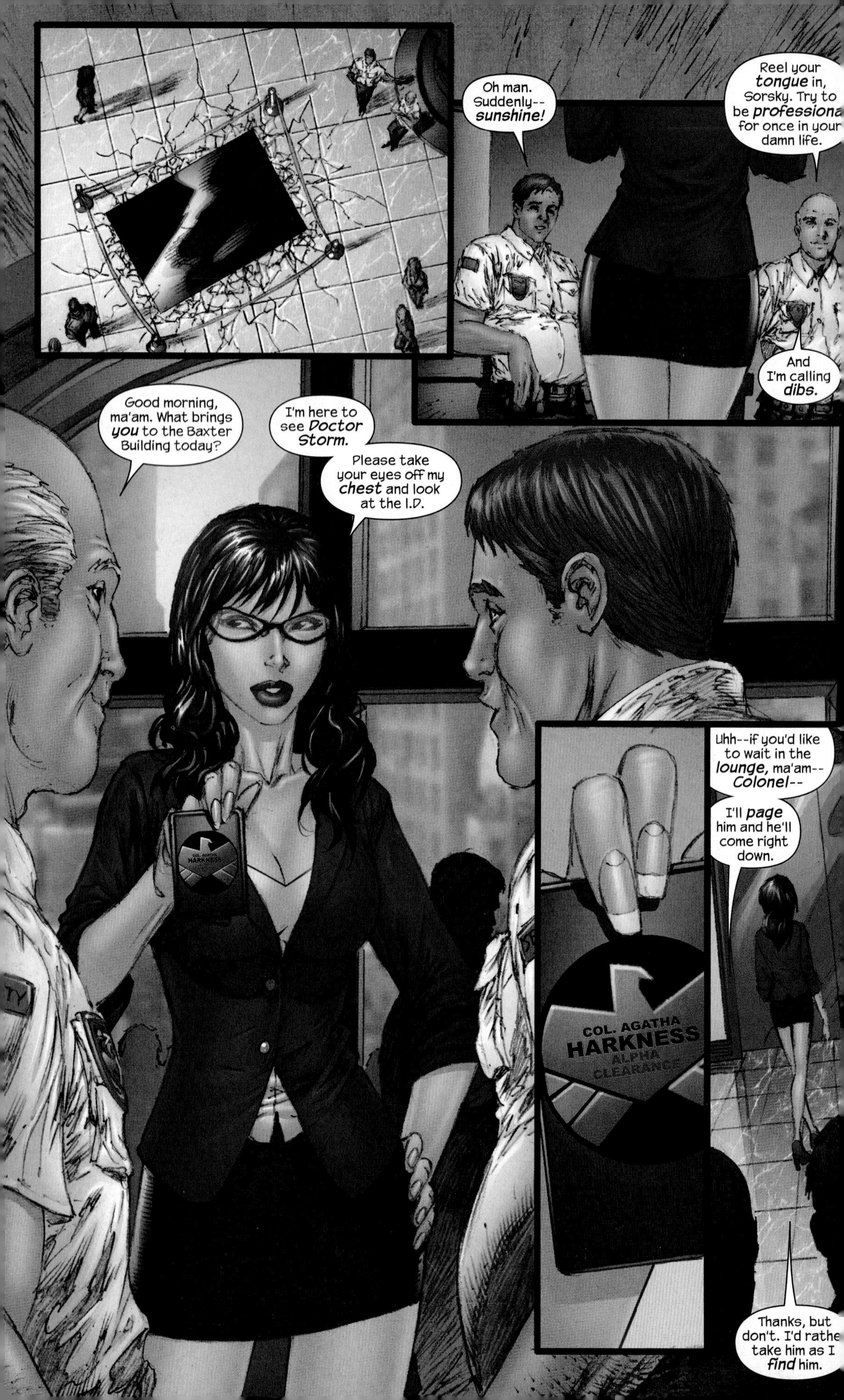

Oh man. Suddenly-- sunshine!
Reel your tongue in, Sorsky. Try to be professiona for once in your damn life.
And I'm calling dibs.
Good morning, ma'am. What brings you to the Baxter Building today?
I'm here to see Doctor Storm.
Please take your eyes off my chest and look at the I.D.
COL. AGATHA HARKNESS ALPHA CLEARANCE
Uhh--if you'd like to wait in the lounge, ma'am-- Colonel--
I'll page him and he'll come right down.
Thanks, but don't. I'd rathe take him as I find him.

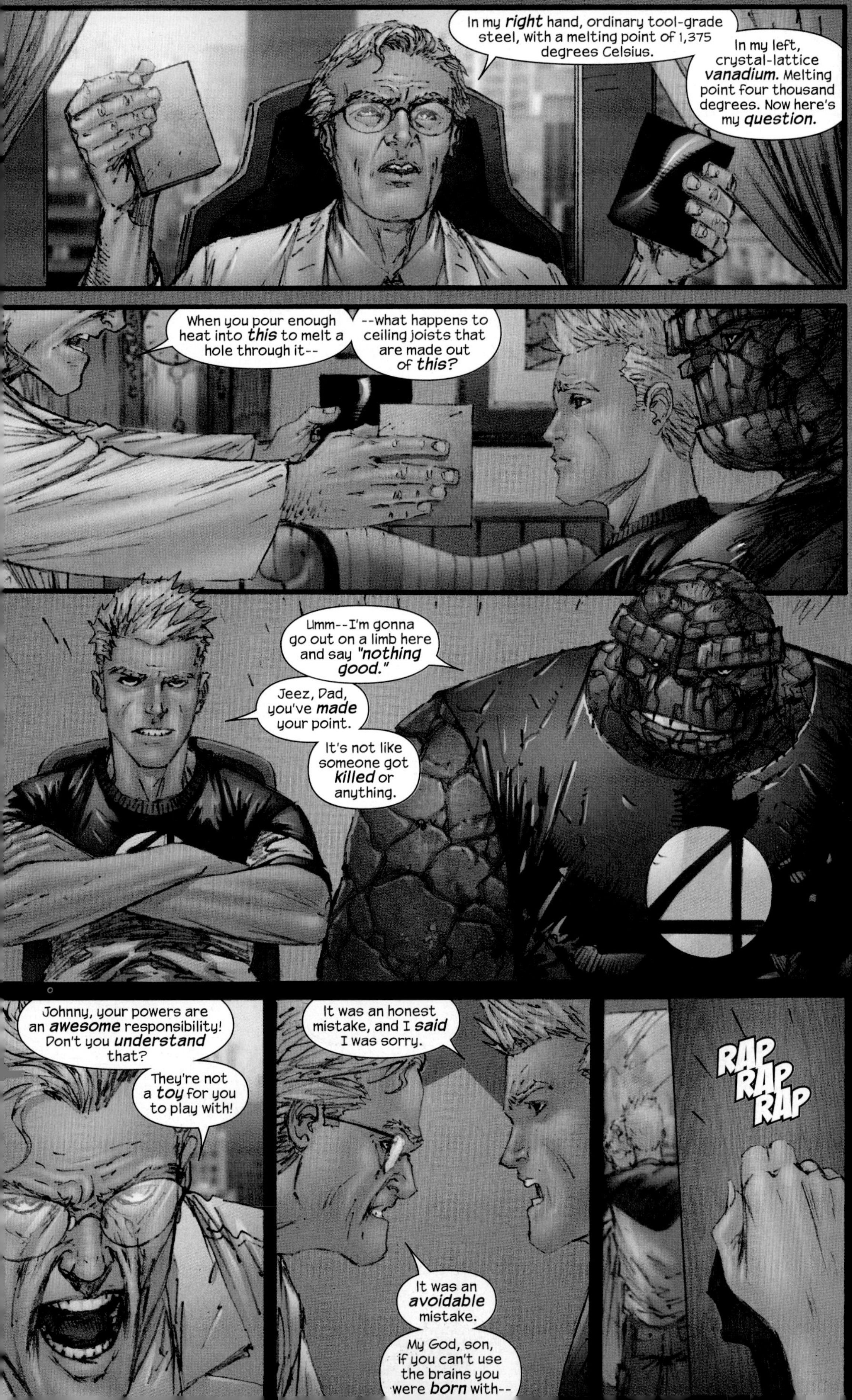
In my right hand, ordinary tool-grade steel, with a melting point of 1,375 degrees Celsius.
In my left, crystal-lattice vanadium. Melting point four thousand degrees. Now here's my question.
When you pour enough heat into this to melt a hole through it--
--what happens to ceiling joists that are made out of this?
Umm--I'm gonna go out on a limb here and say "nothing good."
Jeez, Dad, you've made your point.
It's not like someone got killed or anything.
Johnny, your powers are an awesome responsibility! Don't you understand that?
They're not a toy for you to play with!
It was an honest mistake, and I said I was sorry.
It was an avoidable mistake.
My God, son, if you can't use the brains you were born with--
RAP RAP RAP

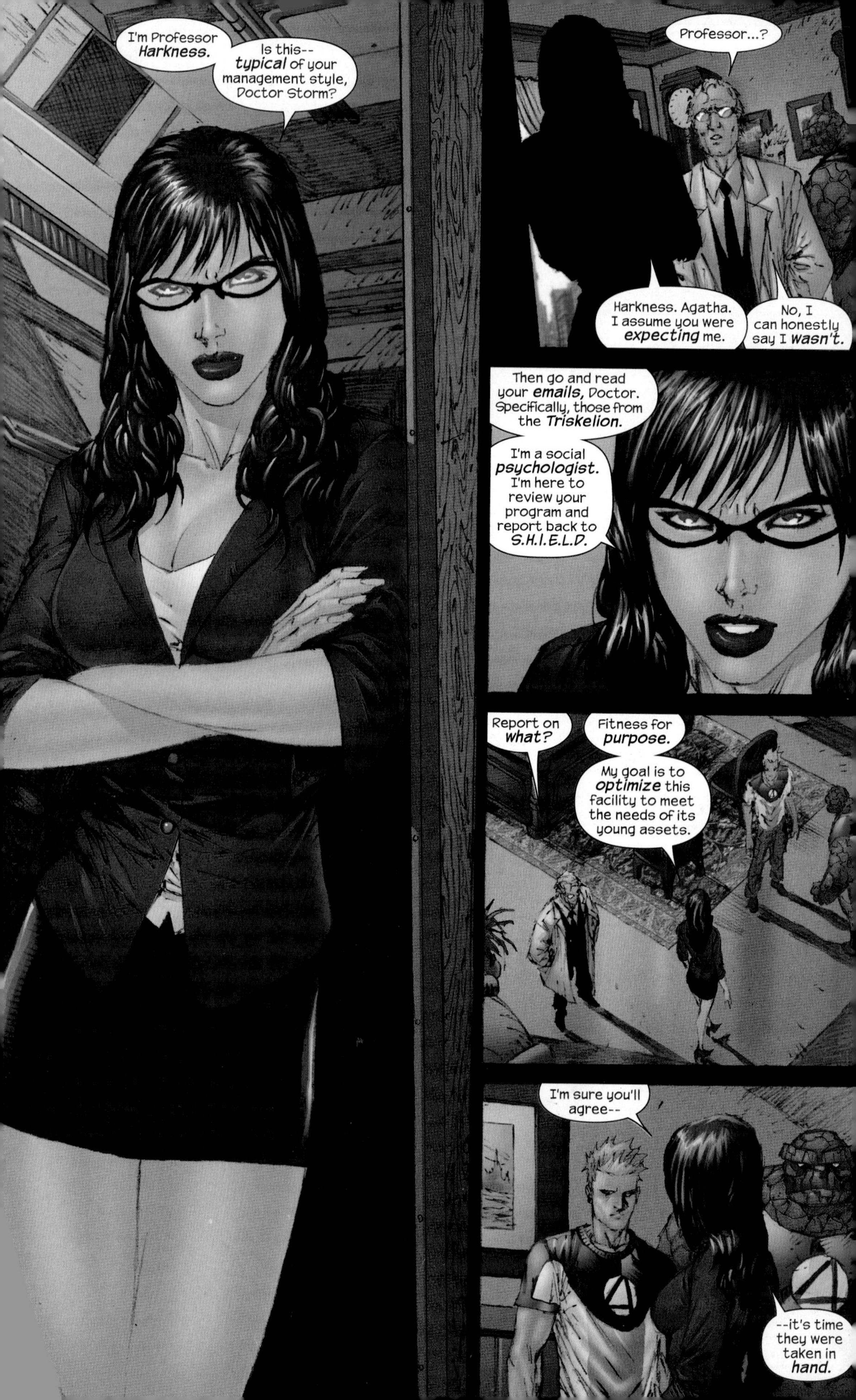
I'm Professor Harkness.
Is this-- typical of your management style, Doctor Storm?
Professor...?
Harkness. Agatha. I assume you were expecting me.
No, I can honestly say I wasn't.
Then go and read your emails, Doctor. Specifically, those from the Triskelion.
I'm a social psychologist. I'm here to review your program and report back to S.H.I.E.L.D.
Report on what?
Fitness for purpose.
My goal is to optimize this facility to meet the needs of its young assets.
I'm sure you'll agree--
--it's time they were taken in hand.

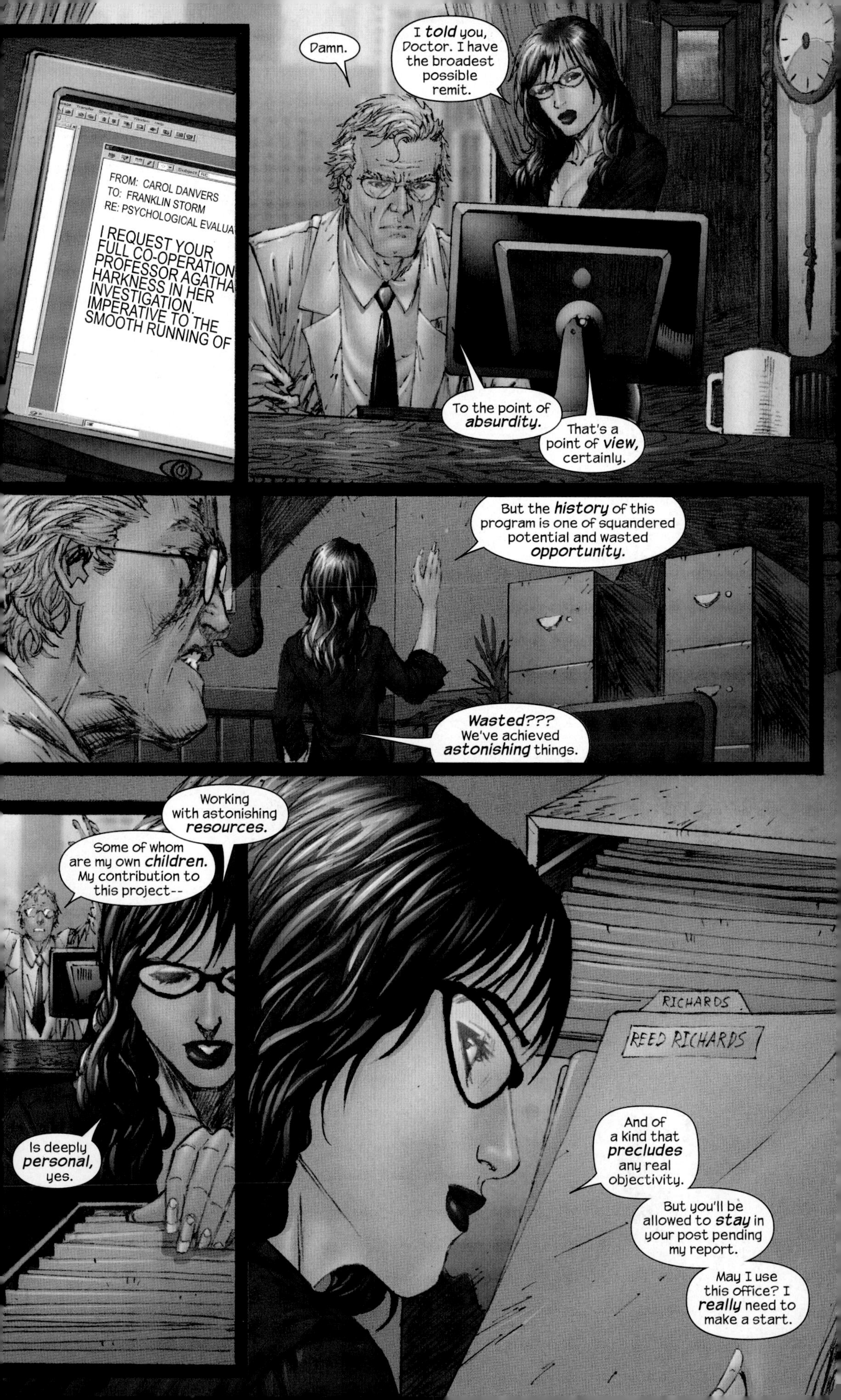

FROM: CAROL DANVERS
TO: FRANKLIN STORM
RE: PSYCHOLOGICAL EVALUA
I REQUEST YOUR FULL CO-OPERATION PROFESSOR AGATHA HARKNESS IN HER INVESTIGATION. IMPERATIVE TO THE SMOOTH RUNNING OF
Damn.
I *told* you, Doctor. I have the broadest possible remit.
To the point of *absurdity*.
That's a point of *view*, certainly.
But the *history* of this program is one of squandered potential and wasted *opportunity*.
Wasted??? We've achieved *astonishing* things.
Working with astonishing *resources*.
Some of whom are my own *children*. My contribution to this project--
Is deeply *personal*, yes.
RICHARDS
REED RICHARDS
And of a kind that *precludes* any real objectivity.
But you'll be allowed to *stay* in your post pending my report.
May I use this office? I *really* need to make a start.

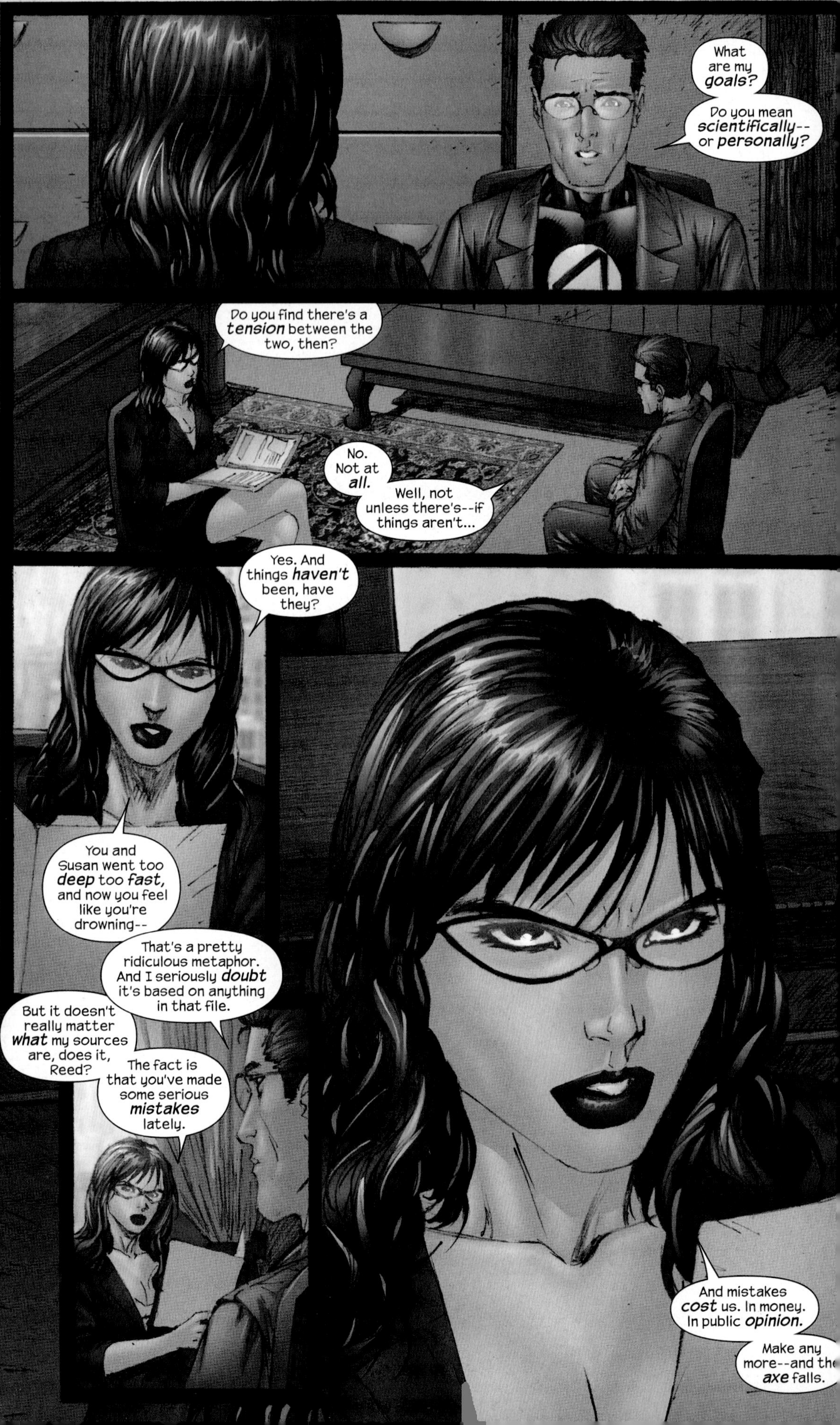

What are my goals?
Do you mean scientifically--or personally?
Do you find there's a tension between the two, then?
No. Not at all.
Well, not unless there's--if things aren't...
Yes. And things haven't been, have they?
You and Susan went too deep too fast, and now you feel like you're drowning--
That's a pretty ridiculous metaphor. And I seriously doubt it's based on anything in that file.
But it doesn't really matter what my sources are, does it, Reed?
The fact is that you've made some serious mistakes lately.
And mistakes cost us. In money. In public opinion.
Make any more--and the axe falls.

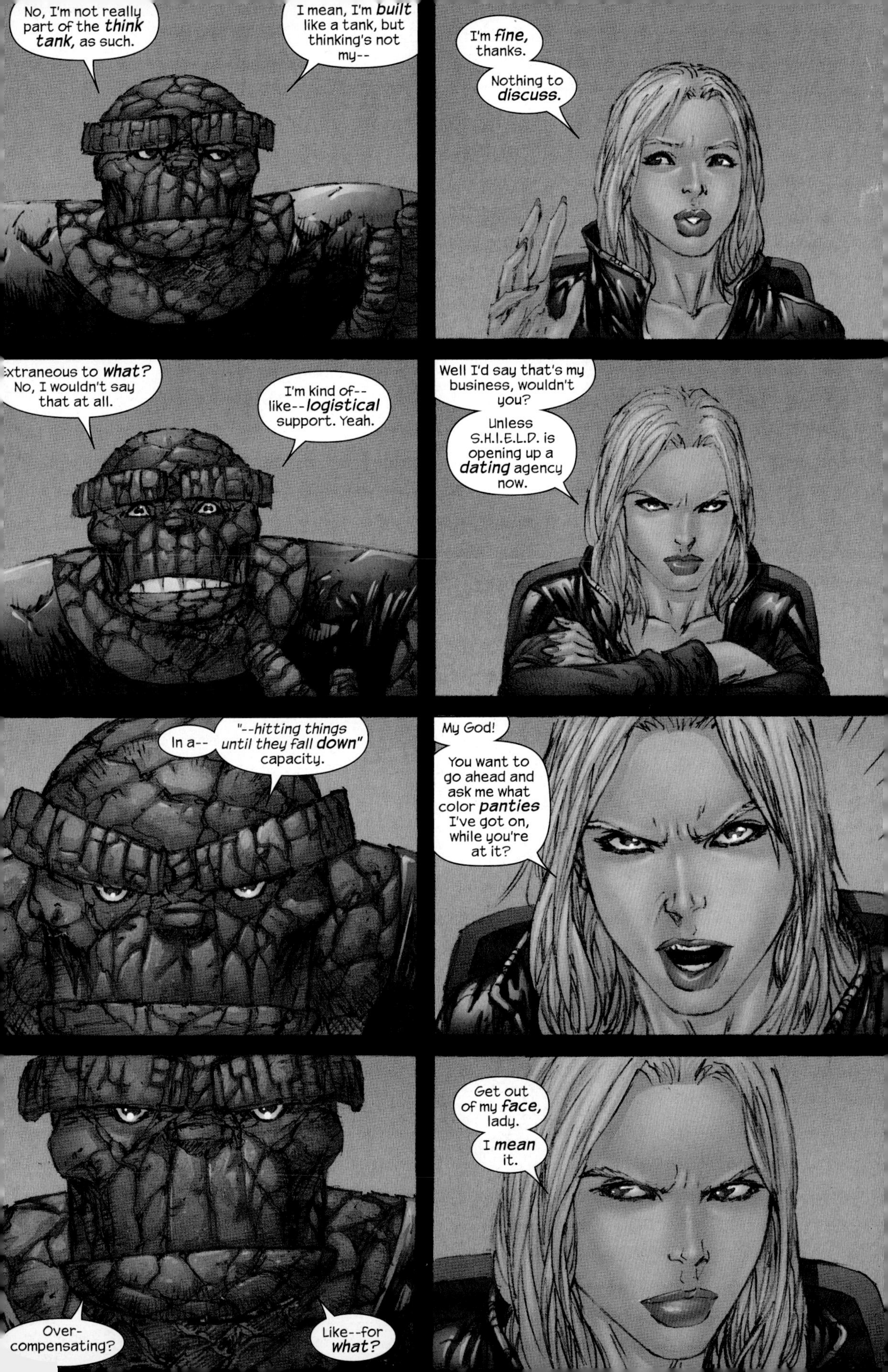

No, I'm not really part of the think tank, as such.
I mean, I'm built like a tank, but thinking's not my--
I'm fine, thanks.
Nothing to discuss.
Extraneous to what? No, I wouldn't say that at all.
I'm kind of--like--logistical support. Yeah.
Well I'd say that's my business, wouldn't you?
Unless S.H.I.E.L.D. is opening up a dating agency now.
In a--
"--hitting things until they fall down" capacity.
My God!
You want to go ahead and ask me what color panties I've got on, while you're at it?
Over-compensating?
Like--for what?
Get out of my face, lady.
I mean it.

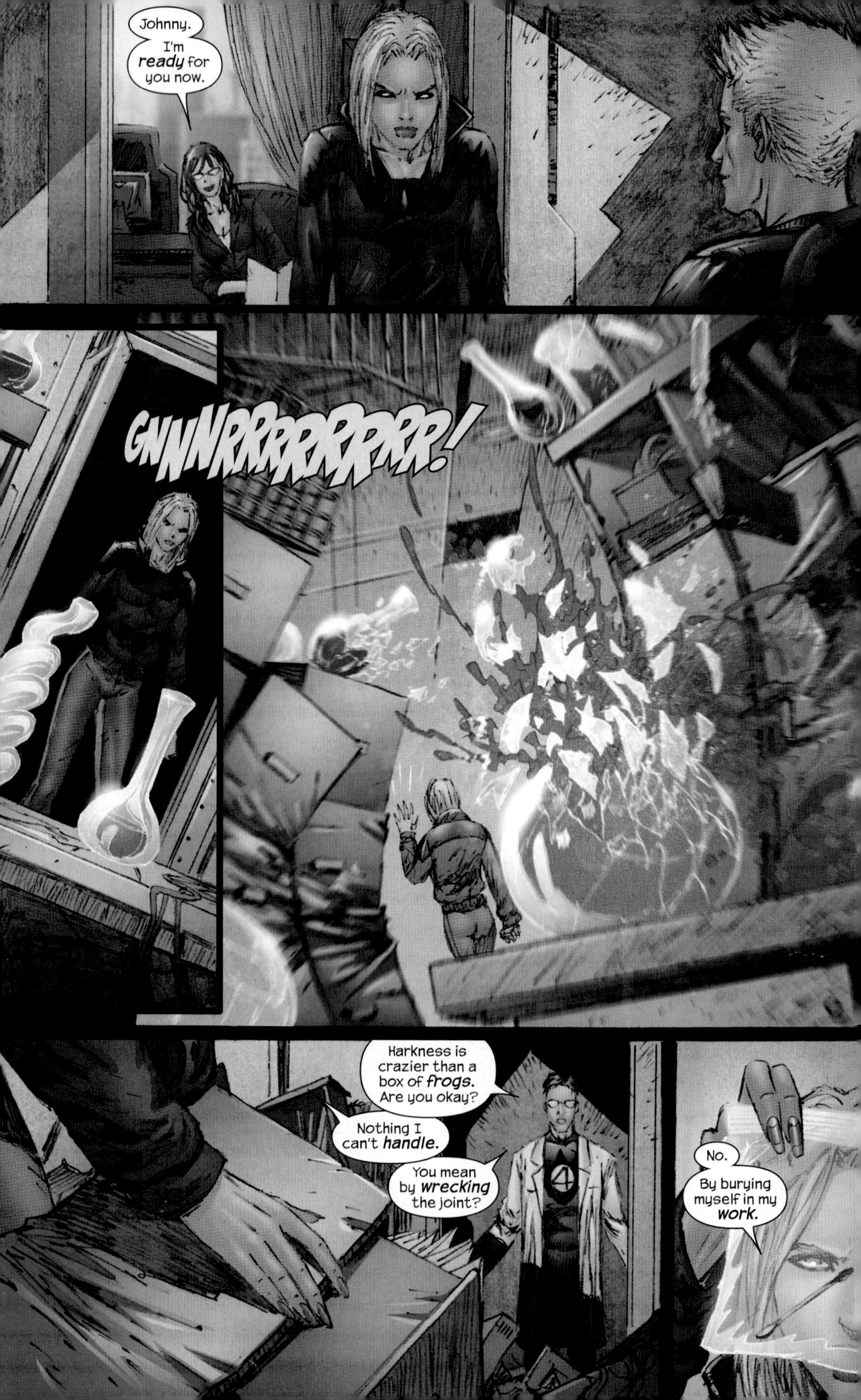
Johnny. I'm ready for you now.
GNNNRRRRRRRRRR!
Harkness is crazier than a box of frogs. Are you okay?
Nothing I can't handle.
You mean by wrecking the joint?
No.
By burying myself in my work.

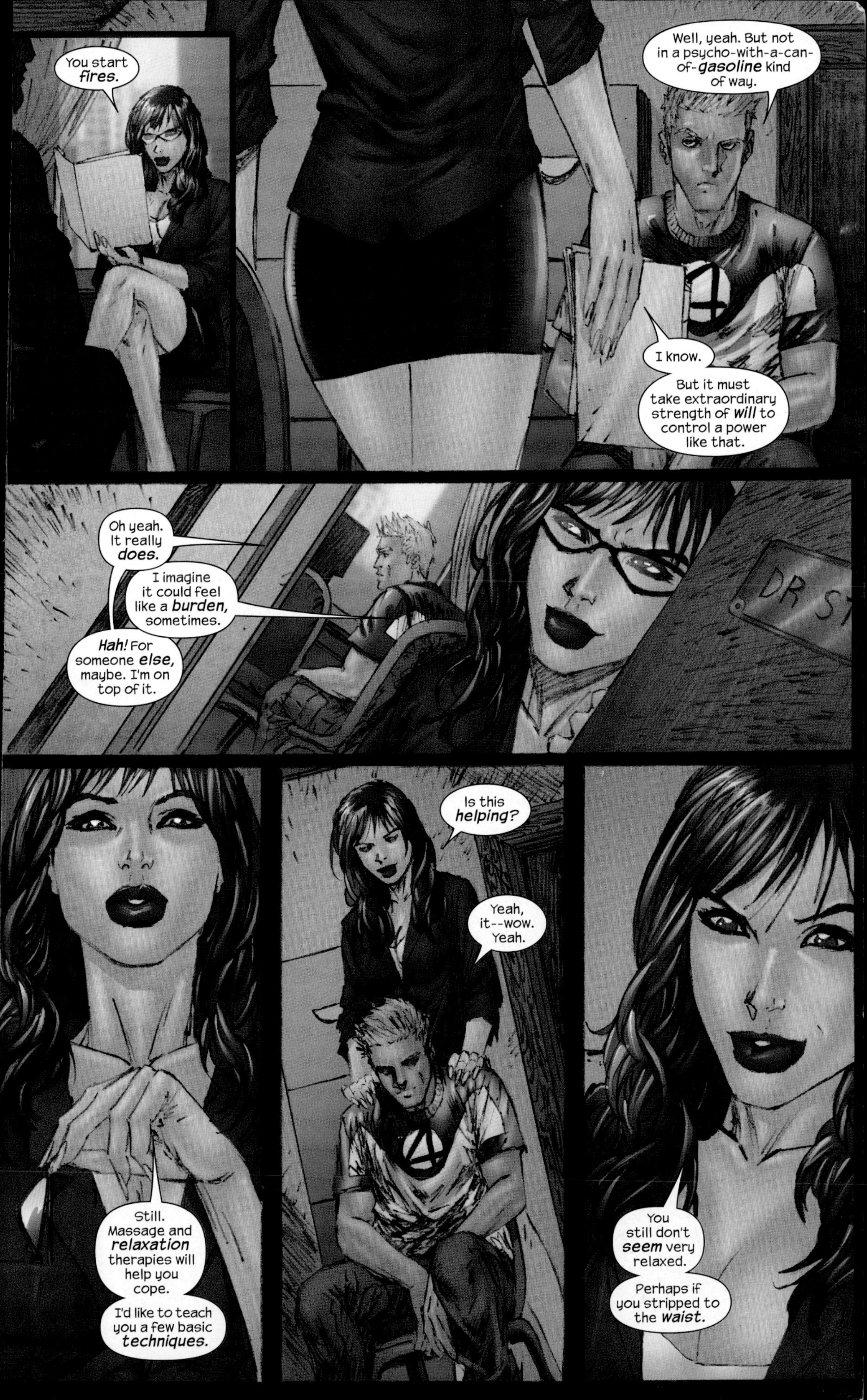
You start *fires.*
Well, yeah. But not in a psycho-with-a-can-of-*gasoline* kind of way.
I know.
But it must take extraordinary strength of *will* to control a power like that.
Oh yeah. It really *does.*
I imagine it could feel like a *burden,* sometimes.
Hah! For someone *else,* maybe. I'm on top of it.
DR ST
Still. Massage and *relaxation* therapies will help you cope.
I'd like to teach you a few basic *techniques.*
Is this *helping?*
Yeah, it--wow. Yeah.
You still don't *seem* very relaxed.
Perhaps if you stripped to the *waist.*

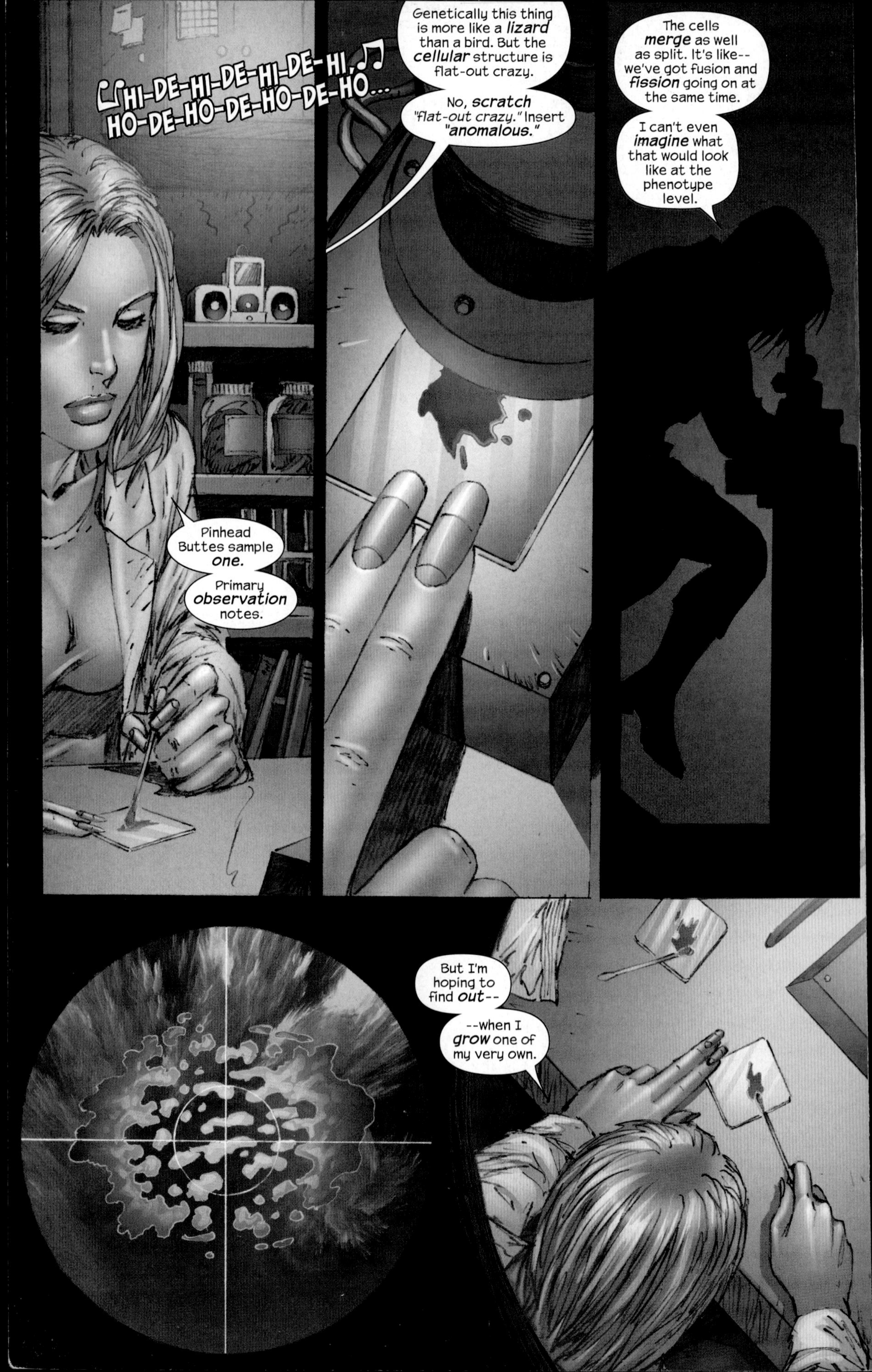

♫HI-DE-HI-DE-HI-DE-HI, ♫ HO-DE-HO-DE-HO-DE-HO...
Pinhead Buttes sample one.
Primary observation notes.
Genetically this thing is more like a lizard than a bird. But the cellular structure is flat-out crazy.
No, scratch "flat-out crazy." Insert "anomalous."
The cells merge as well as split. It's like--we've got fusion and fission going on at the same time.
I can't even imagine what that would look like at the phenotype level.
But I'm hoping to find out--
--when I grow one of my very own.

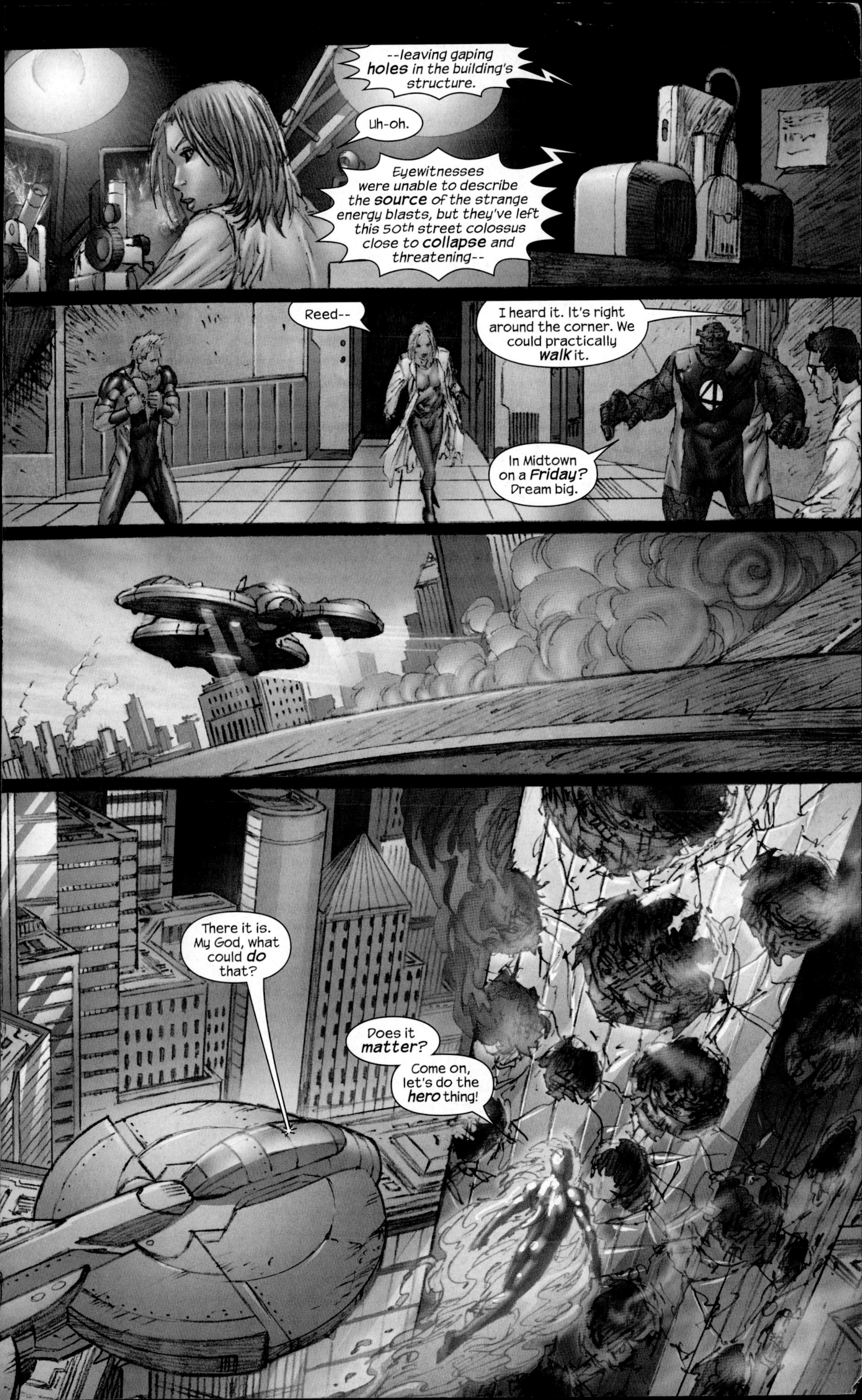
--leaving gaping holes in the building's structure.
Uh-oh.
Eyewitnesses were unable to describe the source of the strange energy blasts, but they've left this 50th street colossus close to collapse and threatening--
Reed--
I heard it. It's right around the corner. We could practically walk it.
In Midtown on a Friday? Dream big.
There it is. My God, what could do that?
Does it matter?
Come on, let's do the hero thing!

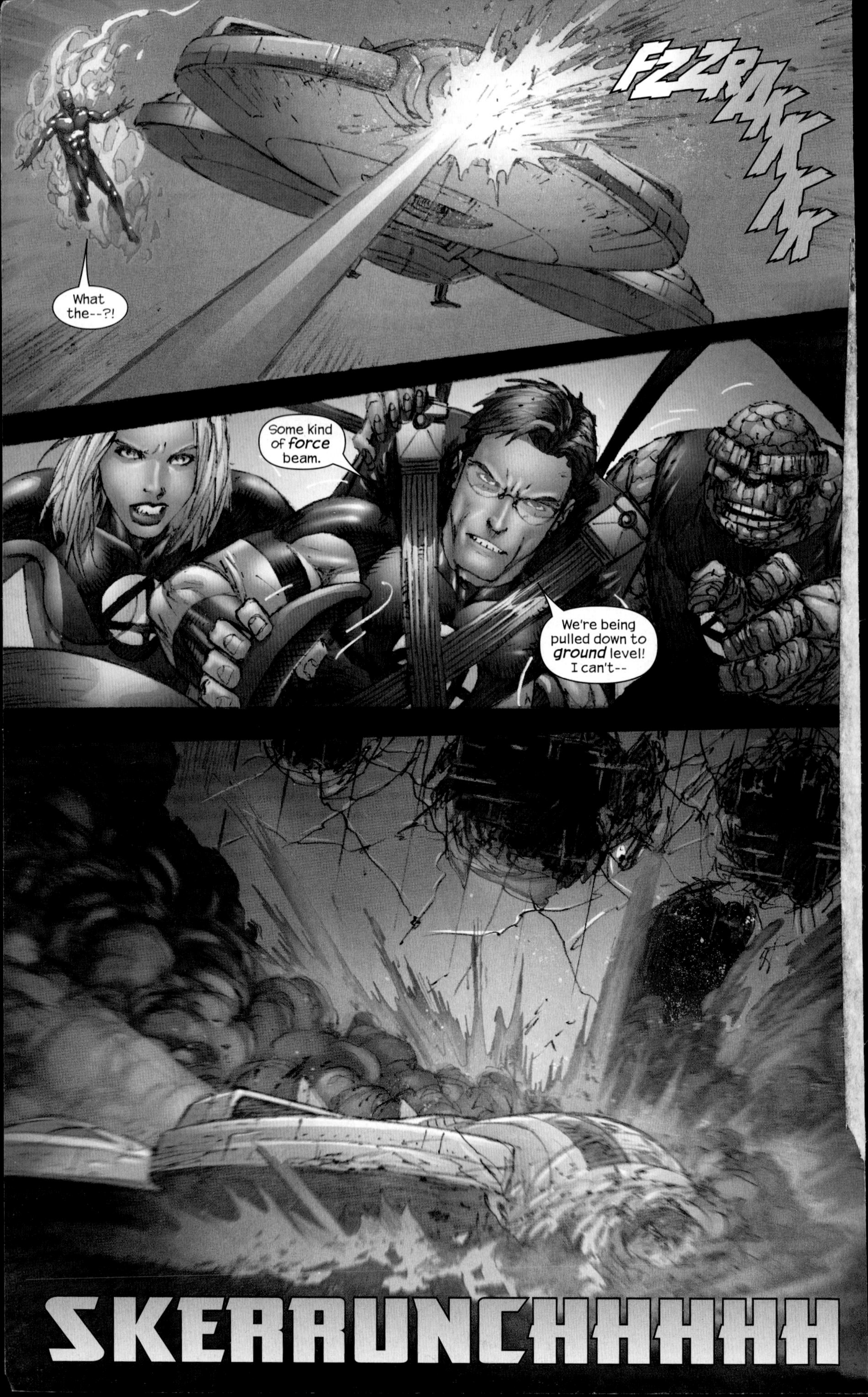
FZZRAKKKK
What the--?!
Some kind of *force* beam.
We're being pulled down to ***ground*** level! I can't--
SKERRUNCHHHHH

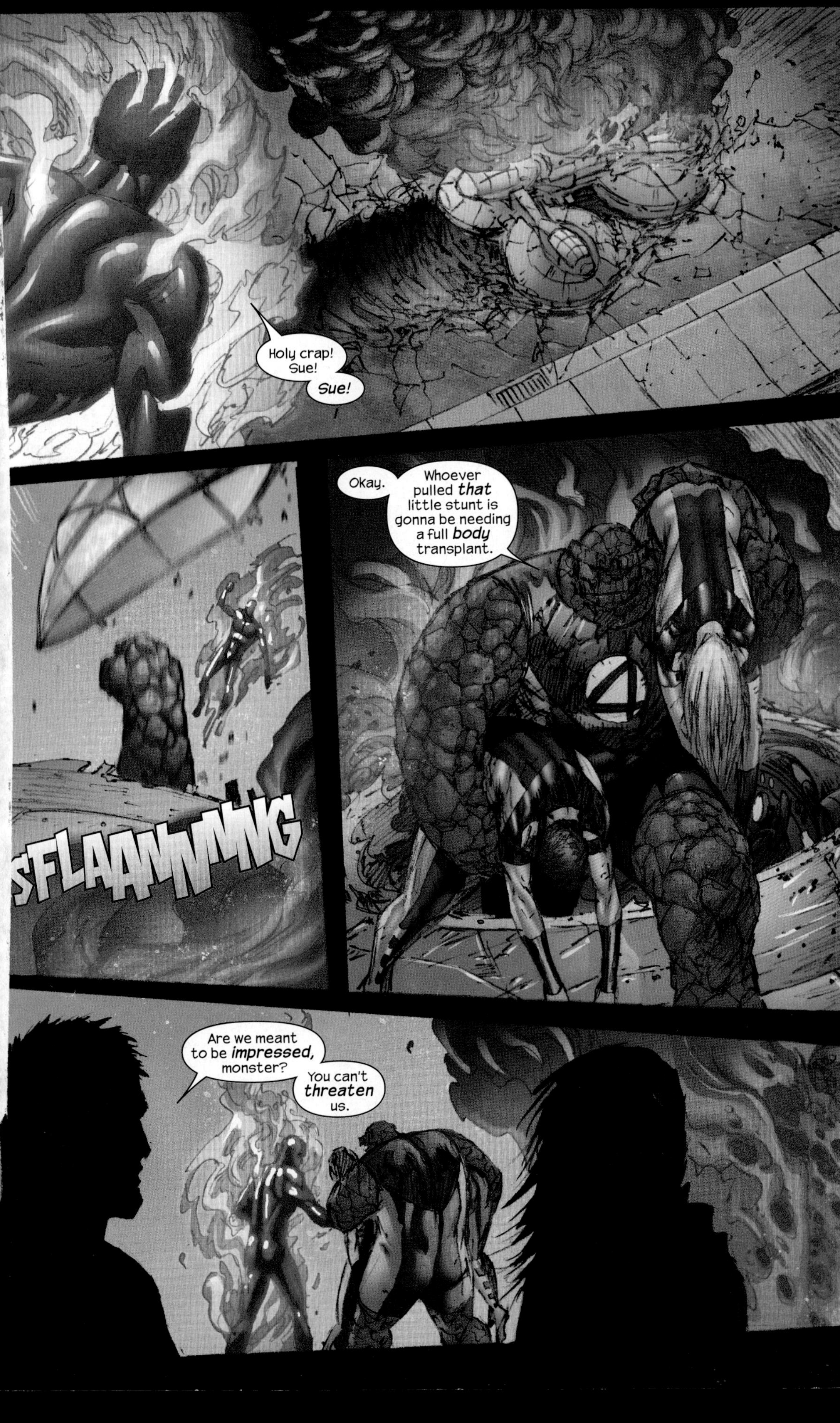
Holy crap! Sue! Sue!
SFLAAMMMNG
Okay.
Whoever pulled that little stunt is gonna be needing a full body transplant.
Are we meant to be impressed, monster?
You can't threaten us.

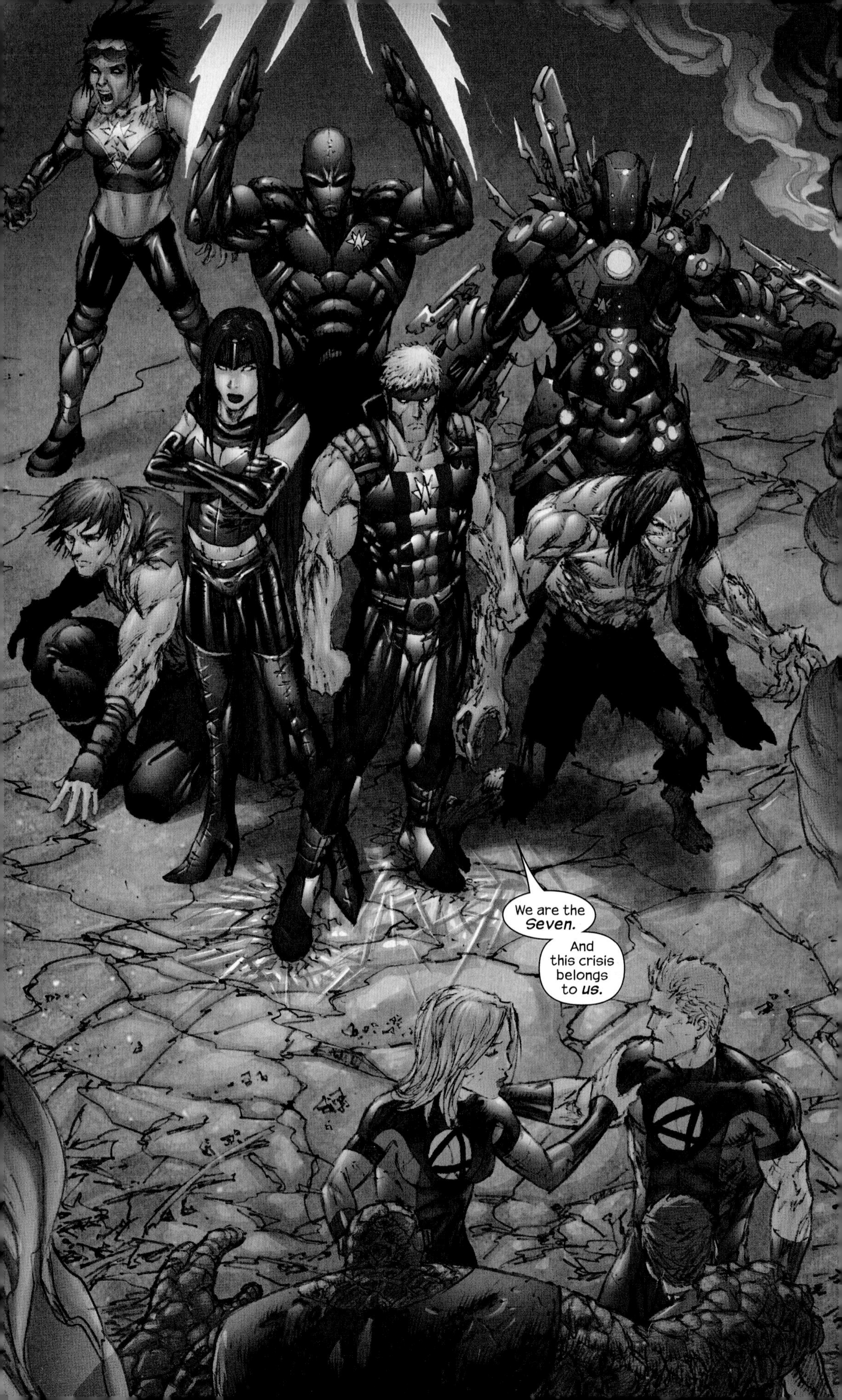
We are the Seven.
And this crisis belongs to us.

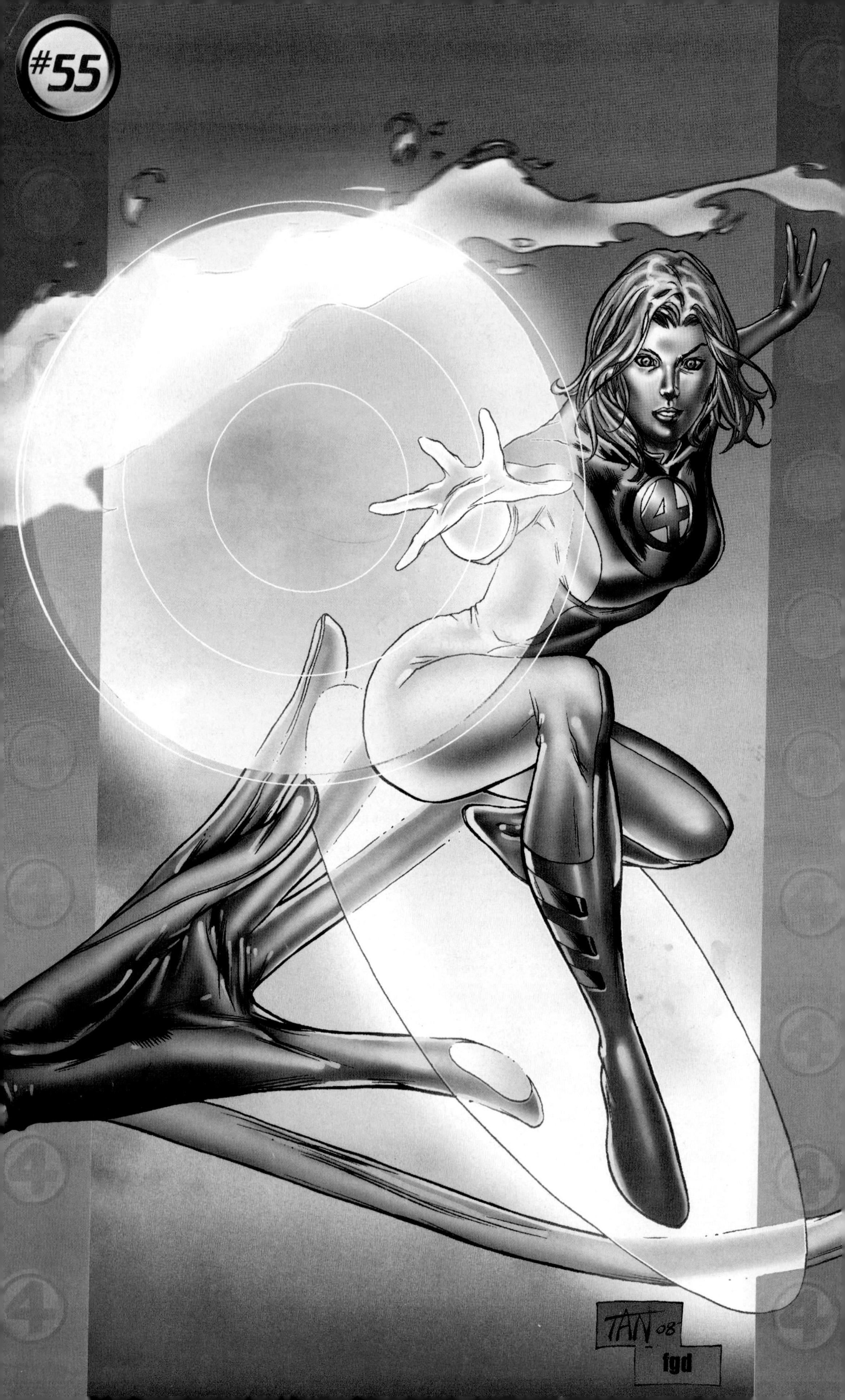
#55
TAN 08
fgd

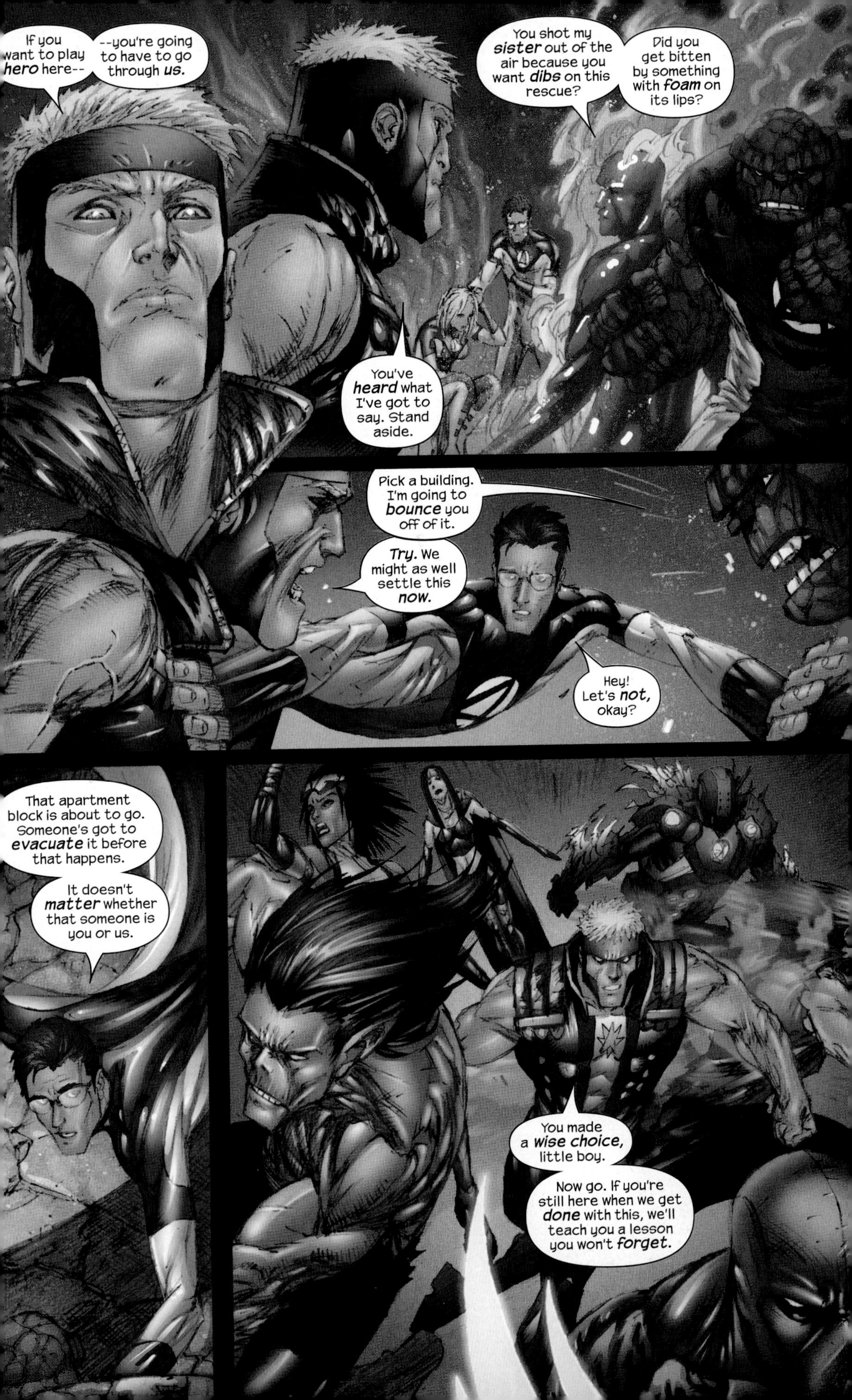

If you want to play hero here--
--you're going to have to go through us.
You shot my sister out of the air because you want dibs on this rescue?
Did you get bitten by something with foam on its lips?
You've heard what I've got to say. Stand aside.
Pick a building. I'm going to bounce you off of it.
Try. We might as well settle this now.
Hey! Let's not, okay?
That apartment block is about to go. Someone's got to evacuate it before that happens.
It doesn't matter whether that someone is you or us.
You made a wise choice, little boy.
Now go. If you're still here when we get done with this, we'll teach you a lesson you won't forget.

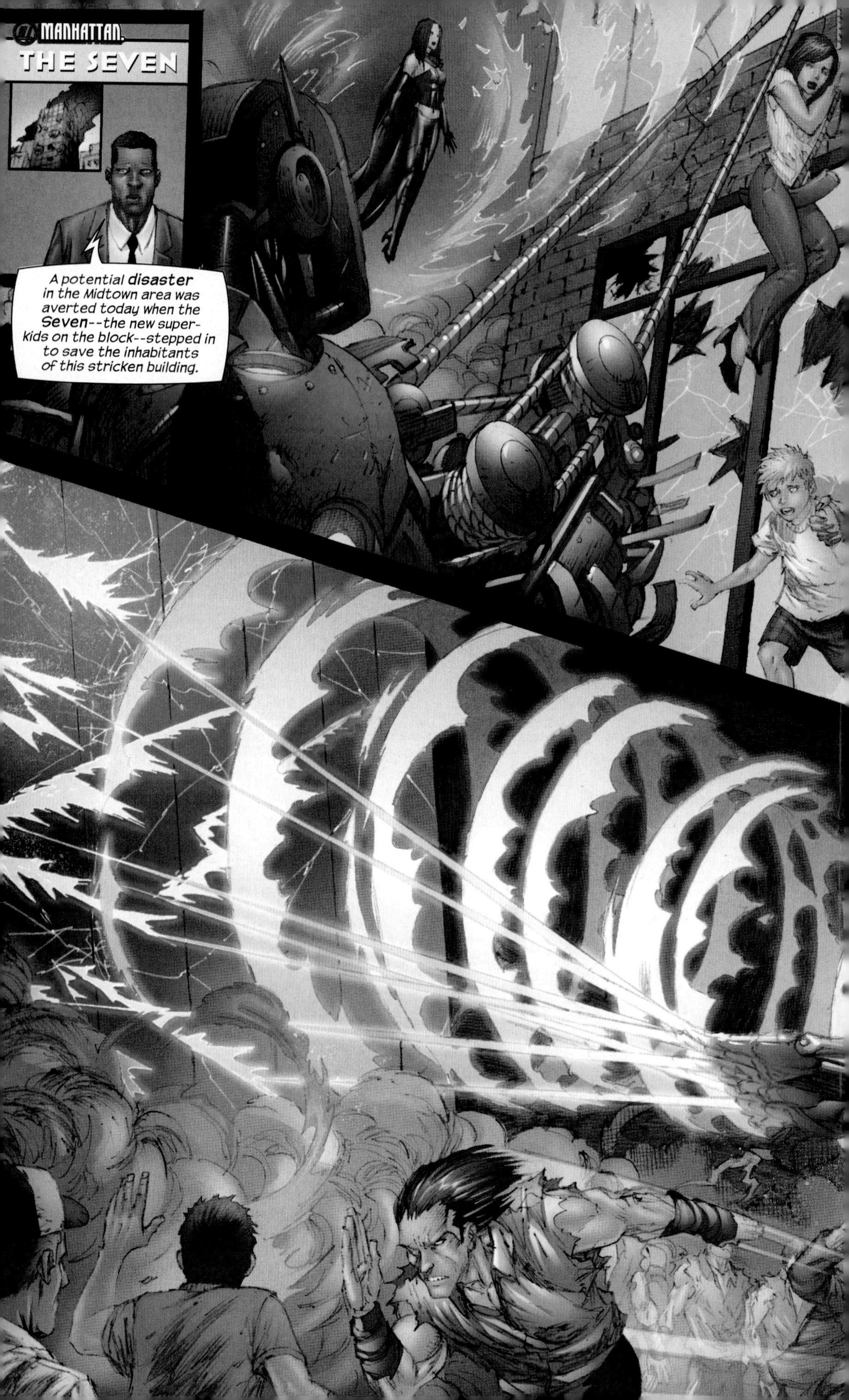
MANHATTAN
THE SEVEN
A potential disaster in the Midtown area was averted today when the Seven--the new super-kids on the block--stepped in to save the inhabitants of this stricken building.

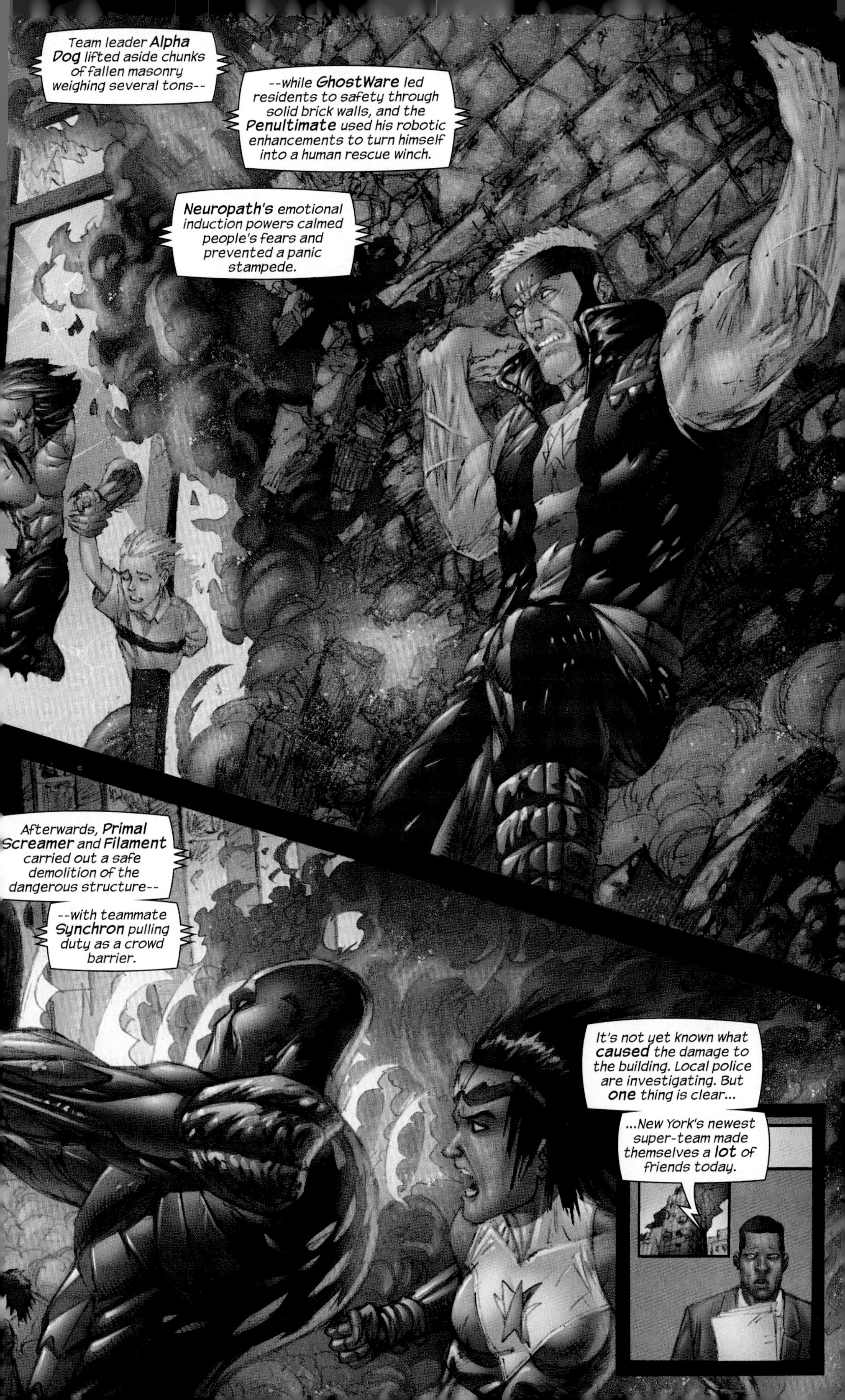
Team leader Alpha Dog lifted aside chunks of fallen masonry weighing several tons--
--while GhostWare led residents to safety through solid brick walls, and the Penultimate used his robotic enhancements to turn himself into a human rescue winch.
Neuropath's emotional induction powers calmed people's fears and prevented a panic stampede.
Afterwards, Primal Screamer and Filament carried out a safe demolition of the dangerous structure--
--with teammate Synchron pulling duty as a crowd barrier.
It's not yet known what caused the damage to the building. Local police are investigating. But one thing is clear...
...New York's newest super-team made themselves a lot of friends today.

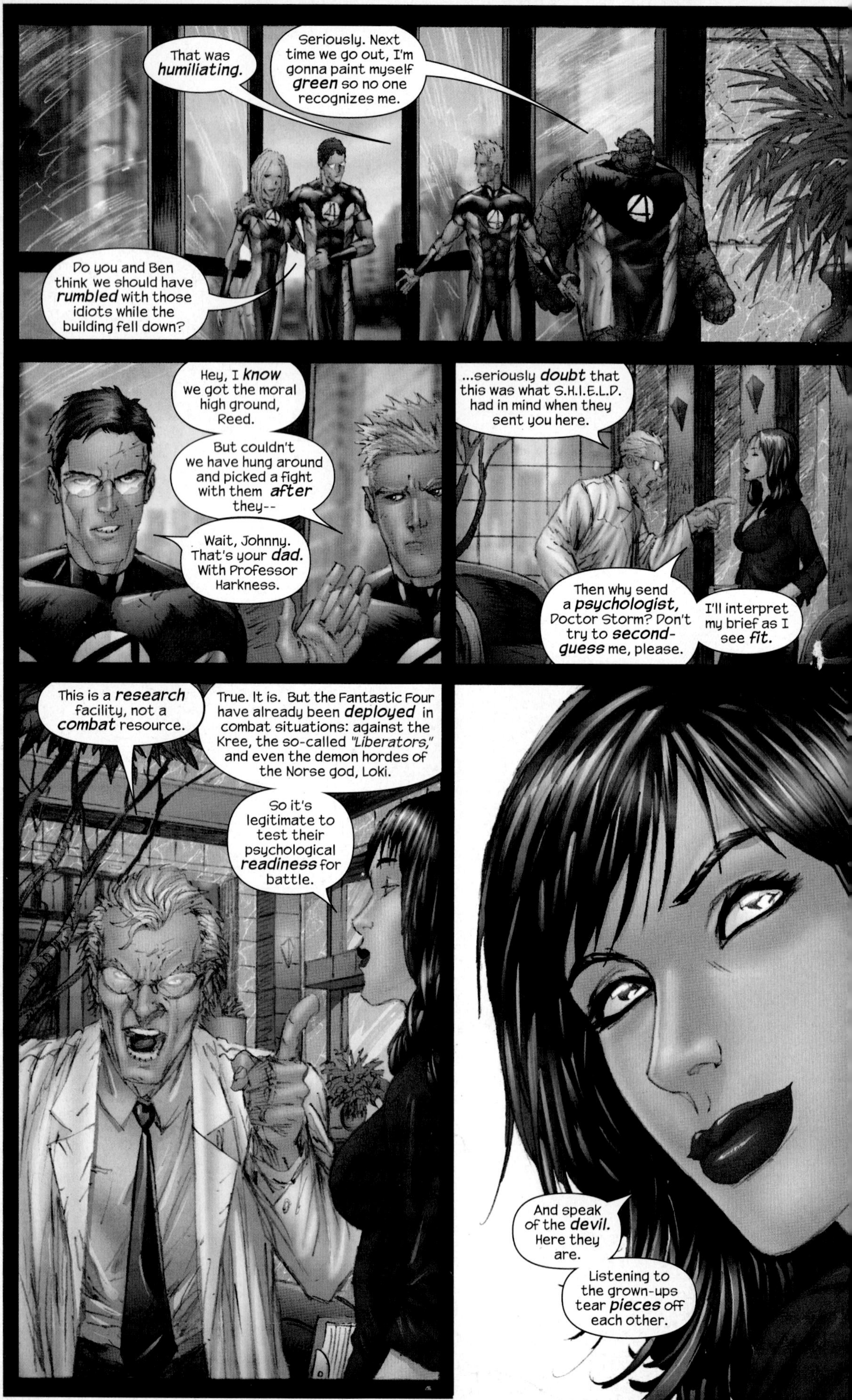
That was humiliating.
Seriously. Next time we go out, I'm gonna paint myself green so no one recognizes me.
Do you and Ben think we should have rumbled with those idiots while the building fell down?
Hey, I know we got the moral high ground, Reed.
But couldn't we have hung around and picked a fight with them after they--
Wait, Johnny. That's your dad. With Professor Harkness.
...seriously doubt that this was what S.H.I.E.L.D. had in mind when they sent you here.
Then why send a psychologist, Doctor Storm? Don't try to second-guess me, please.
I'll interpret my brief as I see fit.
This is a research facility, not a combat resource.
True. It is. But the Fantastic Four have already been deployed in combat situations: against the Kree, the so-called "Liberators," and even the demon hordes of the Norse god, Loki.
So it's legitimate to test their psychological readiness for battle.
And speak of the devil. Here they are.
Listening to the grown-ups tear pieces off each other.

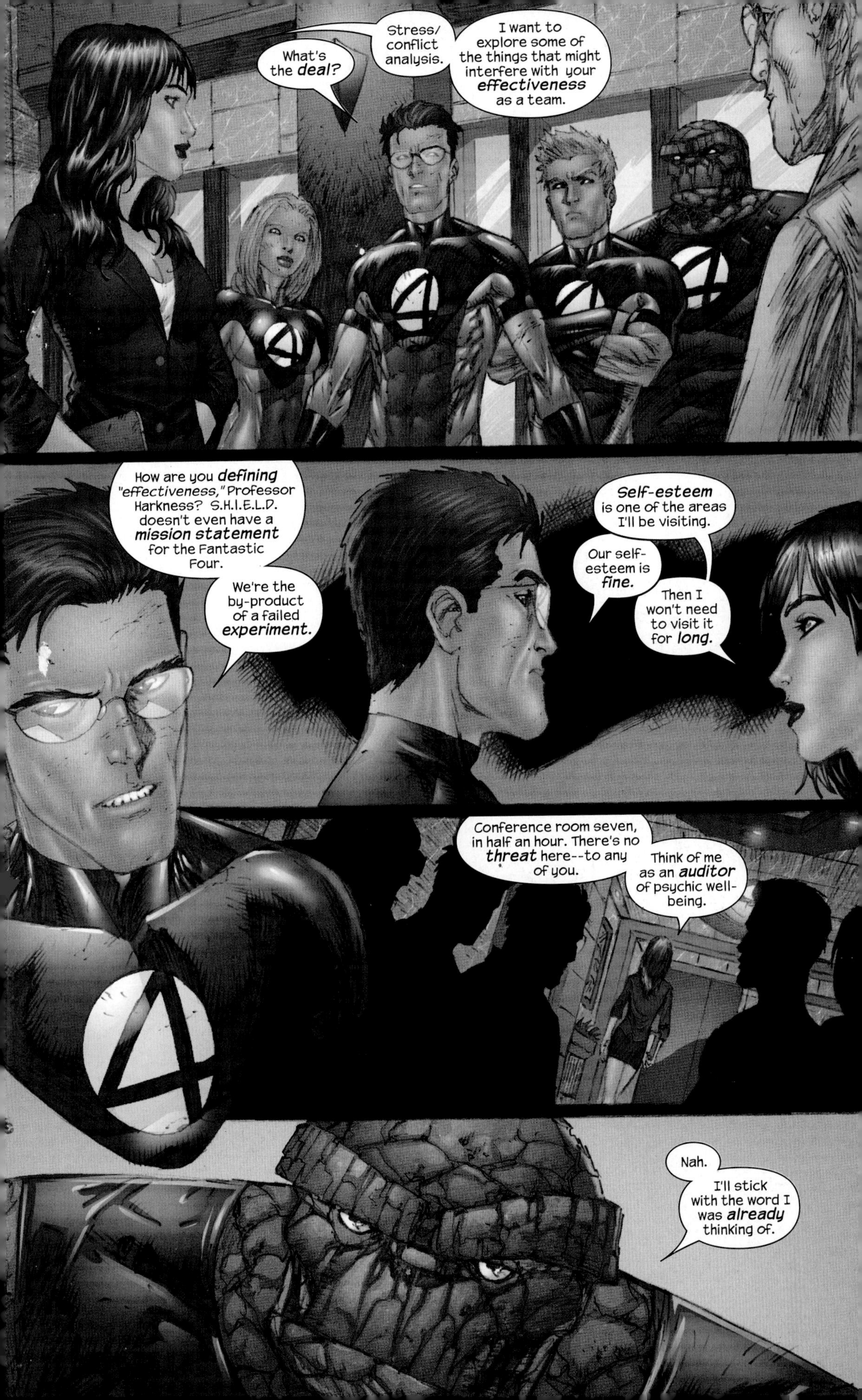
What's the *deal*?
Stress/ conflict analysis.
I want to explore some of the things that might interfere with your *effectiveness* as a team.
How are you *defining* "*effectiveness*," Professor Harkness? S.H.I.E.L.D. doesn't even have a *mission statement* for the Fantastic Four.
We're the by-product of a failed *experiment*.
Self-esteem is one of the areas I'll be visiting.
Our self-esteem is *fine*.
Then I won't need to visit it for *long*.
Conference room seven, in half an hour. There's no *threat* here--to any of you.
Think of me as an *auditor* of psychic well-being.
Nah.
I'll stick with the word I was *already* thinking of.

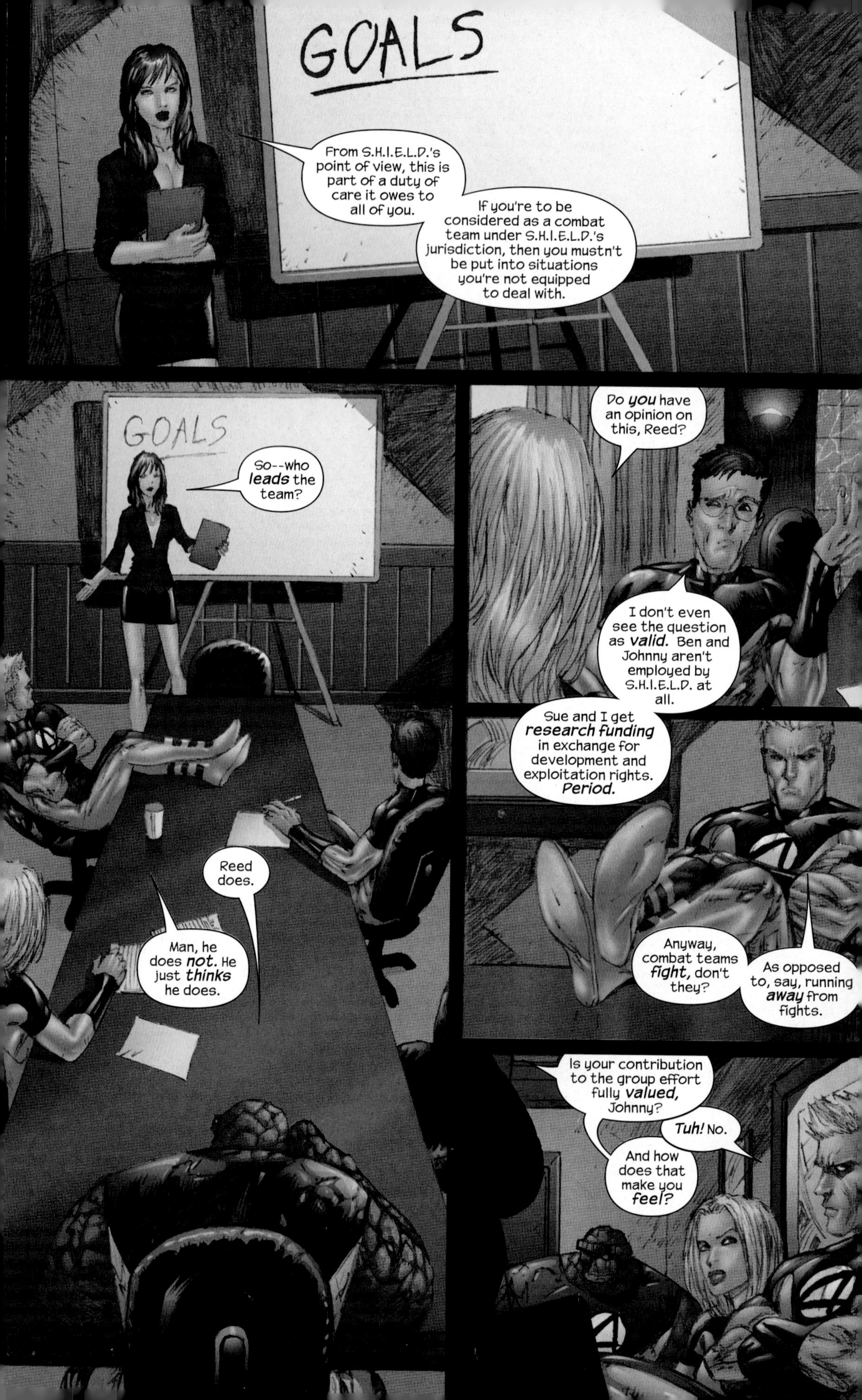
GOALS
From S.H.I.E.L.D.'s point of view, this is part of a duty of care it owes to all of you.
If you're to be considered as a combat team under S.H.I.E.L.D.'s jurisdiction, then you mustn't be put into situations you're not equipped to deal with.
GOALS
So--who leads the team?
Reed does.
Man, he does not. He just thinks he does.
Do you have an opinion on this, Reed?
I don't even see the question as valid. Ben and Johnny aren't employed by S.H.I.E.L.D. at all.
Sue and I get research funding in exchange for development and exploitation rights. Period.
Anyway, combat teams fight, don't they?
As opposed to, say, running away from fights.
Is your contribution to the group effort fully valued, Johnny?
Tuh! No.
And how does that make you feel?

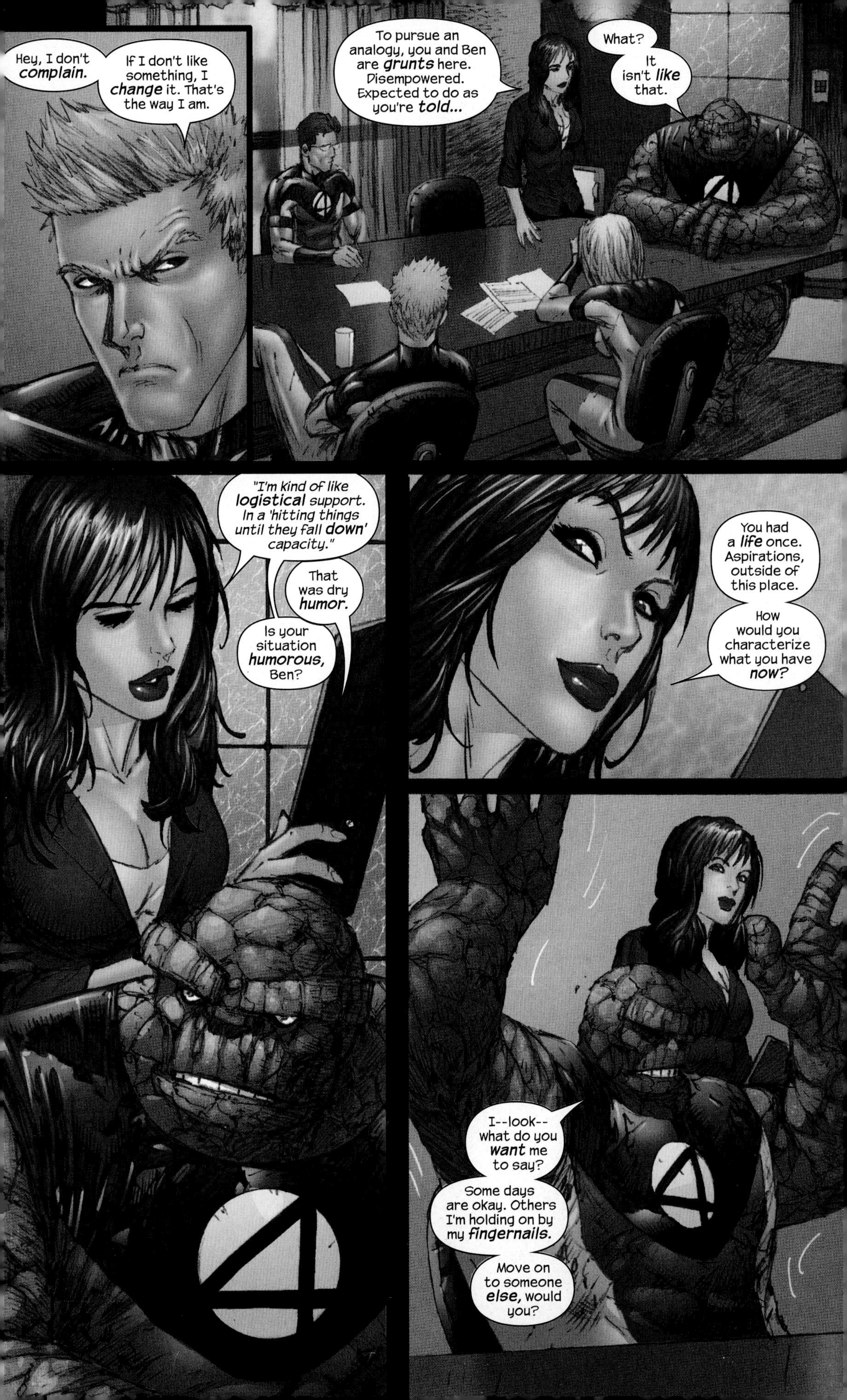

Hey, I don't complain.
If I don't like something, I change it. That's the way I am.
To pursue an analogy, you and Ben are grunts here. Disempowered. Expected to do as you're told...
What?
It isn't like that.
"I'm kind of like logistical support. In a 'hitting things until they fall down' capacity."
That was dry humor.
Is your situation humorous, Ben?
You had a life once. Aspirations, outside of this place.
How would you characterize what you have now?
I--look-- what do you want me to say?
Some days are okay. Others I'm holding on by my fingernails.
Move on to someone else, would you?

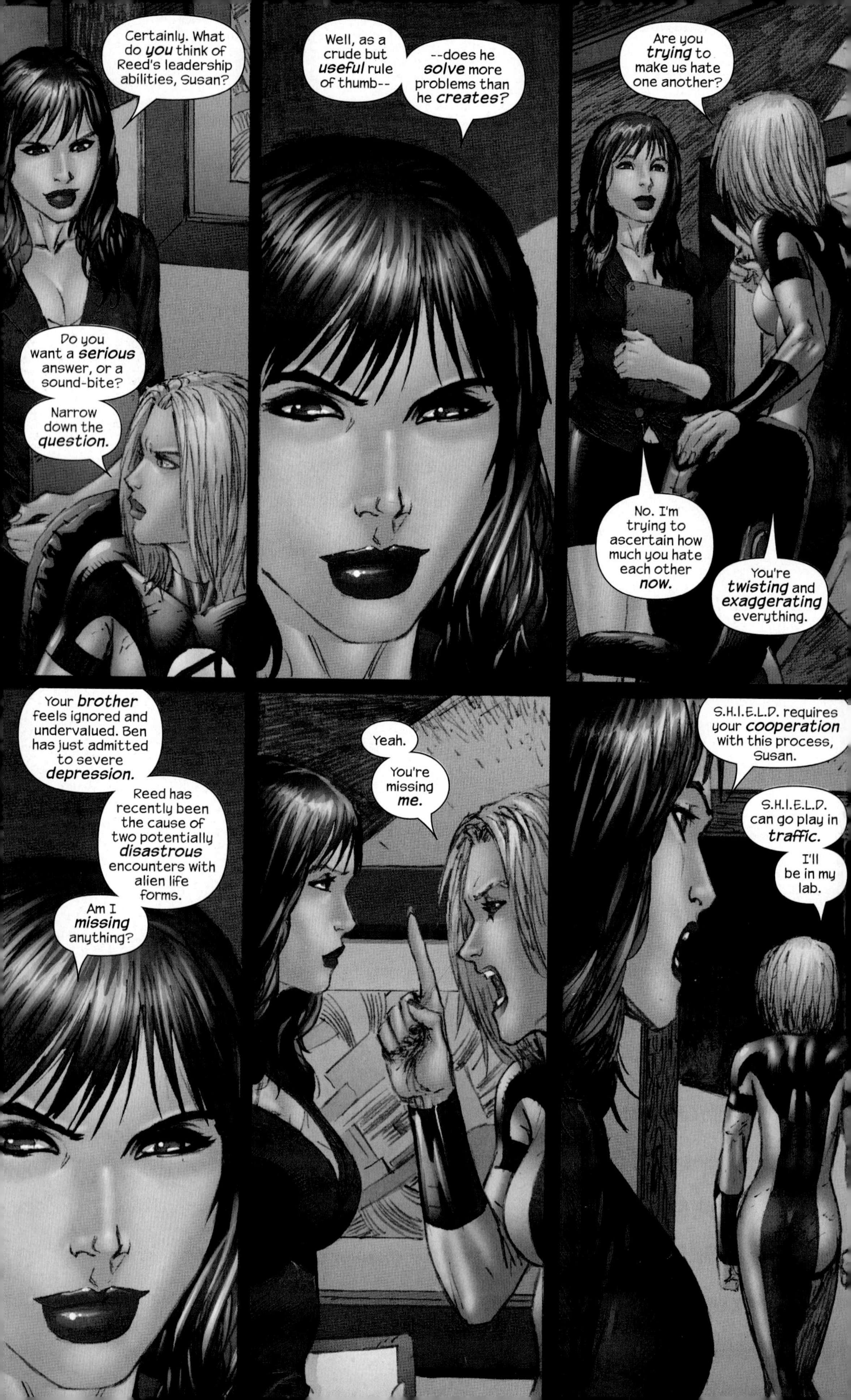
Certainly. What do you think of Reed's leadership abilities, Susan?
Do you want a serious answer, or a sound-bite?
Narrow down the question.
Well, as a crude but useful rule of thumb--
--does he solve more problems than he creates?
Are you trying to make us hate one another?
No. I'm trying to ascertain how much you hate each other now.
You're twisting and exaggerating everything.
Your brother feels ignored and undervalued. Ben has just admitted to severe depression.
Reed has recently been the cause of two potentially disastrous encounters with alien life forms.
Am I missing anything?
Yeah.
You're missing me.
S.H.I.E.L.D. requires your cooperation with this process, Susan.
S.H.I.E.L.D. can go play in traffic.
I'll be in my lab.

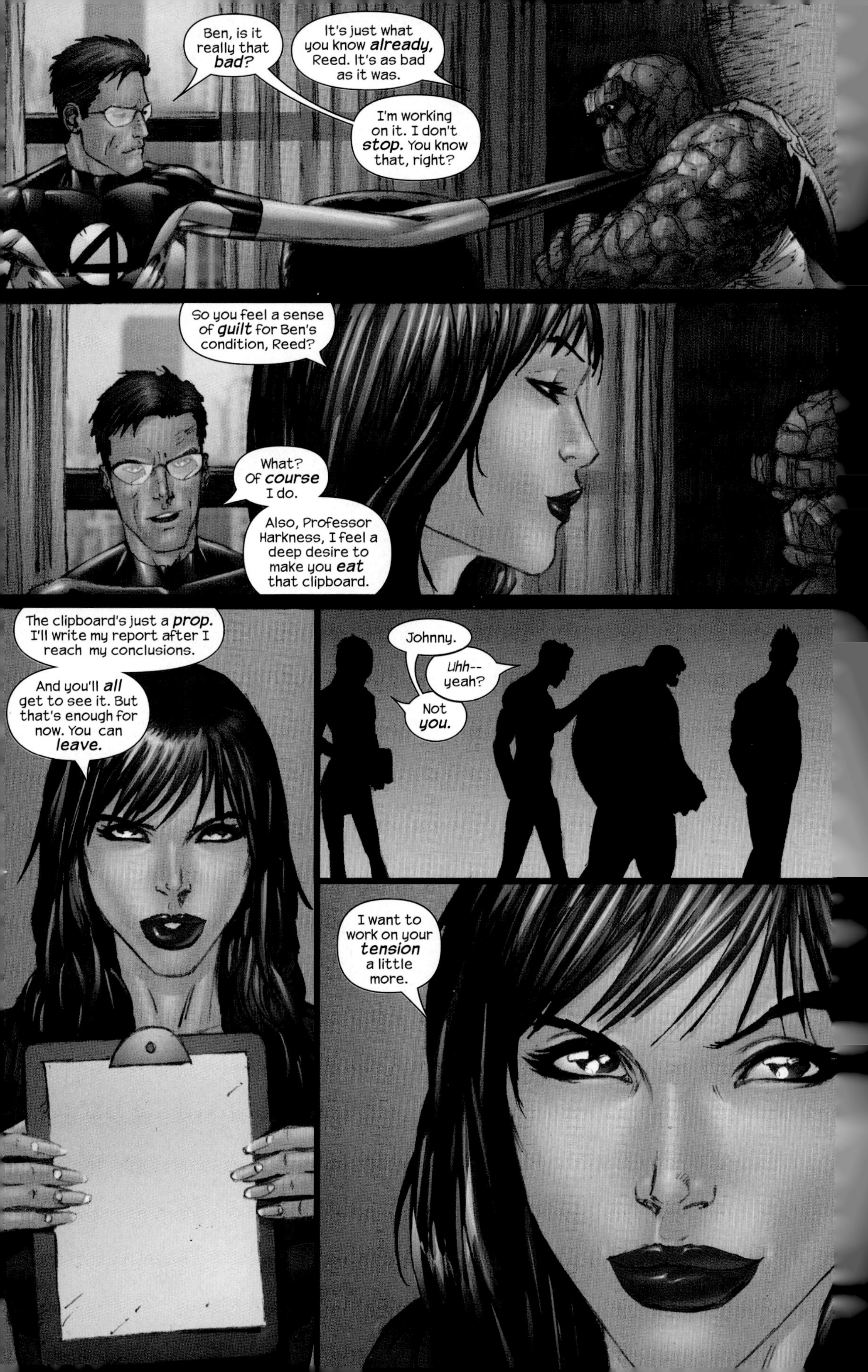
Ben, is it really that *bad?*
It's just what you know *already,* Reed. It's as bad as it was.
I'm working on it. I don't *stop.* You know that, right?
So you feel a sense of *guilt* for Ben's condition, Reed?
What? Of *course* I do.
Also, Professor Harkness, I feel a deep desire to make you *eat* that clipboard.
The clipboard's just a *prop.* I'll write my report after I reach my conclusions.
And you'll *all* get to see it. But that's enough for now. You can *leave.*
Johnny.
Uhh-- yeah?
Not *you.*
I want to work on your *tension* a little more.

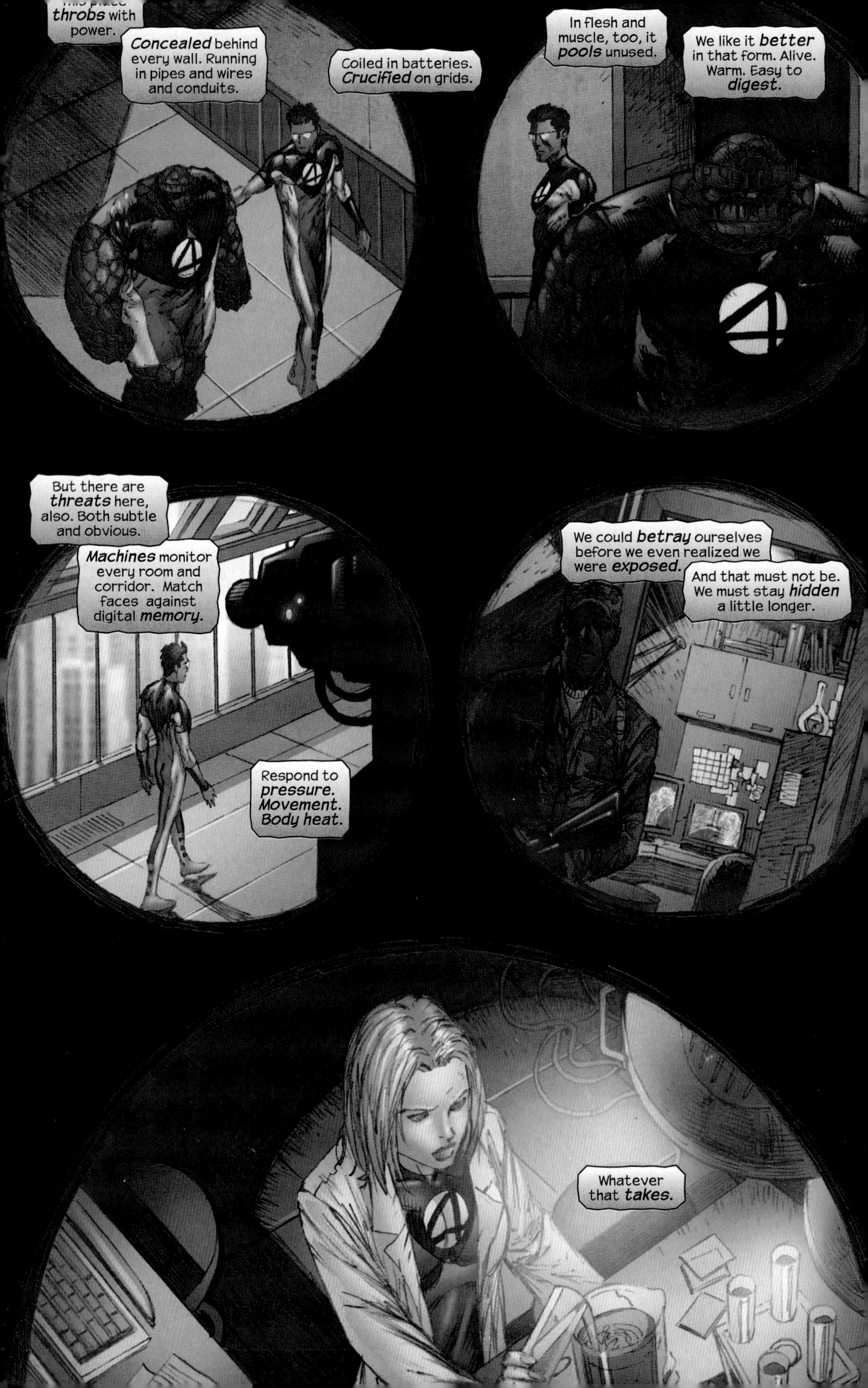
This place throbs with power.
Concealed behind every wall. Running in pipes and wires and conduits.
Coiled in batteries. Crucified on grids.
In flesh and muscle, too, it pools unused.
We like it better in that form. Alive. Warm. Easy to digest.
But there are threats here, also. Both subtle and obvious.
Machines monitor every room and corridor. Match faces against digital memory.
Respond to pressure. Movement. Body heat.
We could betray ourselves before we even realized we were exposed.
And that must not be. We must stay hidden a little longer.
Whatever that takes.

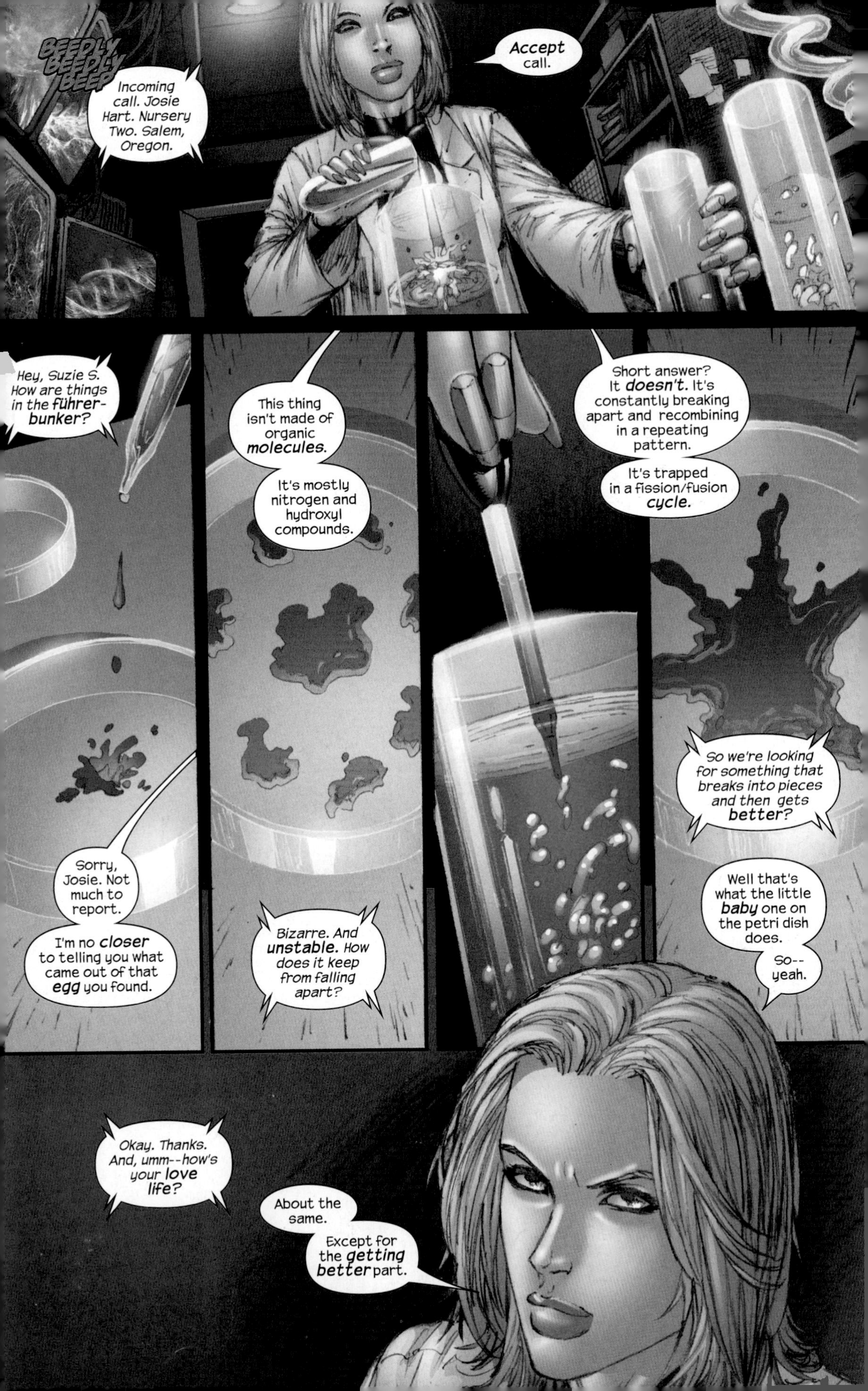
BEEDLY BEEDLY BEEP
Incoming call. Josie Hart. Nursery Two. Salem, Oregon.
Accept call.
Hey, Suzie S. How are things in the führer-bunker?
Sorry, Josie. Not much to report.
I'm no closer to telling you what came out of that egg you found.
This thing isn't made of organic molecules.
It's mostly nitrogen and hydroxyl compounds.
Bizarre. And unstable. How does it keep from falling apart?
Short answer? It doesn't. It's constantly breaking apart and recombining in a repeating pattern.
It's trapped in a fission/fusion cycle.
So we're looking for something that breaks into pieces and then gets better?
Well that's what the little baby one on the petri dish does.
So--yeah.
Okay. Thanks. And, umm--how's your love life?
About the same.
Except for the getting better part.

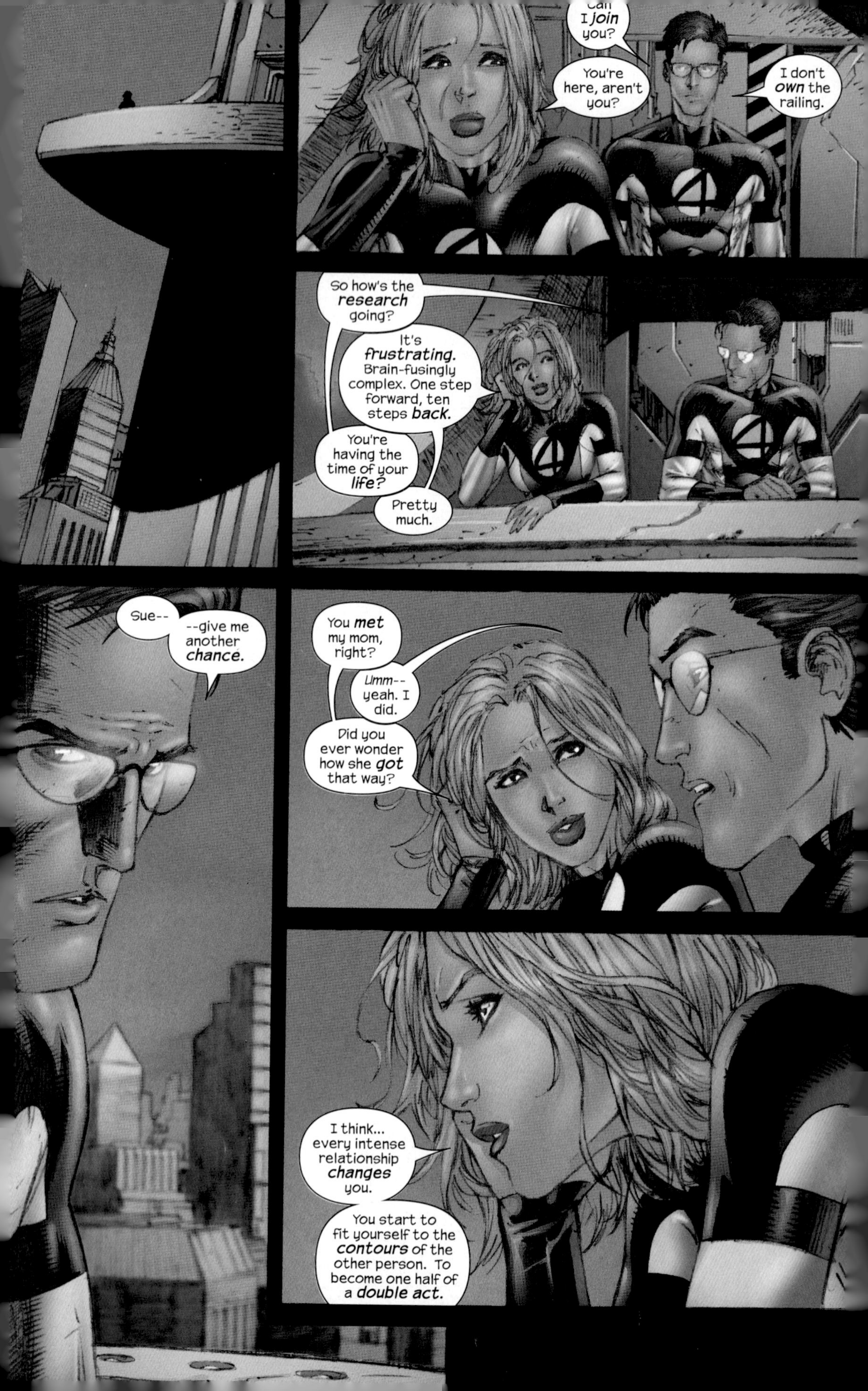

Can I join you?
You're here, aren't you?
I don't own the railing.
So how's the research going?
It's frustrating. Brain-fusingly complex. One step forward, ten steps back.
You're having the time of your life?
Pretty much.
Sue--
--give me another chance.
You met my mom, right?
Umm--yeah. I did.
Did you ever wonder how she got that way?
I think... every intense relationship changes you.
You start to fit yourself to the contours of the other person. To become one half of a double act.

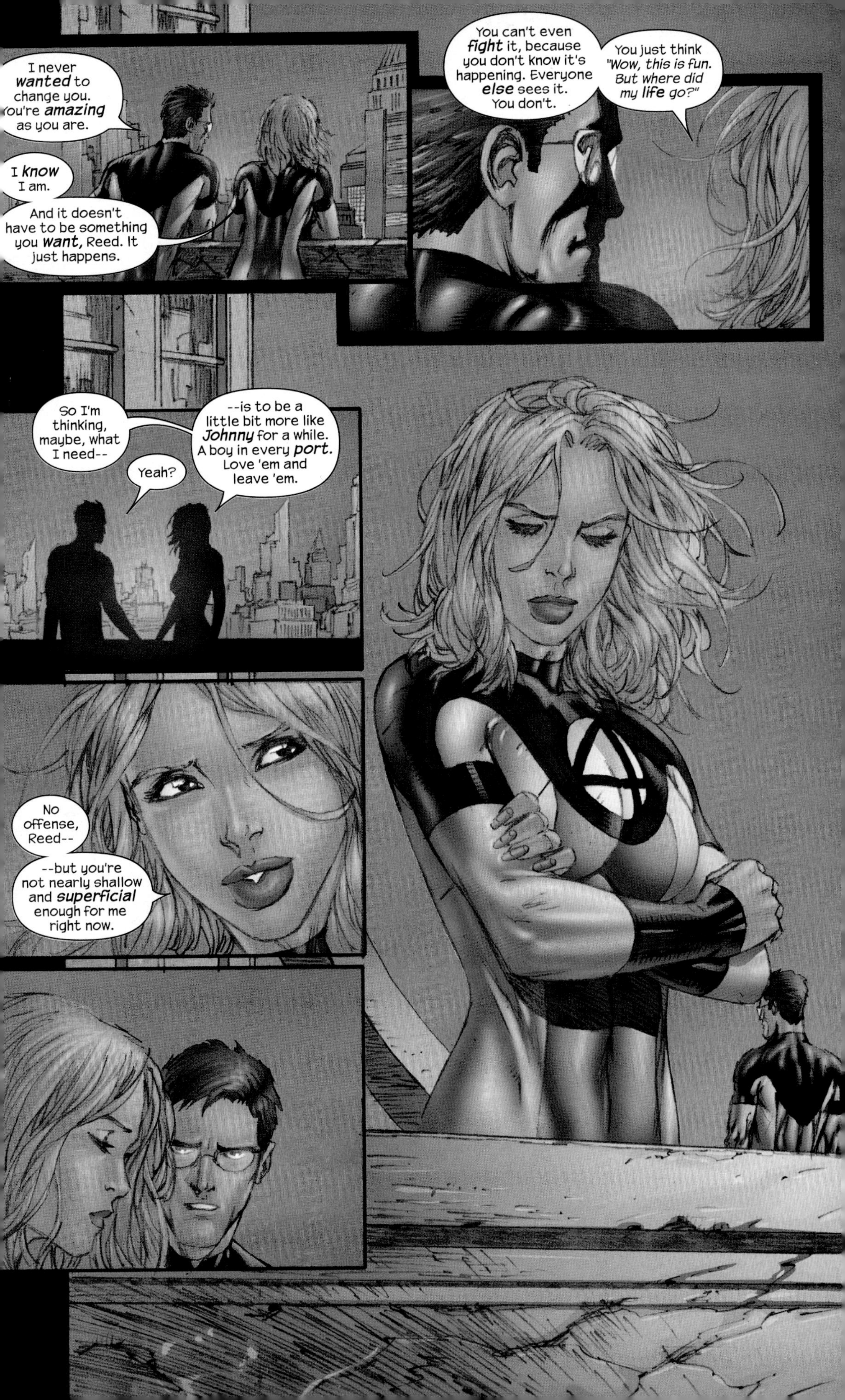

I never wanted to change you. You're amazing as you are.
I know I am.
And it doesn't have to be something you want, Reed. It just happens.
You can't even fight it, because you don't know it's happening. Everyone else sees it. You don't.
You just think "Wow, this is fun. But where did my life go?"
So I'm thinking, maybe, what I need--
Yeah?
--is to be a little bit more like Johnny for a while. A boy in every port. Love 'em and leave 'em.
No offense, Reed--
--but you're not nearly shallow and superficial enough for me right now.

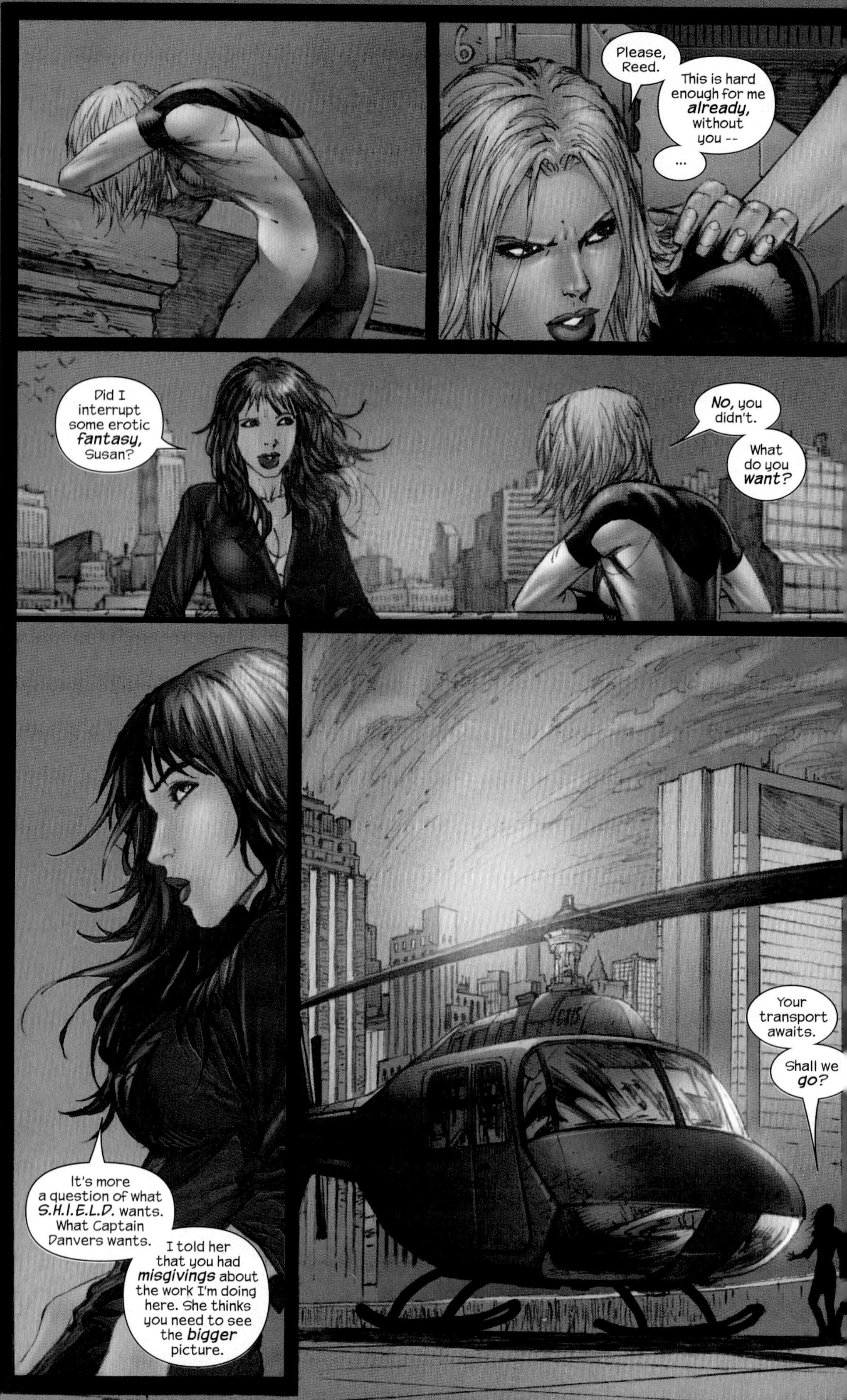
Please, Reed.
This is hard enough for me *already,* without you --
...
Did I interrupt some erotic *fantasy,* Susan?
No, you didn't.
What do you *want?*
It's more a question of what *S.H.I.E.L.D.* wants. What Captain Danvers wants.
I told her that you had *misgivings* about the work I'm doing here. She thinks you need to see the *bigger* picture.
Your transport awaits.
Shall we *go?*

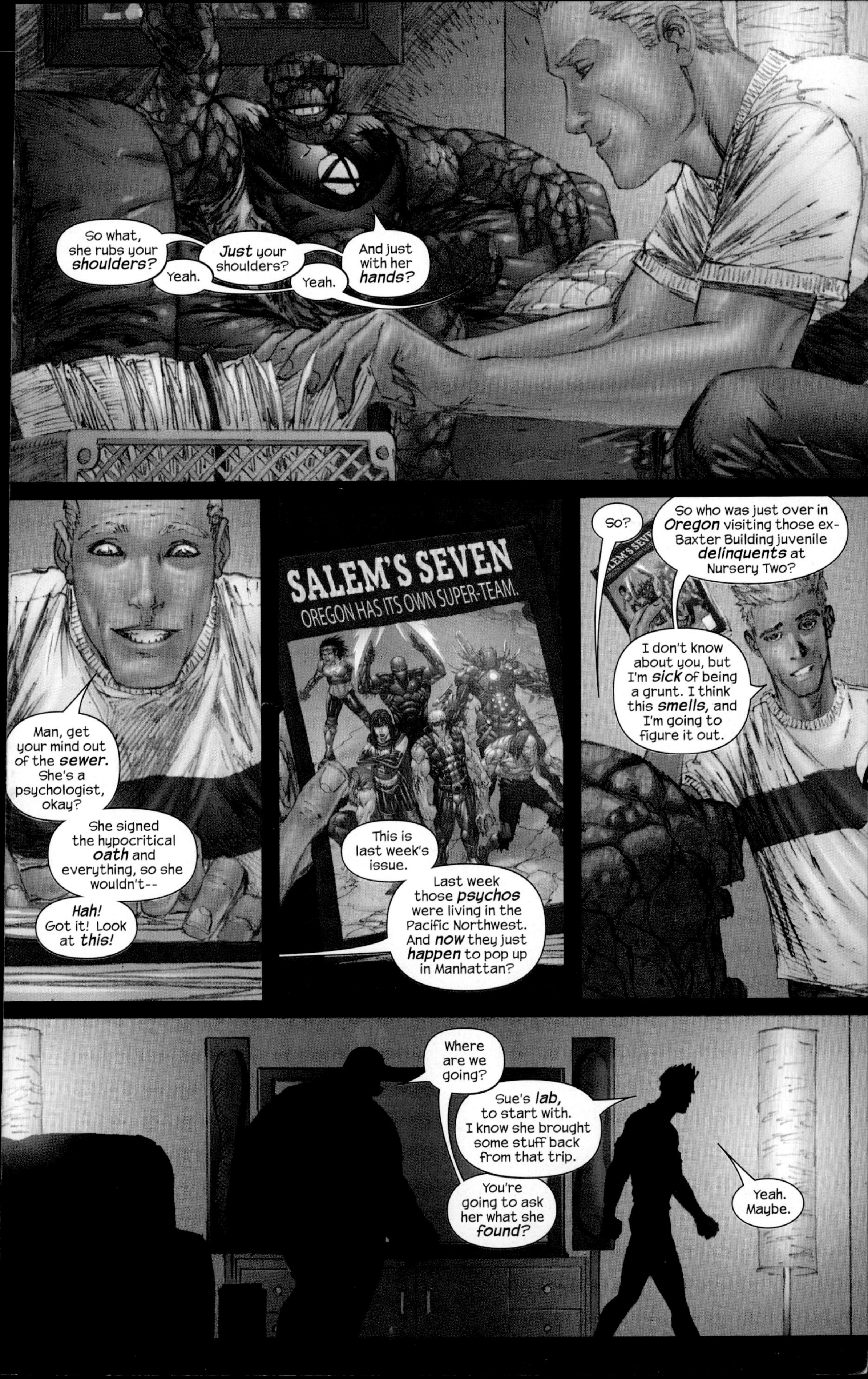

So what, she rubs your shoulders?
Yeah.
Just your shoulders?
Yeah.
And just with her hands?
Man, get your mind out of the sewer. She's a psychologist, okay?
She signed the hypocritical oath and everything, so she wouldn't--
Hah! Got it! Look at this!
SALEM'S SEVEN
OREGON HAS ITS OWN SUPER-TEAM.
This is last week's issue.
Last week those psychos were living in the Pacific Northwest. And now they just happen to pop up in Manhattan?
So?
So who was just over in Oregon visiting those ex-Baxter Building juvenile delinquents at Nursery Two?
I don't know about you, but I'm sick of being a grunt. I think this smells, and I'm going to figure it out.
Where are we going?
Sue's lab, to start with. I know she brought some stuff back from that trip.
You're going to ask her what she found?
Yeah. Maybe.

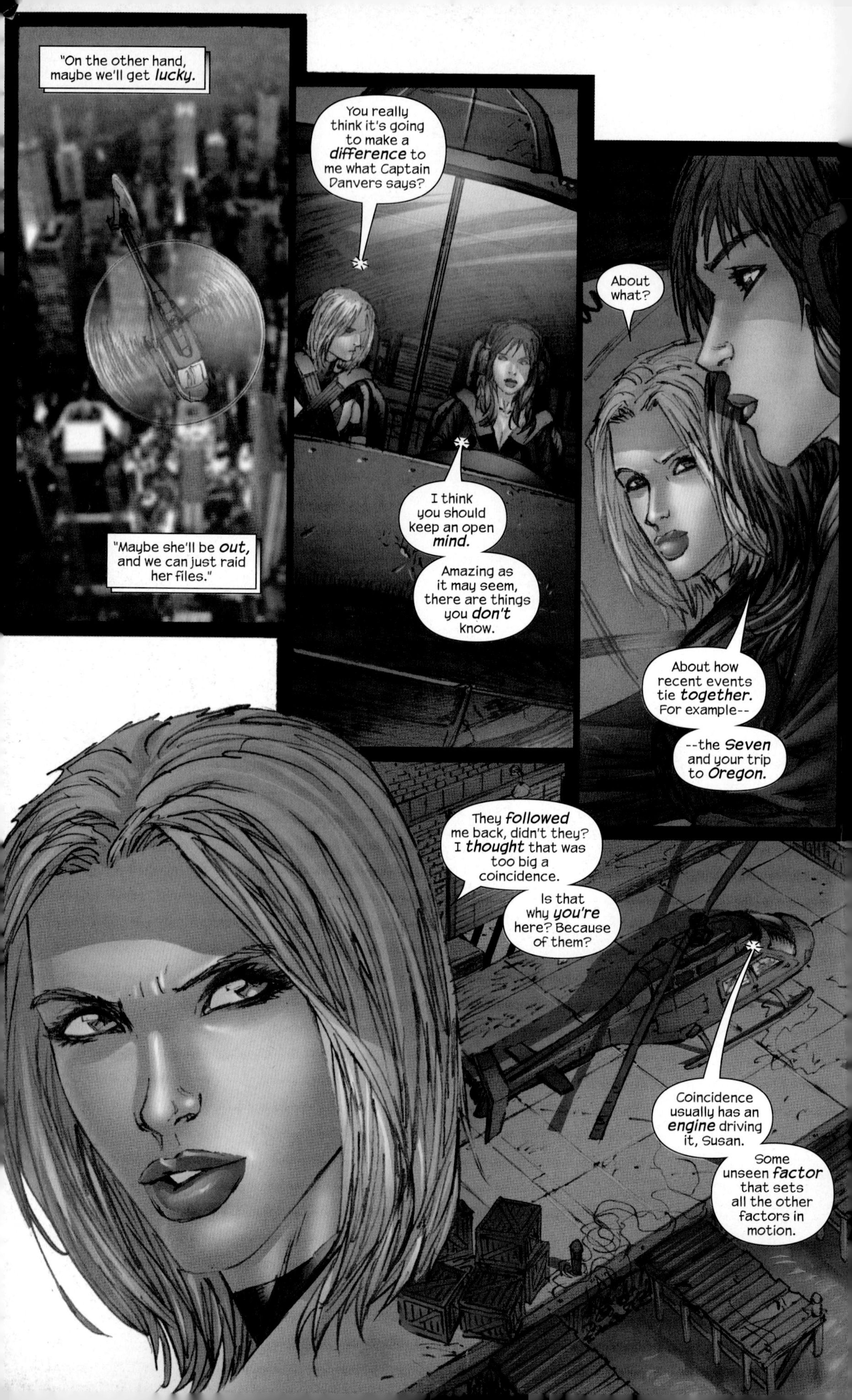
"On the other hand, maybe we'll get *lucky.*
"Maybe she'll be *out,* and we can just raid her files."
You really think it's going to make a *difference* to me what Captain Danvers says?
I think you should keep an open *mind.*
Amazing as it may seem, there are things you *don't* know.
About what?
About how recent events tie *together.* For example--
--the *Seven* and your trip to *Oregon.*
They *followed* me back, didn't they? I *thought* that was too big a coincidence.
Is that why *you're* here? Because of them?
Coincidence usually has an *engine* driving it, Susan.
Some unseen *factor* that sets all the other factors in motion.

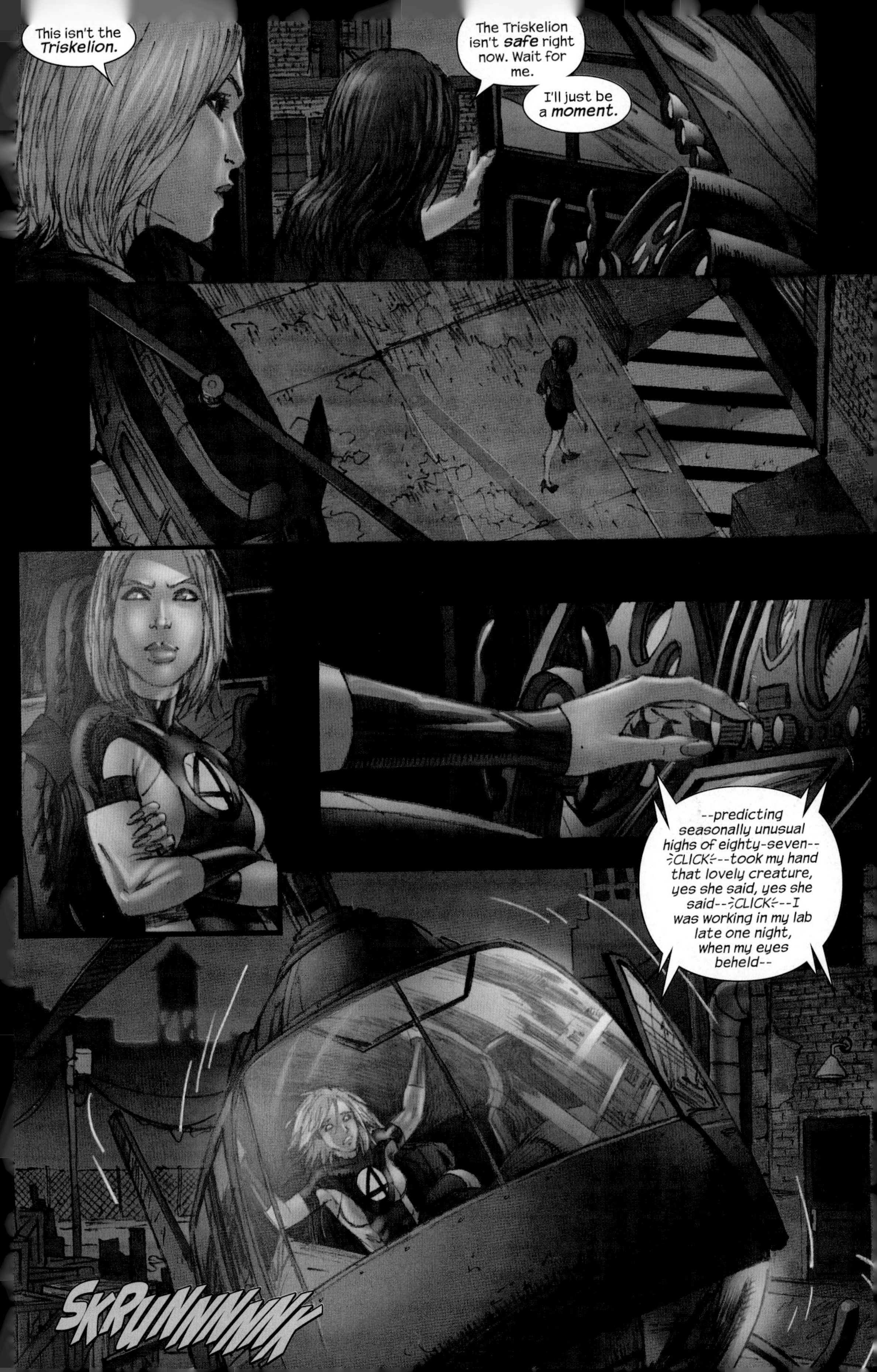

This isn't the *Triskelion.*
The Triskelion isn't *safe* right now. Wait for me.
I'll just be a *moment.*
--predicting seasonally unusual highs of eighty-seven-- ⇒CLICK⇐--took my hand that lovely creature, yes she said, yes she said--⇒CLICK⇐--I was working in my lab late one night, when my eyes beheld--
SKRUNNNNNK

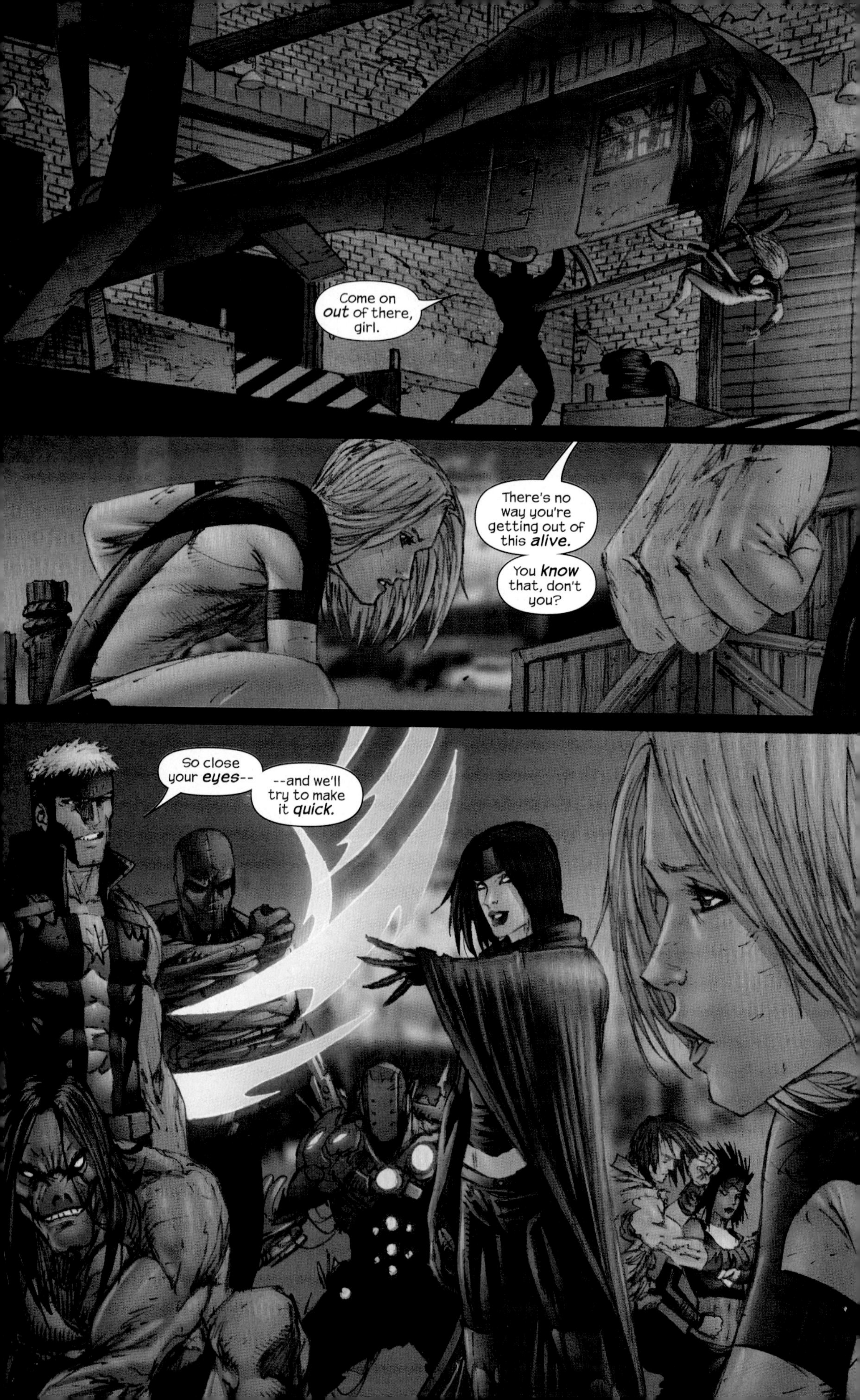
Come on *out* of there, girl.
There's no way you're getting out of this *alive.*
You *know* that, don't you?
So close your *eyes*--
--and we'll try to make it *quick.*

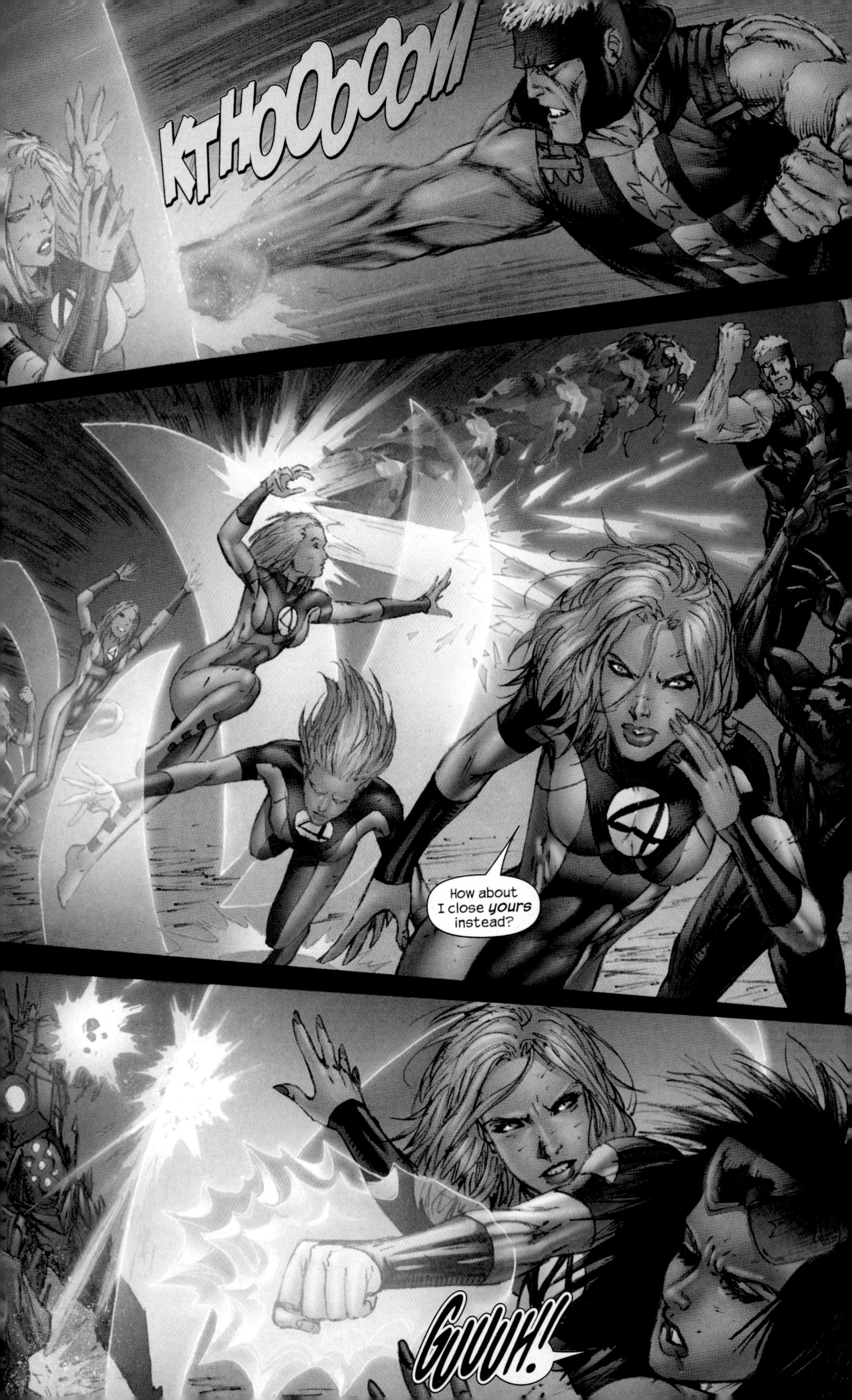
KTHOOOOOM
How about I close *yours* instead?
GUUH!

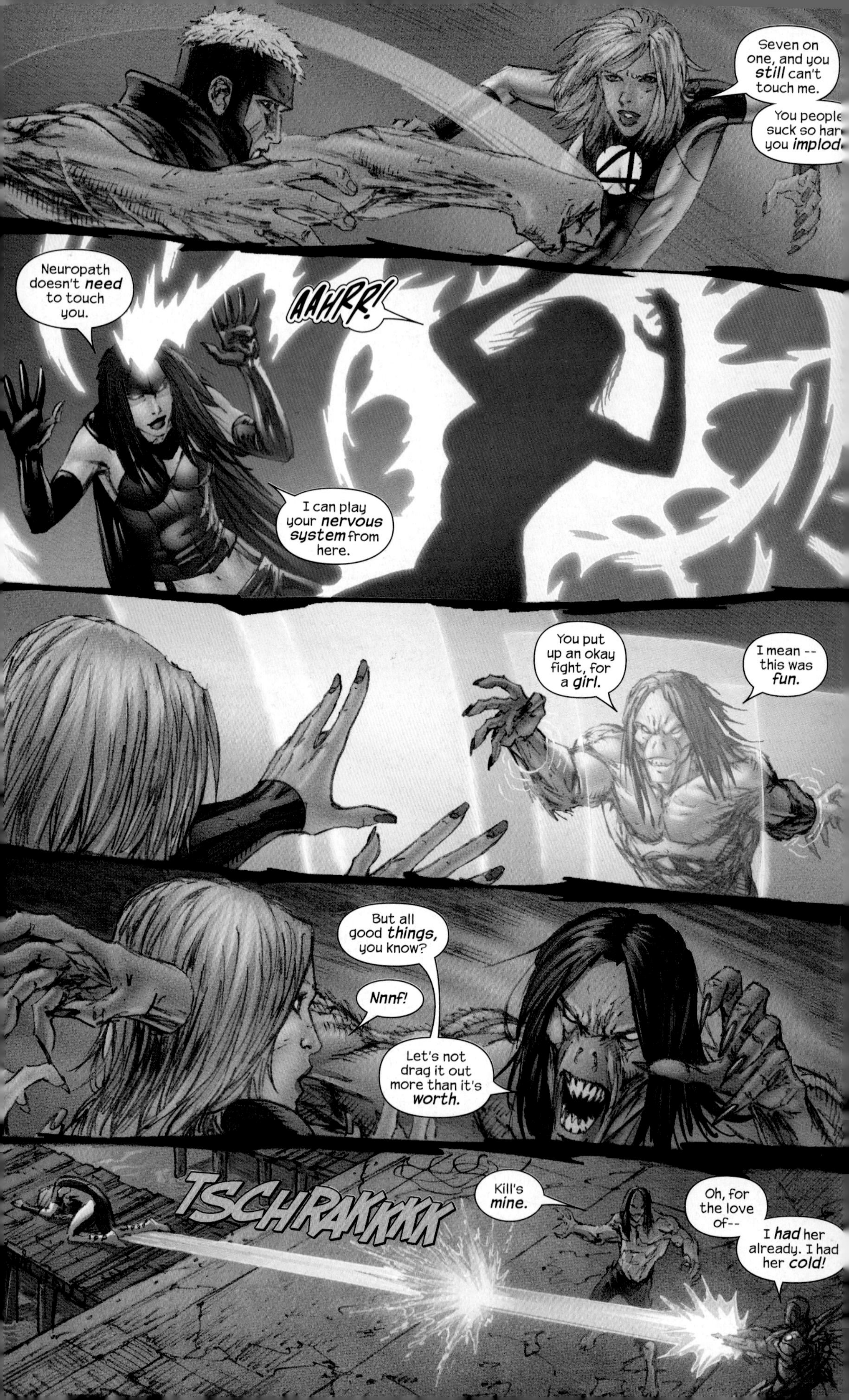

Seven on one, and you *still* can't touch me.
You people suck so hard you *implod*
Neuropath doesn't *need* to touch you.
AAHRR!
I can play your *nervous system* from here.
You put up an okay fight, for a *girl.*
I mean -- this was *fun.*
But all good *things,* you know?
Nnnf!
Let's not drag it out more than it's *worth.*
TSCHRAKKKK
Kill's *mine.*
Oh, for the love of--
I *had* her already. I had her *cold!*

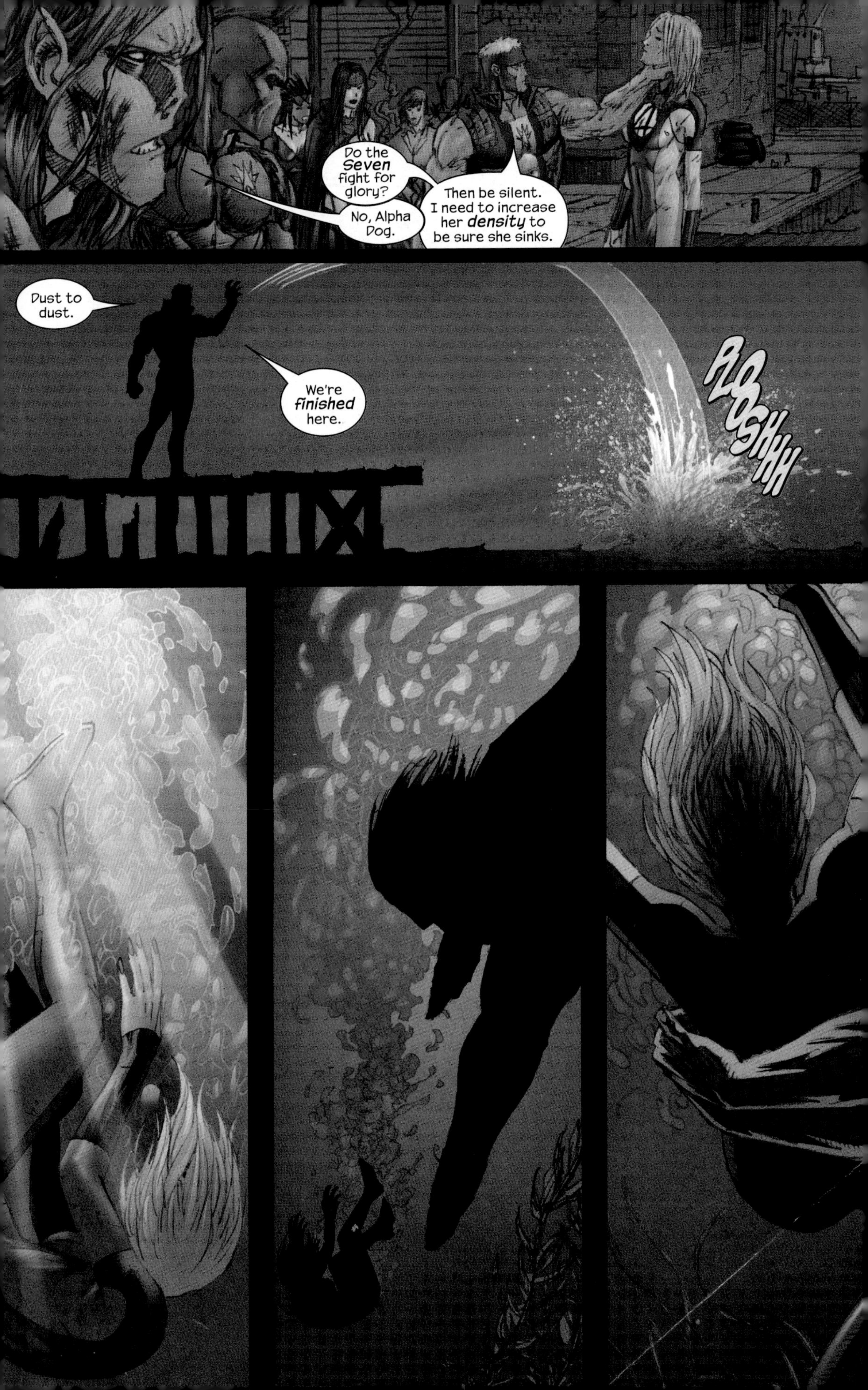
Do the Seven fight for glory?
No, Alpha Dog.
Then be silent. I need to increase her density to be sure she sinks.
Dust to dust.
We're finished here.
PLOOSHHH

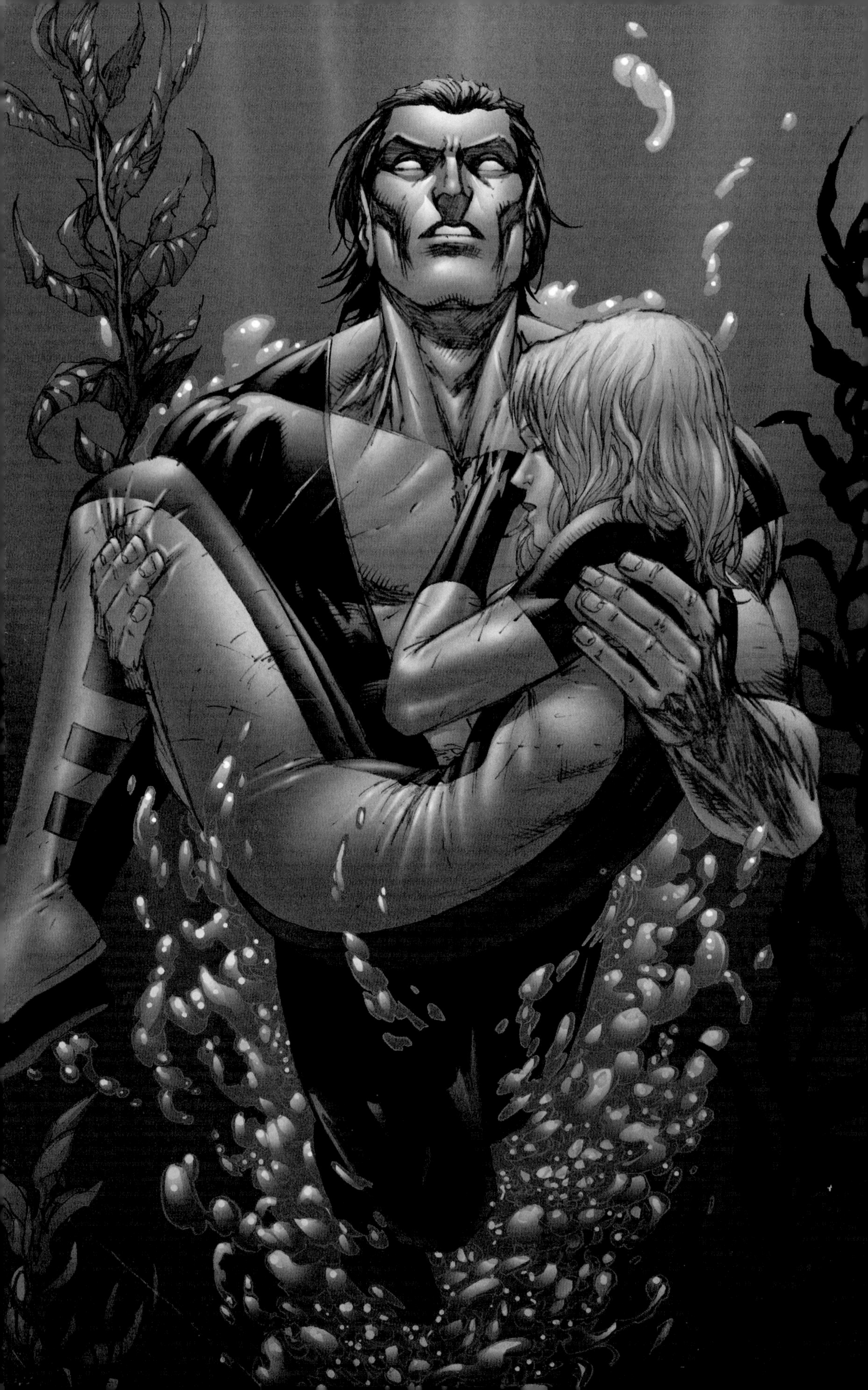

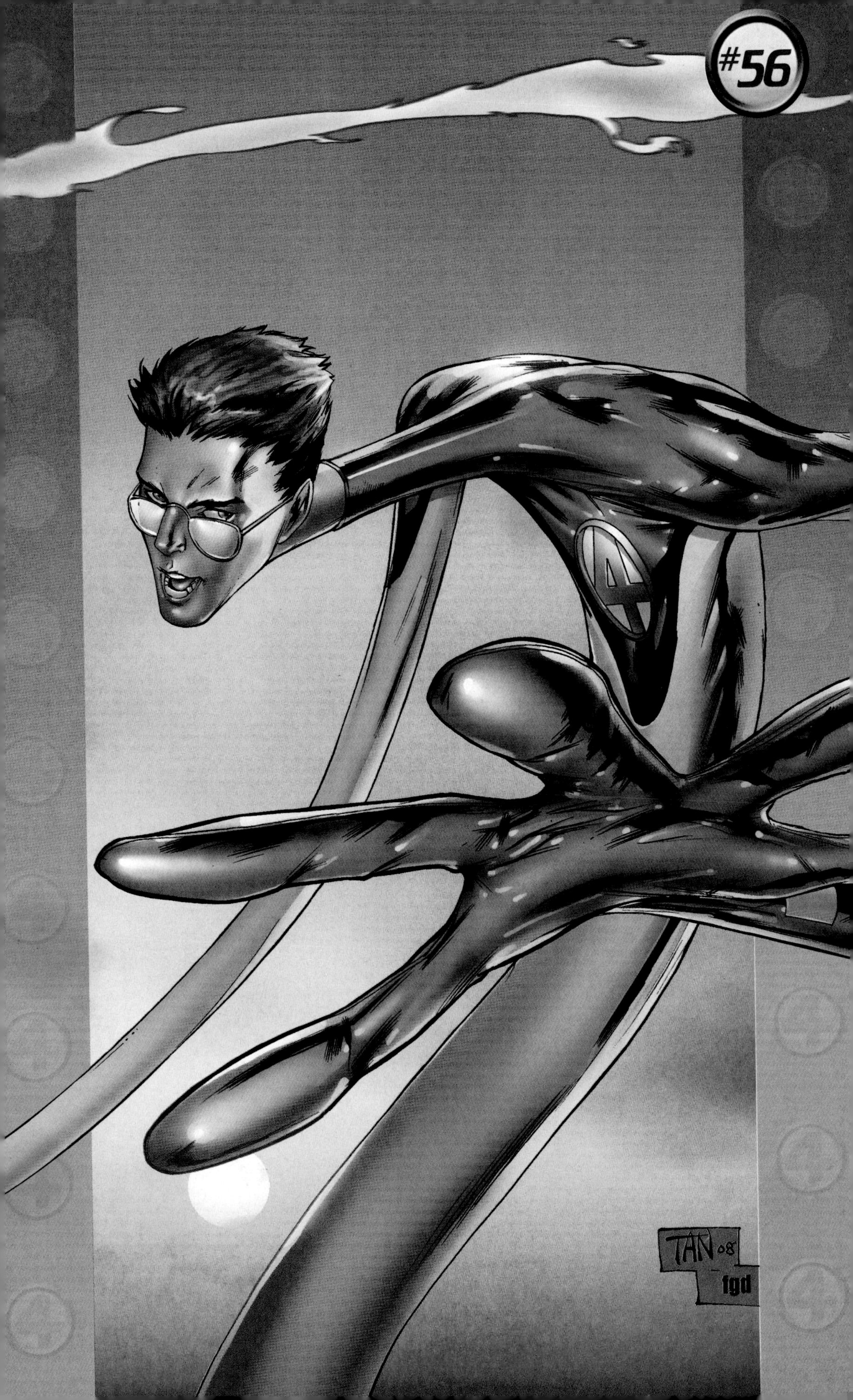
#56
TAN 08
fgd

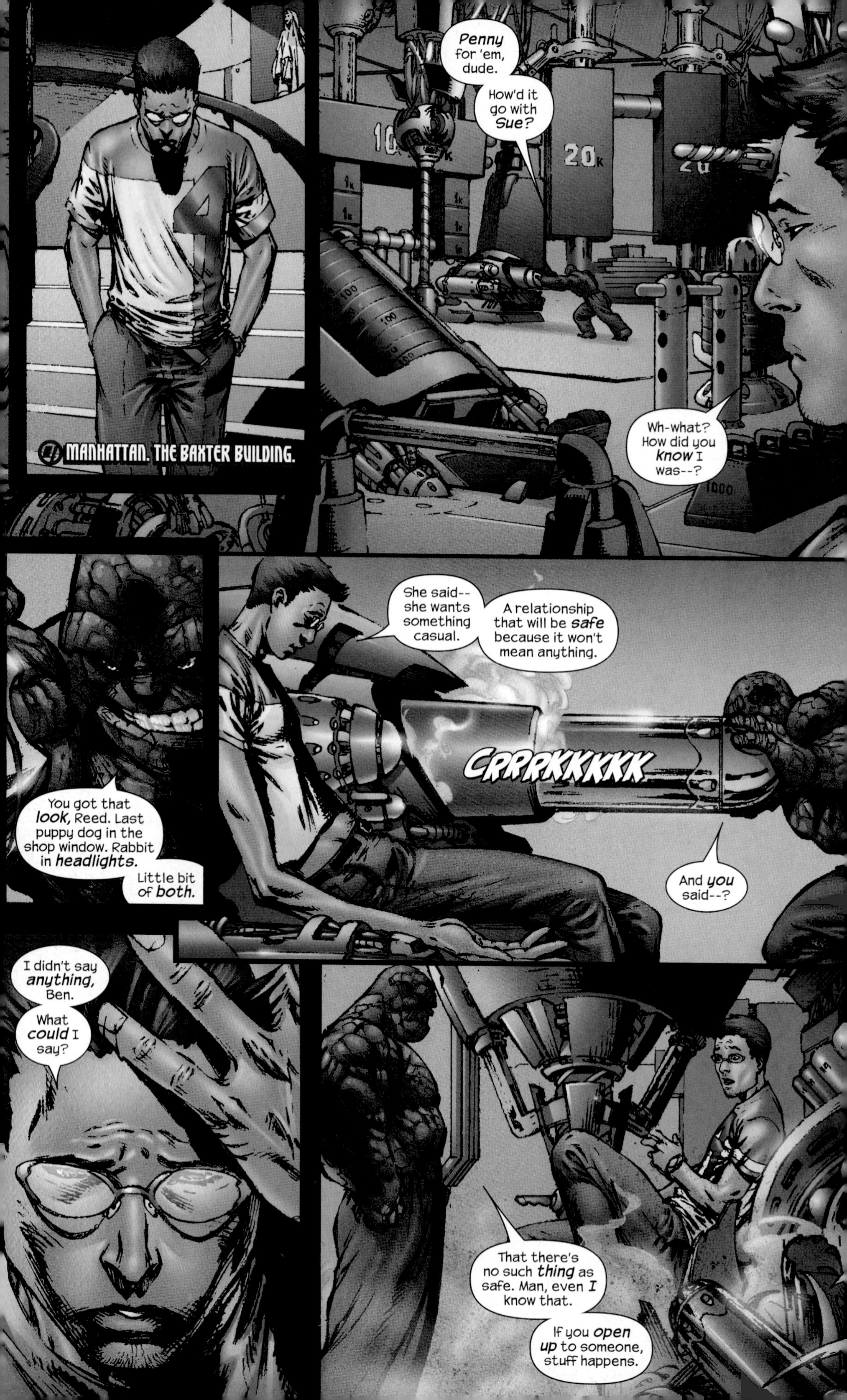
MANHATTAN. THE BAXTER BUILDING.
Penny for 'em, dude.
How'd it go with Sue?
Wh-what? How did you know I was--?
She said--she wants something casual.
A relationship that will be safe because it won't mean anything.
CRRRKKKKK
You got that look, Reed. Last puppy dog in the shop window. Rabbit in headlights.
Little bit of both.
And you said--?
I didn't say anything, Ben.
What could I say?
That there's no such thing as safe. Man, even I know that.
If you open up to someone, stuff happens.

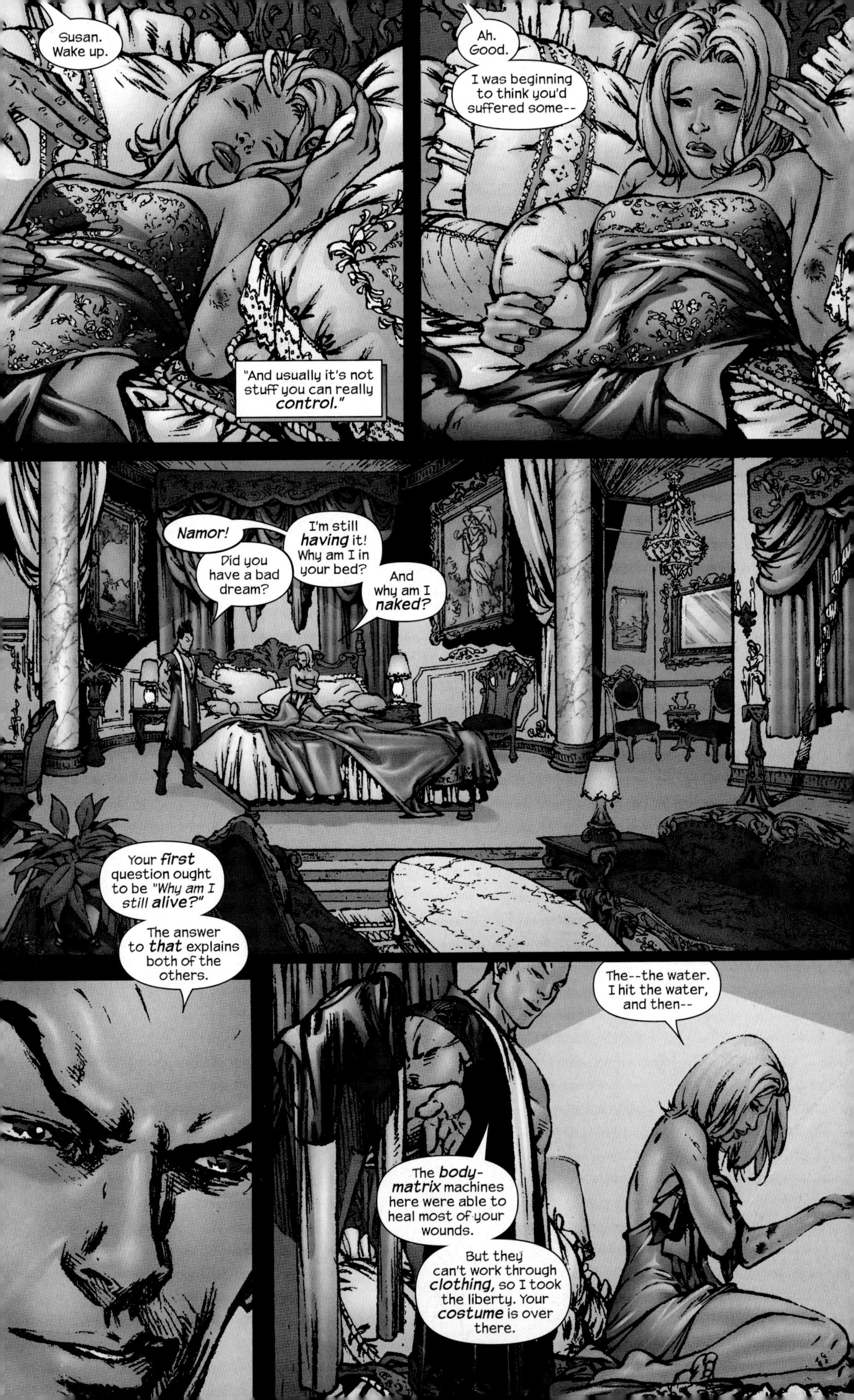
Susan.
Wake up.
"And usually it's not stuff you can really *control.*"
Ah.
Good.
I was beginning to think you'd suffered some--
Namor!
I'm still *having* it! Why am I in your bed?
Did you have a bad dream?
And why am I *naked?*
Your *first* question ought to be *"Why am I still alive?"*
The answer to *that* explains both of the others.
The--the water. I hit the water, and then--
The *body-matrix* machines here were able to heal most of your wounds.
But they can't work through *clothing,* so I took the liberty. Your *costume* is over there.

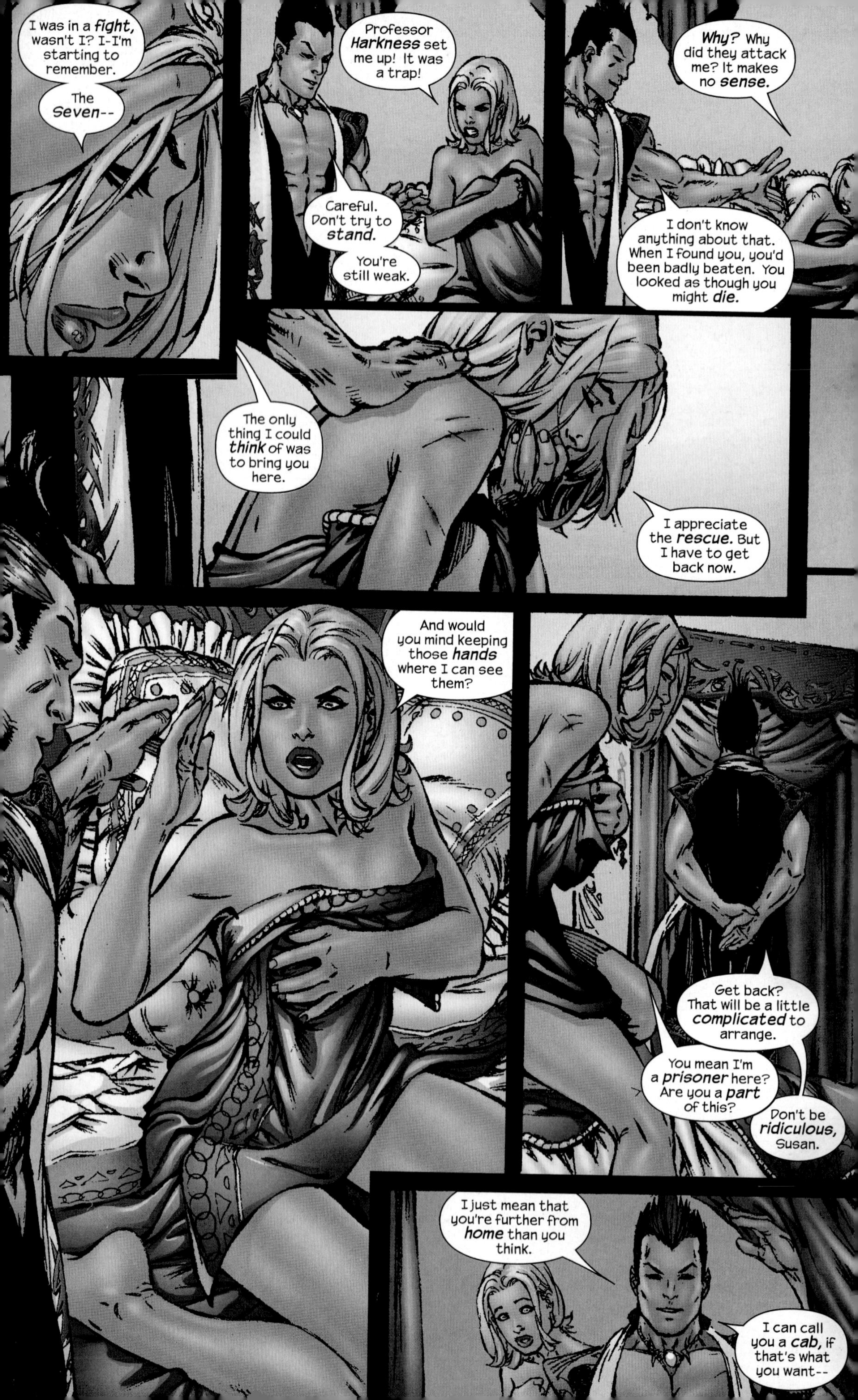
I was in a fight, wasn't I? I-I'm starting to remember.
The Seven--
Professor Harkness set me up! It was a trap!
Careful. Don't try to stand.
You're still weak.
Why? Why did they attack me? It makes no sense.
I don't know anything about that. When I found you, you'd been badly beaten. You looked as though you might die.
The only thing I could think of was to bring you here.
I appreciate the rescue. But I have to get back now.
And would you mind keeping those hands where I can see them?
Get back? That will be a little complicated to arrange.
You mean I'm a prisoner here? Are you a part of this?
Don't be ridiculous, Susan.
I just mean that you're further from home than you think.
I can call you a cab, if that's what you want--

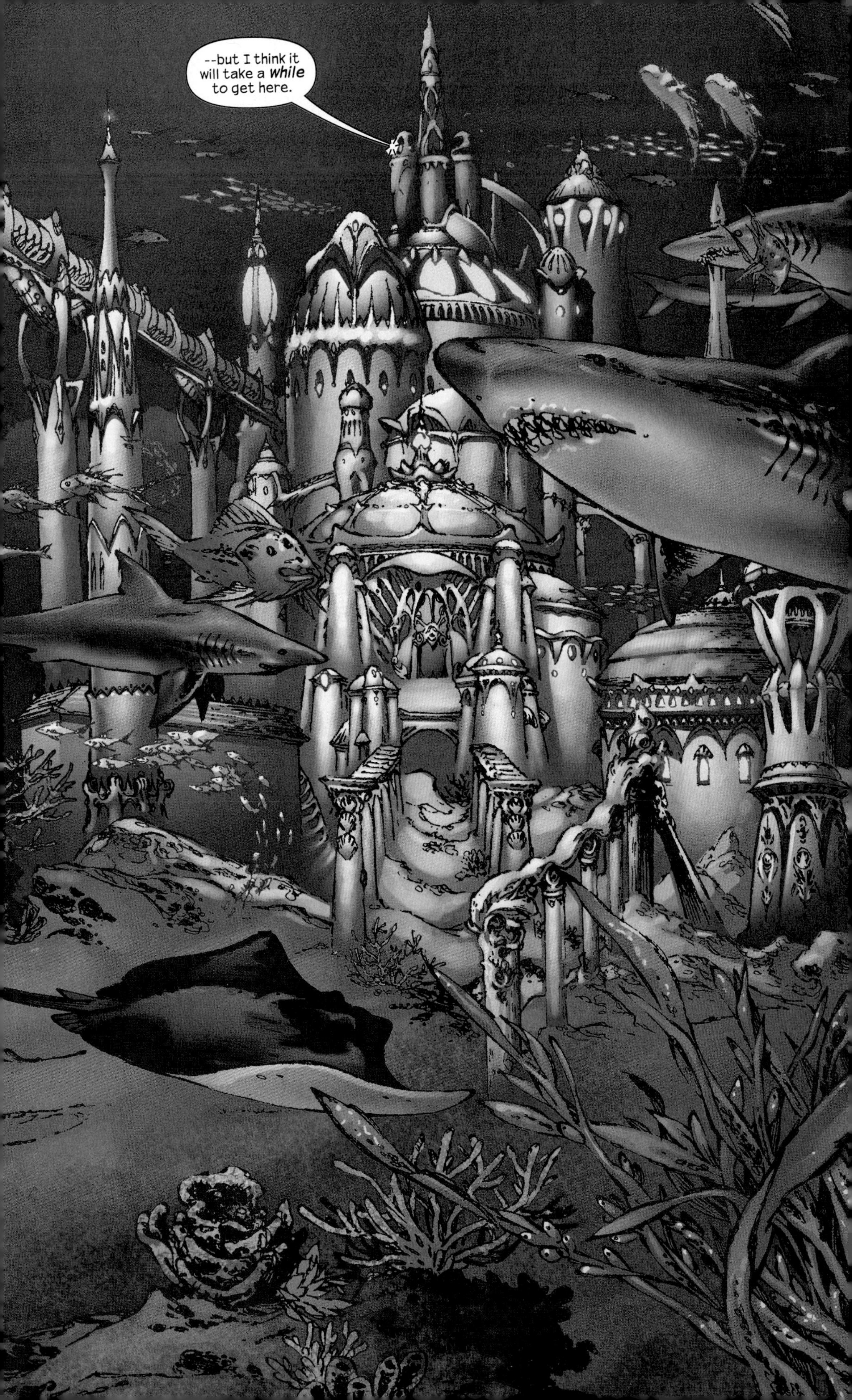
--but I think it will take a *while* to get here.

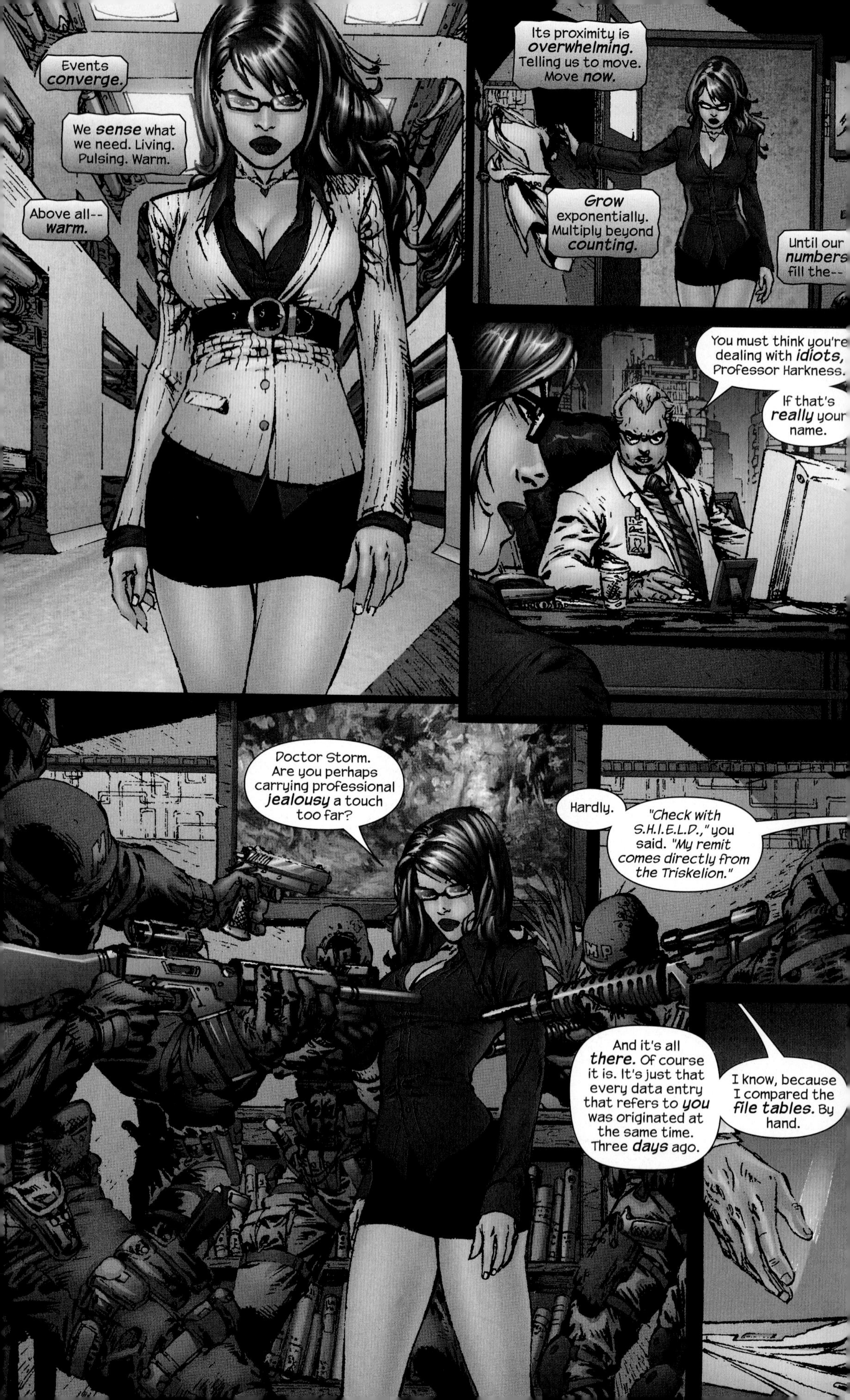
Events converge.
We sense what we need. Living. Pulsing. Warm.
Above all-- warm.
Its proximity is overwhelming. Telling us to move. Move now.
Grow exponentially. Multiply beyond counting.
Until our numbers fill the--
You must think you're dealing with idiots, Professor Harkness.
If that's really your name.
Doctor Storm. Are you perhaps carrying professional jealousy a touch too far?
Hardly.
"Check with S.H.I.E.L.D.," you said. "My remit comes directly from the Triskelion."
And it's all there. Of course it is. It's just that every data entry that refers to you was originated at the same time. Three days ago.
I know, because I compared the file tables. By hand.

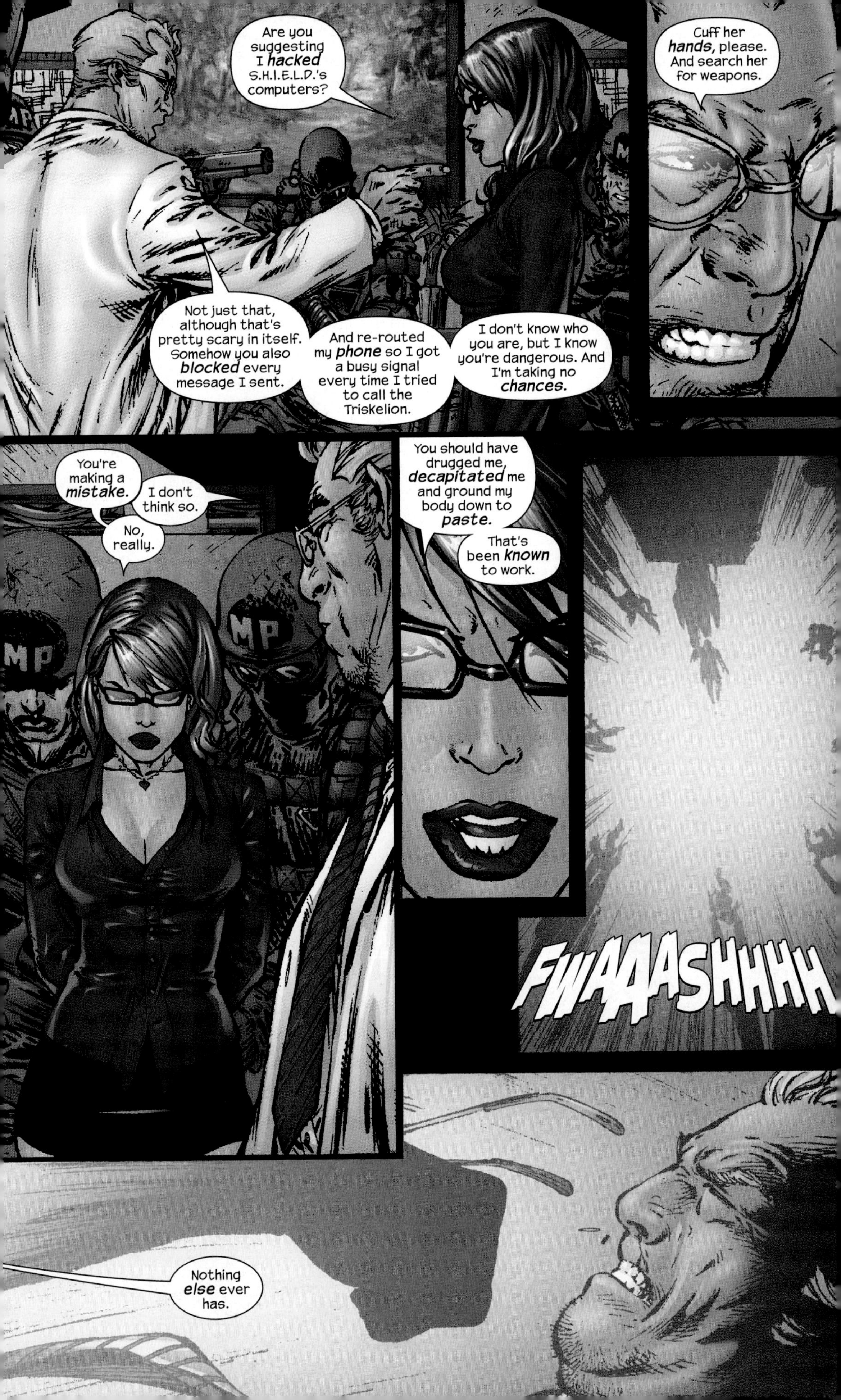

Are you suggesting I hacked S.H.I.E.L.D.'s computers?
Cuff her hands, please. And search her for weapons.
Not just that, although that's pretty scary in itself. Somehow you also blocked every message I sent.
And re-routed my phone so I got a busy signal every time I tried to call the Triskelion.
I don't know who you are, but I know you're dangerous. And I'm taking no chances.
You're making a mistake.
I don't think so.
No, really.
MP
MP
You should have drugged me, decapitated me and ground my body down to paste.
That's been known to work.
FWAAASHHHH
Nothing else ever has.

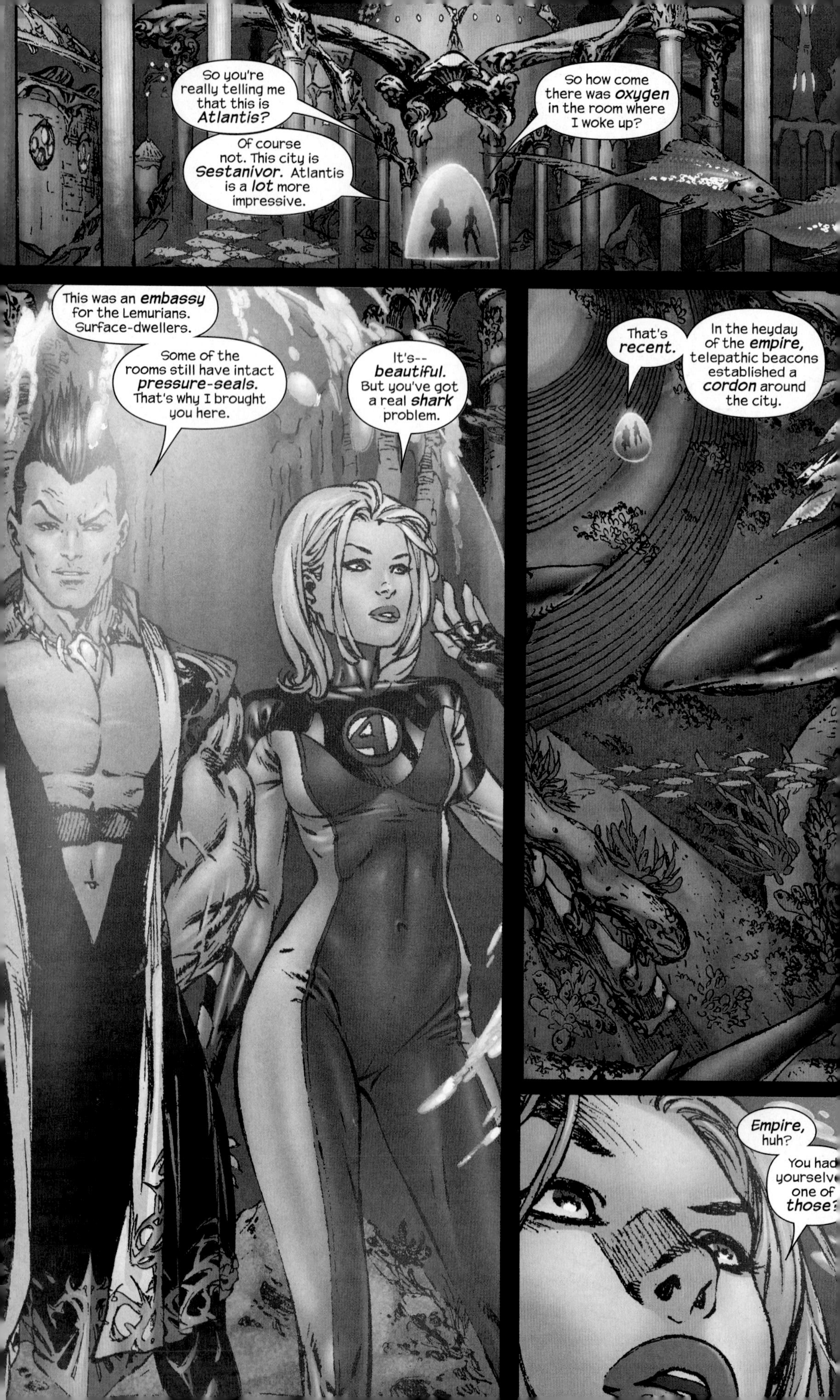
So you're really telling me that this is *Atlantis?*
Of course not. This city is *Sestanivor.* Atlantis is a *lot* more impressive.
So how come there was *oxygen* in the room where I woke up?
This was an *embassy* for the Lemurians. Surface-dwellers.
Some of the rooms still have intact *pressure-seals.* That's why I brought you here.
It's-- *beautiful.* But you've got a real *shark* problem.
That's *recent.*
In the heyday of the *empire,* telepathic beacons established a *cordon* around the city.
Empire, huh?
You had yourselv one of *those?*

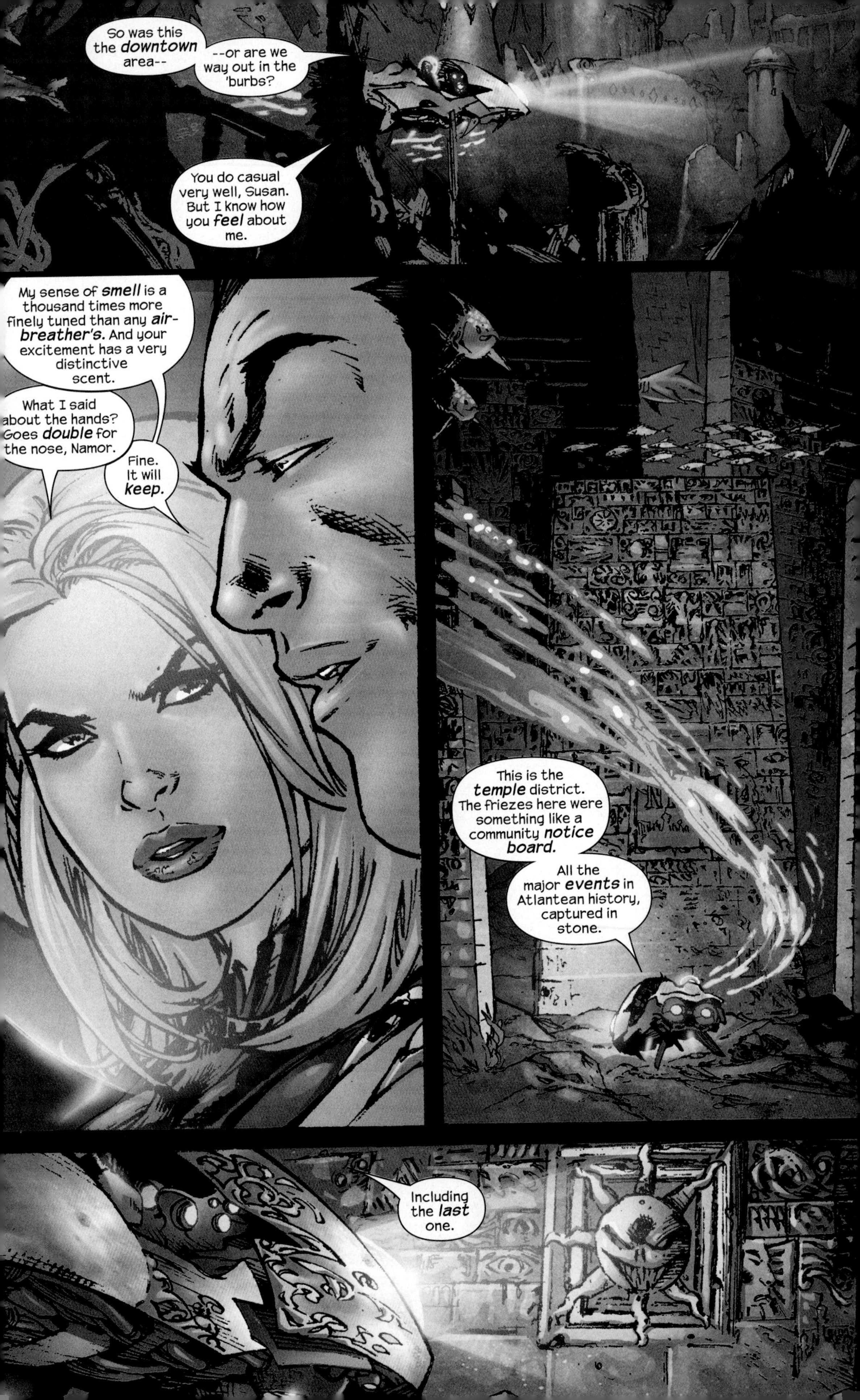
So was this the *downtown* area--
--or are we way out in the 'burbs?
You do casual very well, Susan. But I know how you *feel* about me.
My sense of *smell* is a thousand times more finely tuned than any *air-breather's.* And your excitement has a very distinctive scent.
What I said about the hands? Goes *double* for the nose, Namor.
Fine. It will *keep.*
This is the *temple* district. The friezes here were something like a community *notice board.*
All the major *events* in Atlantean history, captured in stone.
Including the *last* one.

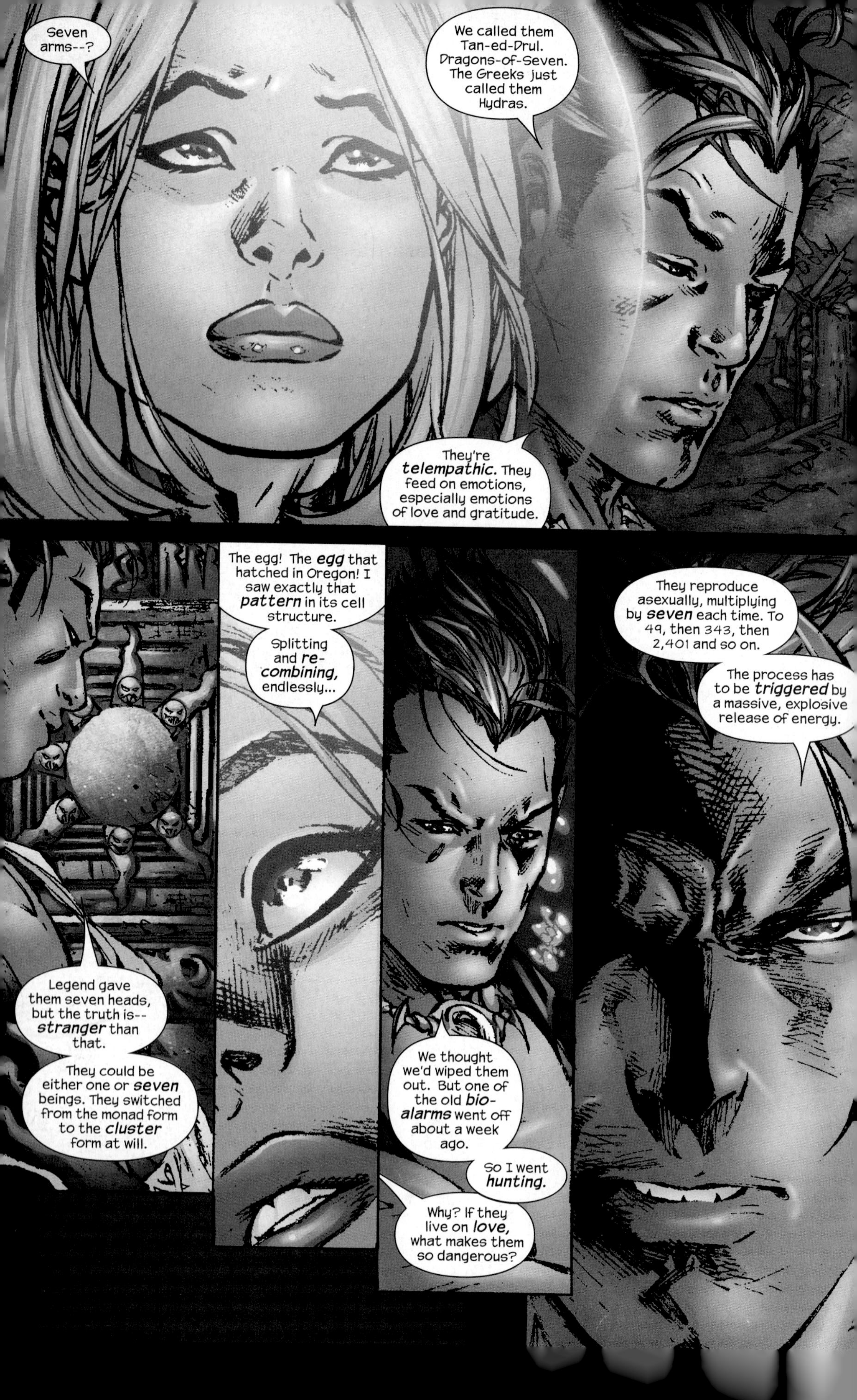

Seven arms--?
We called them Tan-ed-Drul. Dragons-of-Seven. The Greeks just called them Hydras.
They're telempathic. They feed on emotions, especially emotions of love and gratitude.
Legend gave them seven heads, but the truth is--stranger than that.
They could be either one or seven beings. They switched from the monad form to the cluster form at will.
The egg! The egg that hatched in Oregon! I saw exactly that pattern in its cell structure.
Splitting and re-combining, endlessly...
We thought we'd wiped them out. But one of the old bio-alarms went off about a week ago.
So I went hunting.
Why? If they live on love, what makes them so dangerous?
They reproduce asexually, multiplying by seven each time. To 49, then 343, then 2,401 and so on.
The process has to be triggered by a massive, explosive release of energy.

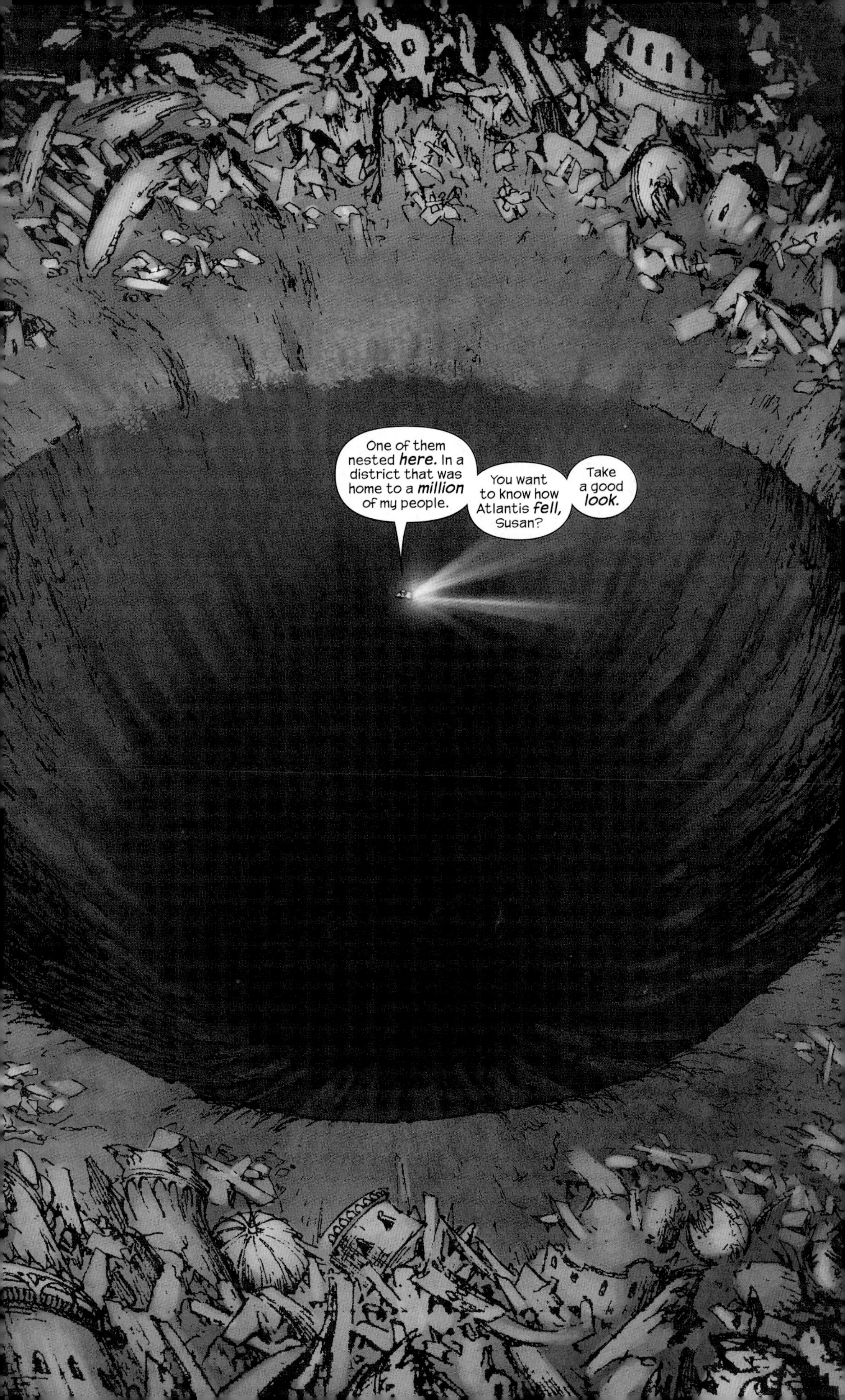
One of them nested *here.* In a district that was home to a *million* of my people.
You want to know how Atlantis *fell,* Susan?
Take a good *look.*

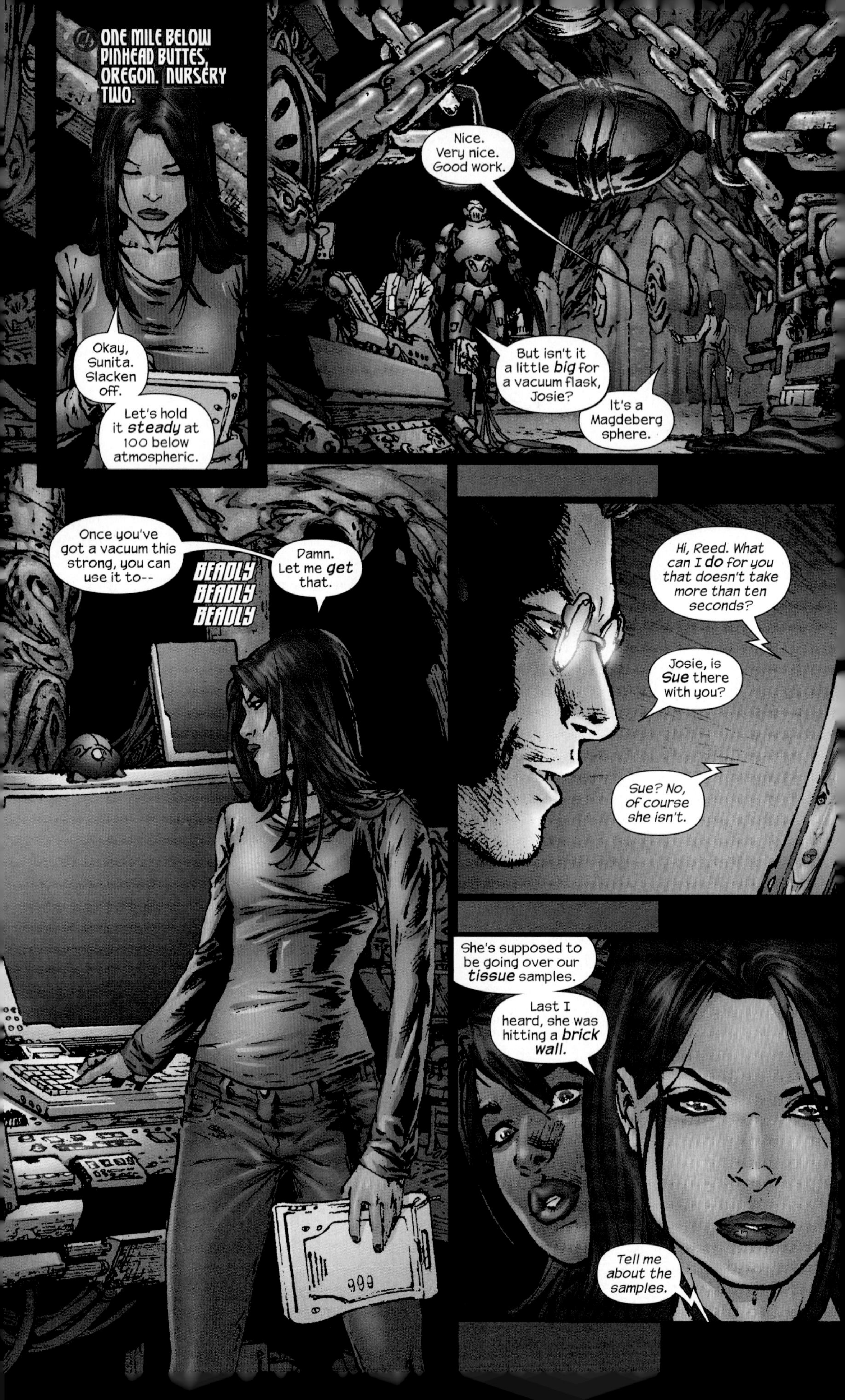
ONE MILE BELOW PINHEAD BUTTES, OREGON. NURSERY TWO.
Okay, Sunita. Slacken off.
Let's hold it steady at 100 below atmospheric.
Nice. Very nice. Good work.
But isn't it a little big for a vacuum flask, Josie?
It's a Magdeberg sphere.
Once you've got a vacuum this strong, you can use it to--
BEADLY BEADLY BEADLY
Damn. Let me get that.
Hi, Reed. What can I do for you that doesn't take more than ten seconds?
Josie, is Sue there with you?
Sue? No, of course she isn't.
She's supposed to be going over our tissue samples.
Last I heard, she was hitting a brick wall.
Tell me about the samples.

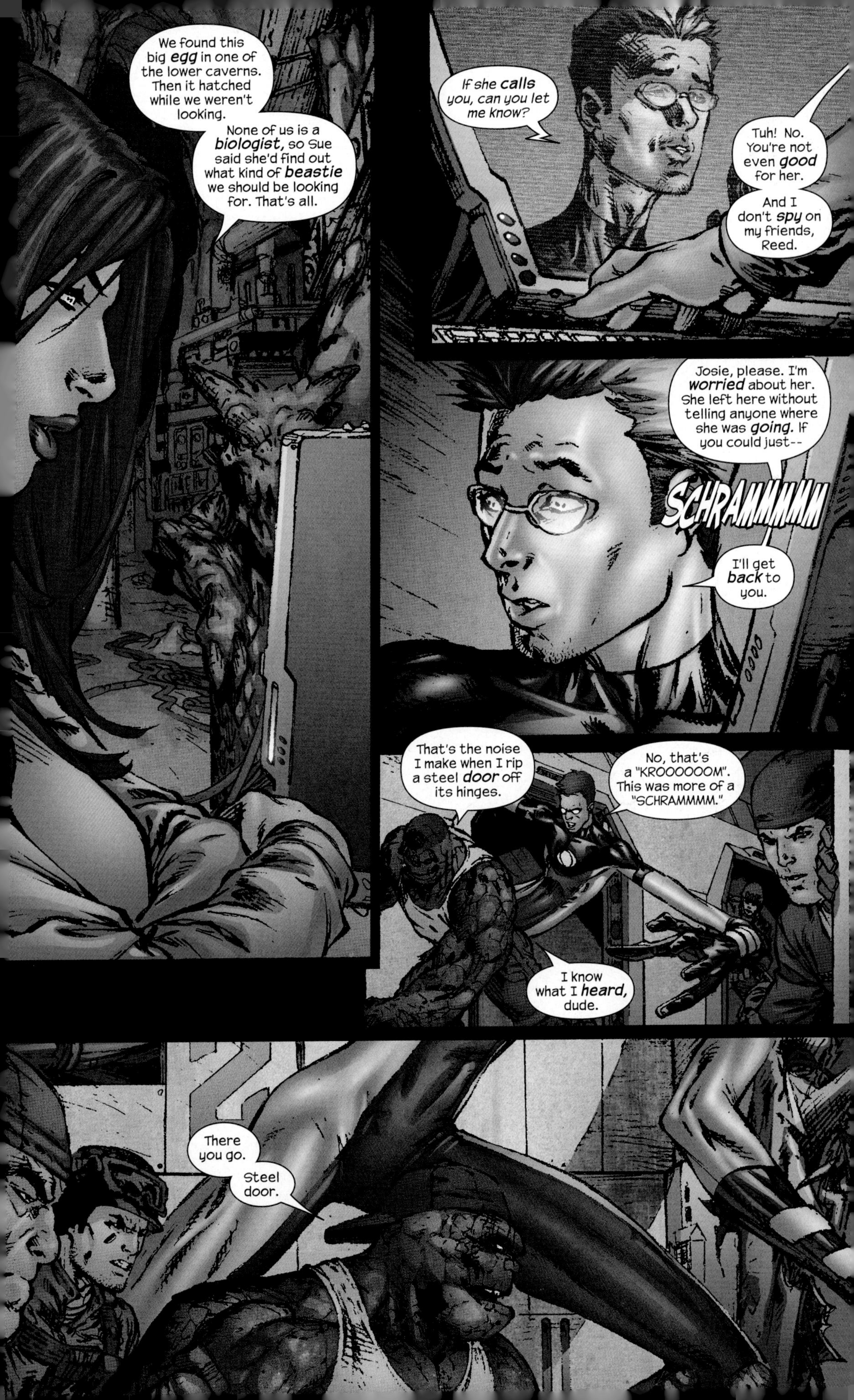
We found this big egg in one of the lower caverns. Then it hatched while we weren't looking.
None of us is a biologist, so Sue said she'd find out what kind of beastie we should be looking for. That's all.
If she calls you, can you let me know?
Tuh! No. You're not even good for her.
And I don't spy on my friends, Reed.
Josie, please. I'm worried about her. She left here without telling anyone where she was going. If you could just--
SCHRAMMMMM
I'll get back to you.
That's the noise I make when I rip a steel door off its hinges.
No, that's a "KROOOOOOM". This was more of a "SCHRAMMMM."
I know what I heard, dude.
There you go.
Steel door.

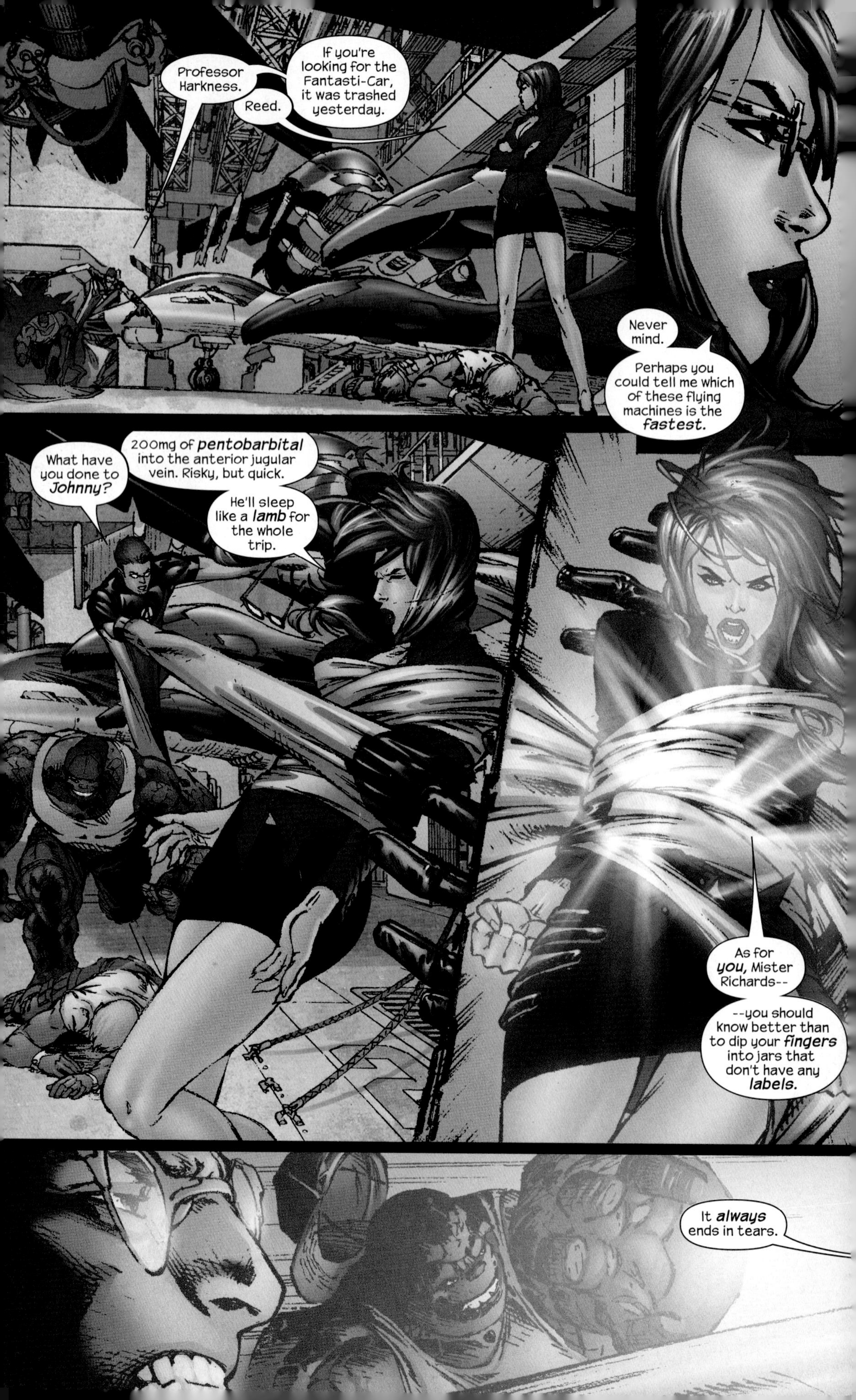

Professor Harkness.
If you're looking for the Fantasti-Car, it was trashed yesterday.
Reed.
Never mind.
Perhaps you could tell me which of these flying machines is the fastest.
What have you done to Johnny?
200mg of pentobarbital into the anterior jugular vein. Risky, but quick.
He'll sleep like a lamb for the whole trip.
As for you, Mister Richards--
--you should know better than to dip your fingers into jars that don't have any labels.
It always ends in tears.

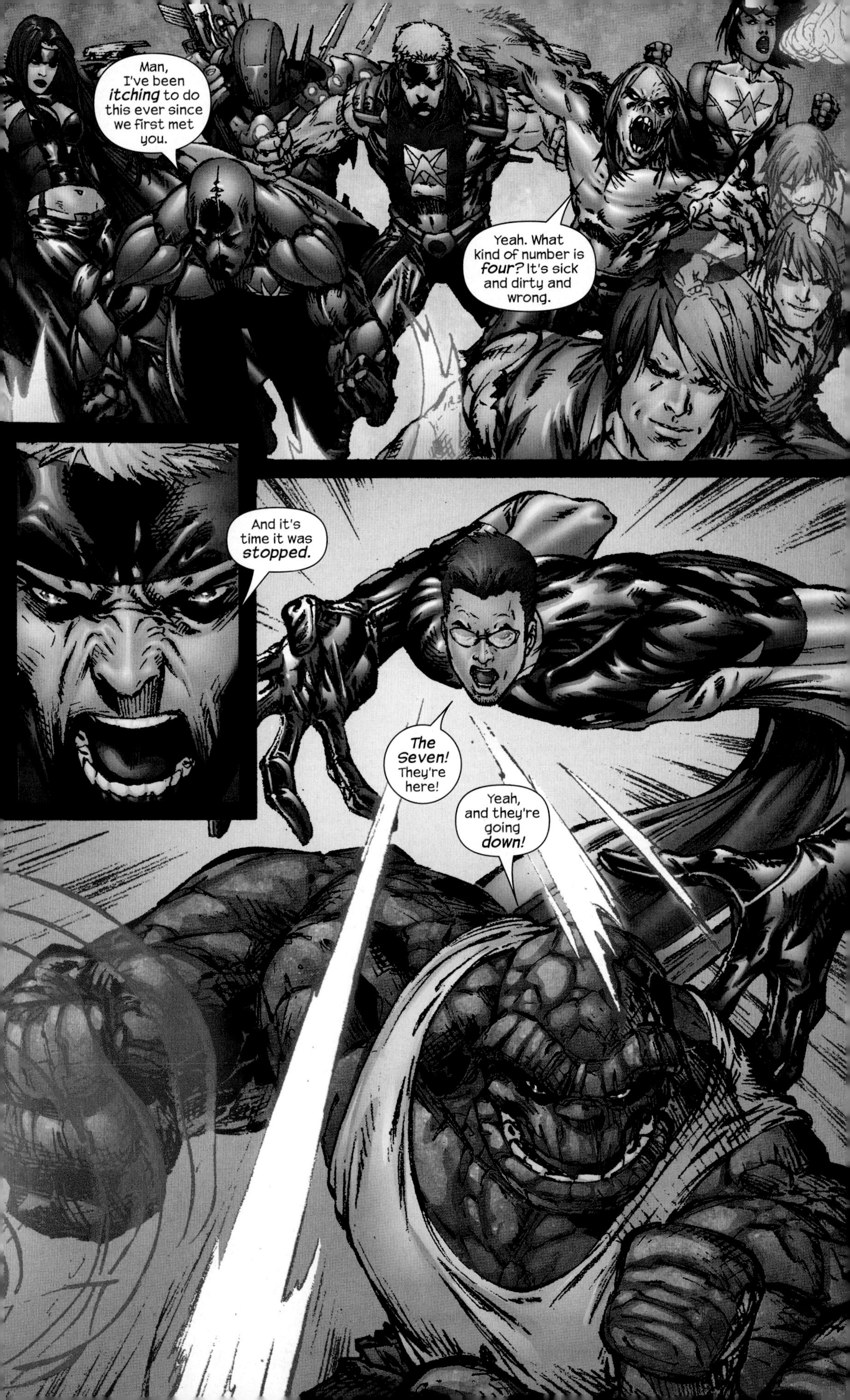

Man, I've been *itching* to do this ever since we first met you.
Yeah. What kind of number is *four?* It's sick and dirty and wrong.
And it's time it was *stopped.*
The Seven! They're here!
Yeah, and they're going *down!*

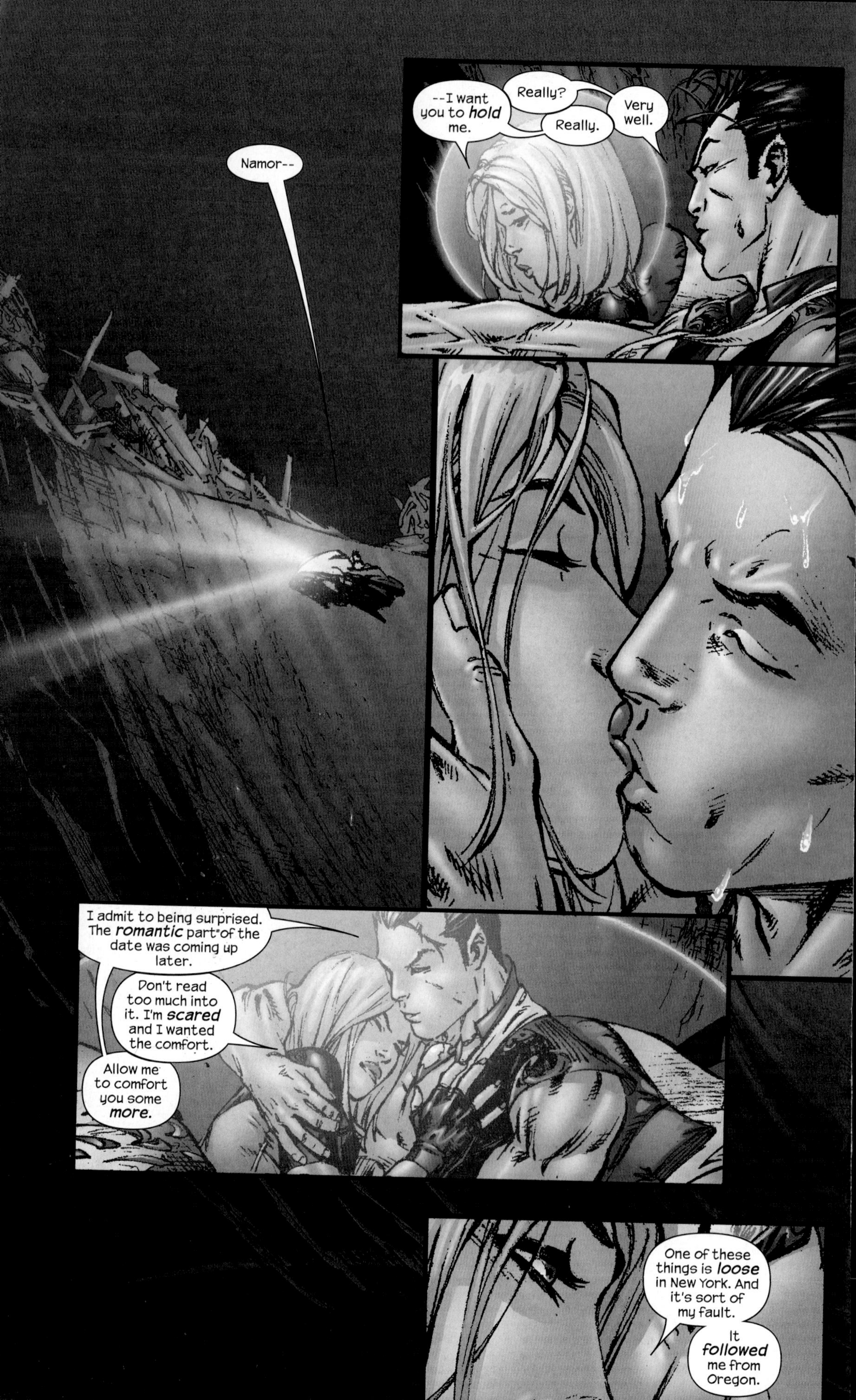
Namor--
--I want you to *hold* me.
Really?
Really.
Very well.
I admit to being surprised. The *romantic* part of the date was coming up later.
Don't read too much into it. I'm *scared* and I wanted the comfort.
Allow me to comfort you some *more.*
One of these things is *loose* in New York. And it's sort of my fault.
It *followed* me from Oregon.

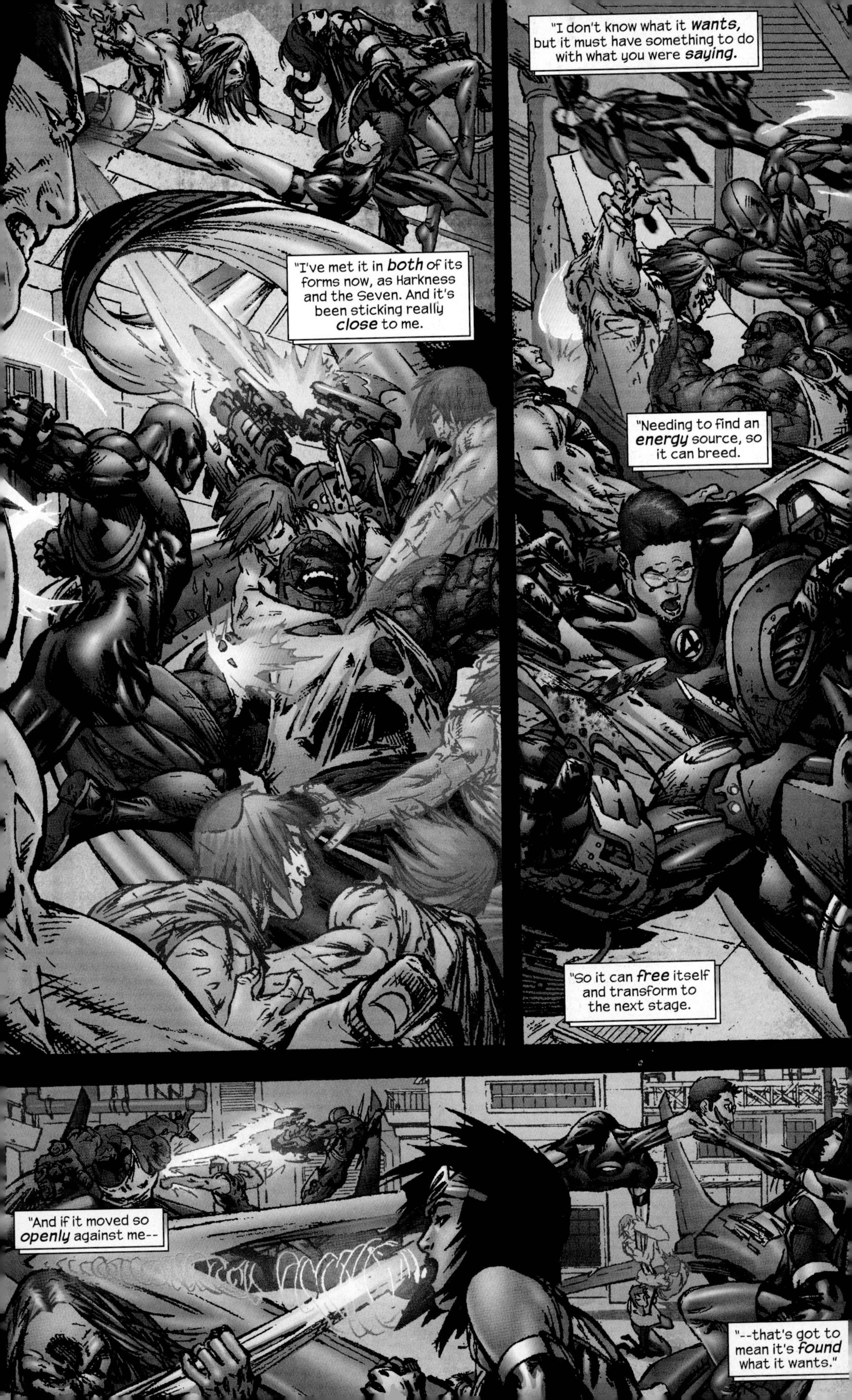
"I've met it in both of its forms now, as Harkness and the Seven. And it's been sticking really close to me.
"I don't know what it wants, but it must have something to do with what you were saying.
"Needing to find an energy source, so it can breed.
"So it can free itself and transform to the next stage.
"And if it moved so openly against me--
"--that's got to mean it's found what it wants."

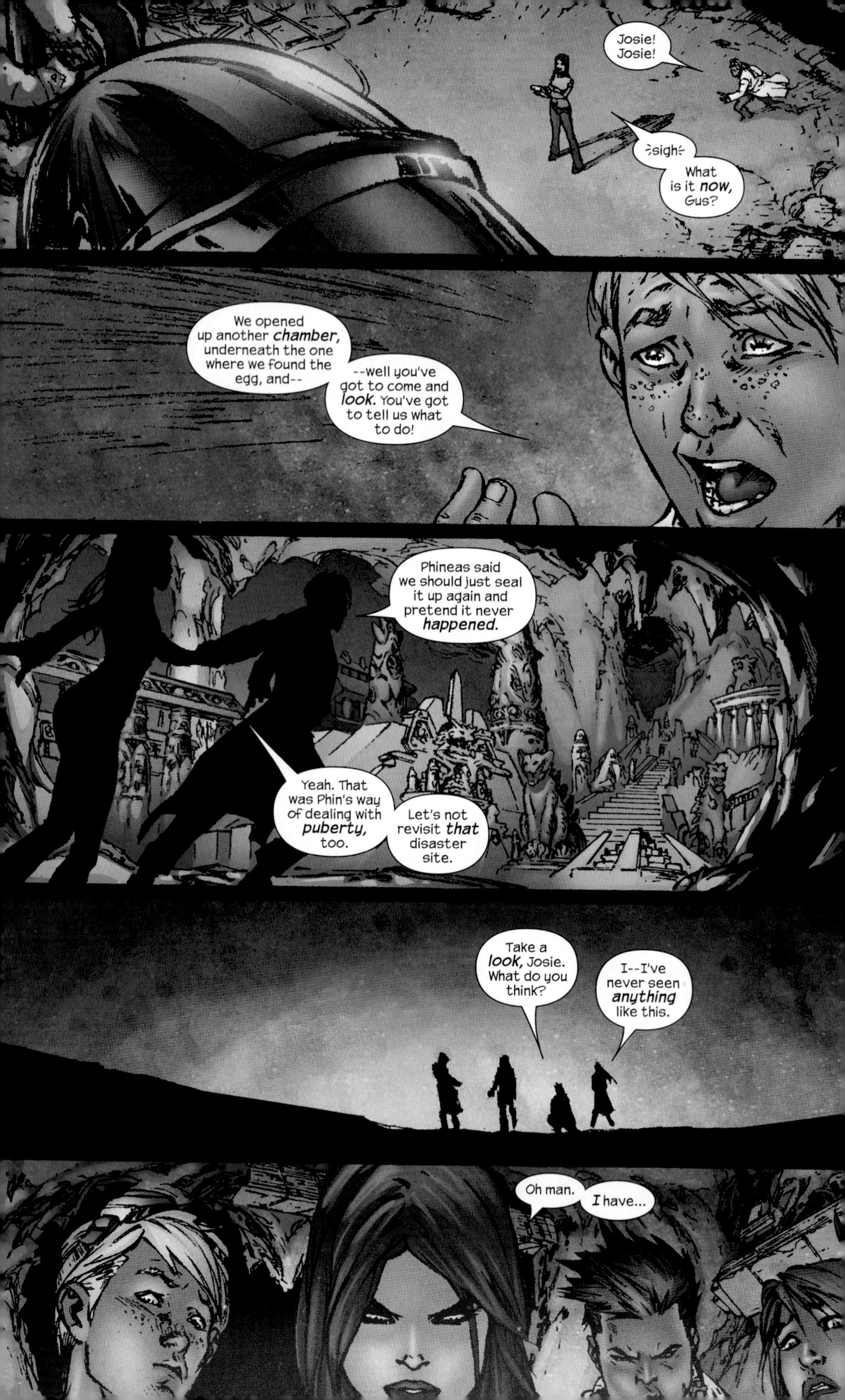
Josie! Josie!
⁓sigh⁓
What is it now, Gus?
We opened up another chamber, underneath the one where we found the egg, and--
--well you've got to come and look. You've got to tell us what to do!
Phineas said we should just seal it up again and pretend it never happened.
Yeah. That was Phin's way of dealing with puberty, too.
Let's not revisit that disaster site.
Take a look, Josie. What do you think?
I--I've never seen anything like this.
Oh man.
I have...

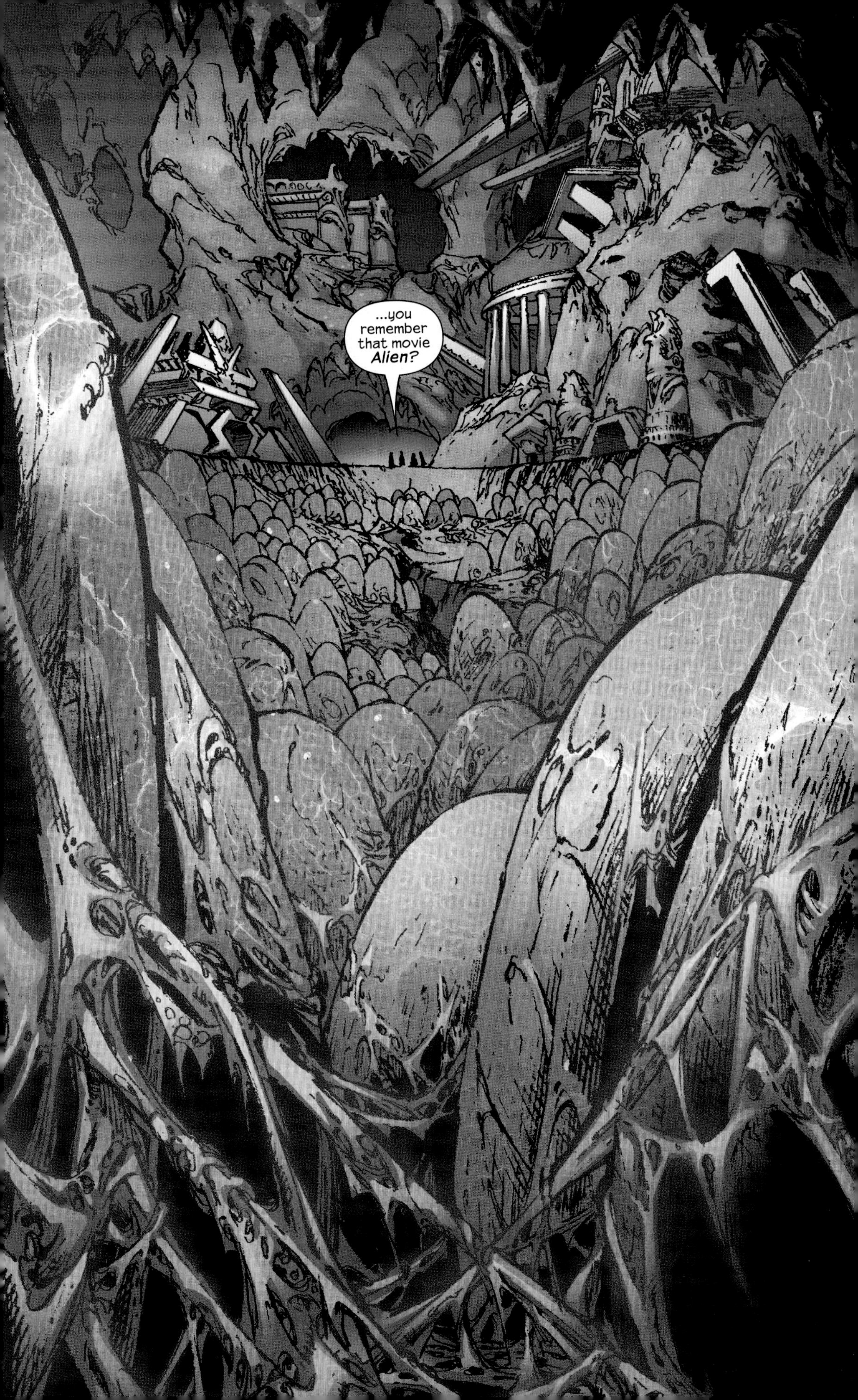
...you remember that movie *Alien*?

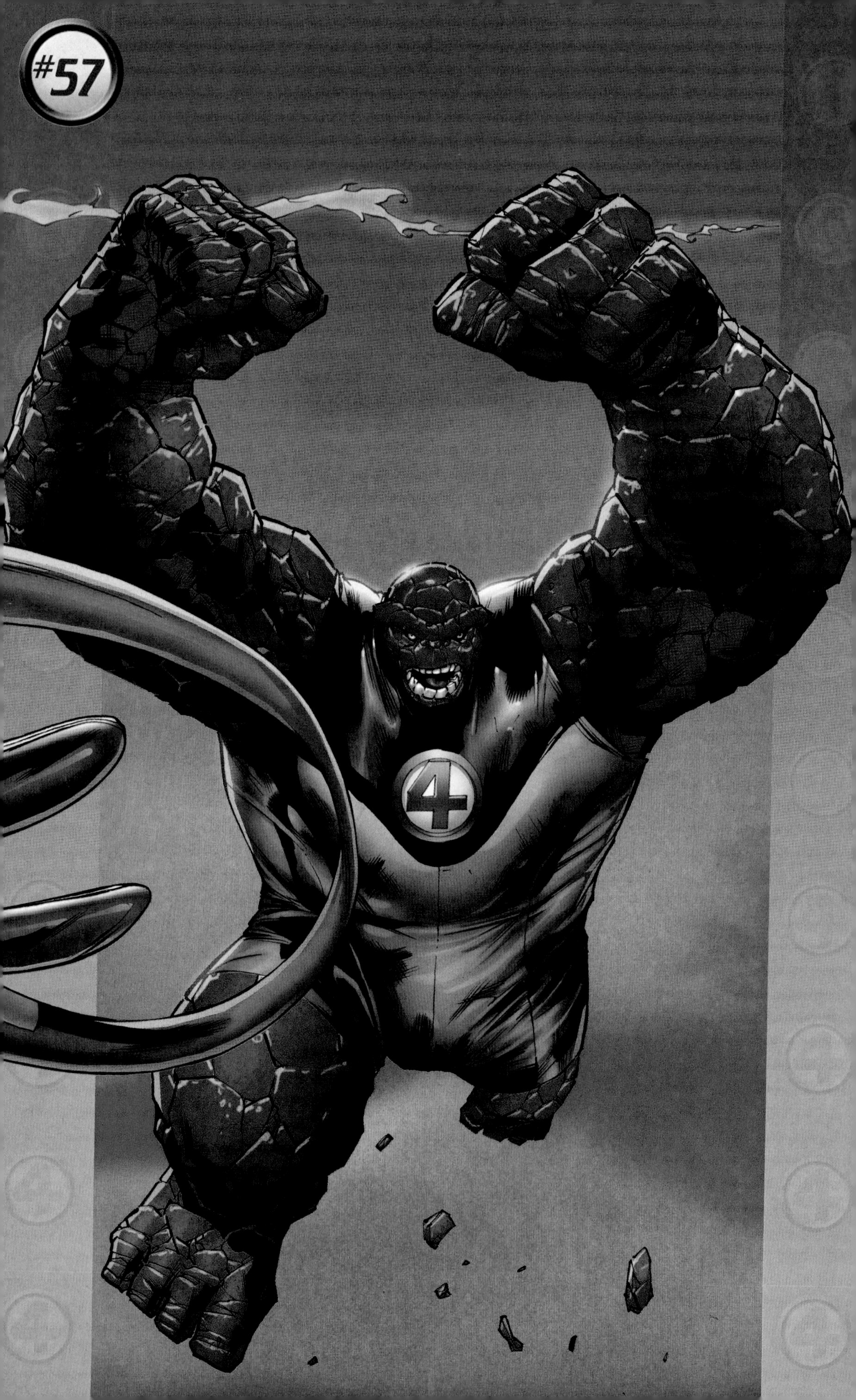
#57

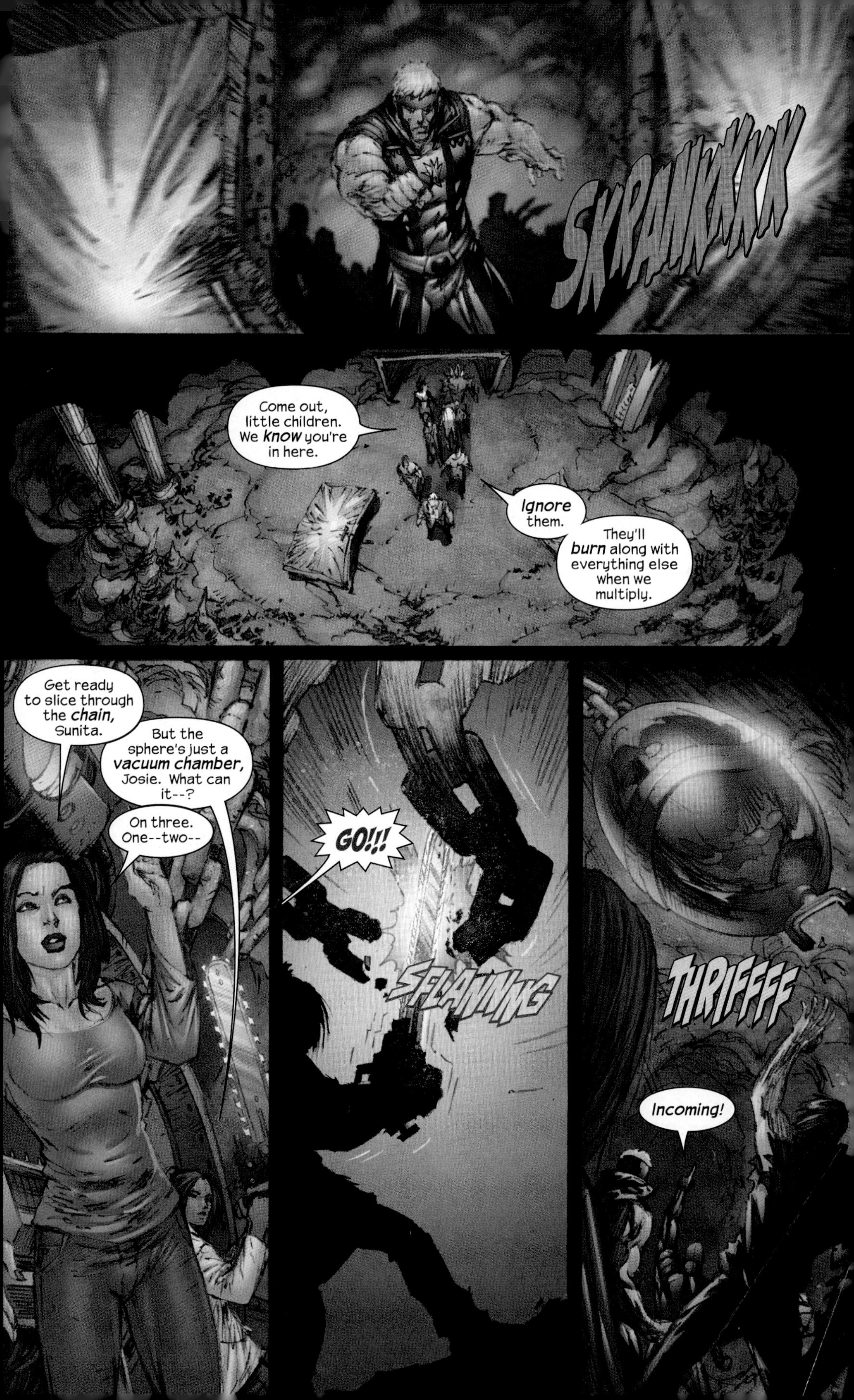
SKRANKKKK
Come out, little children. We *know* you're in here.
Ignore them.
They'll *burn* along with everything else when we multiply.
Get ready to slice through the *chain,* Sunita.
But the sphere's just a *vacuum chamber,* Josie. What can it--?
On three. One--two--
GO!!!
SFLANNNG
THRIFFFF
Incoming!

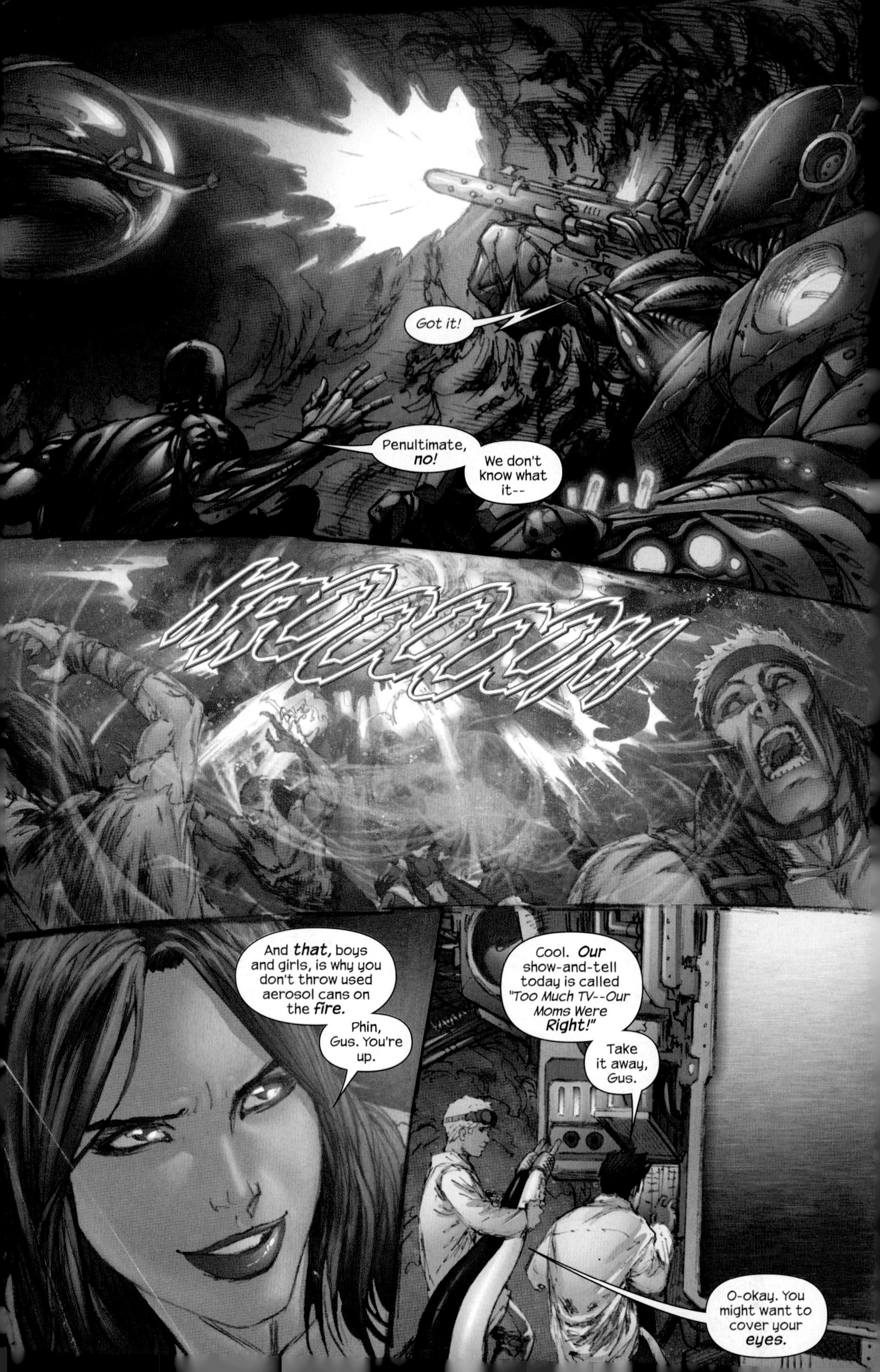

Got it!
Penultimate, *no!*
We don't know what it--
KRA-BOOOOM
And *that,* boys and girls, is why you don't throw used aerosol cans on the *fire.*
Phin, Gus. You're up.
Cool. *Our* show-and-tell today is called *"Too Much TV--Our Moms Were Right!"*
Take it away, Gus.
O-okay. You might want to cover your *eyes.*

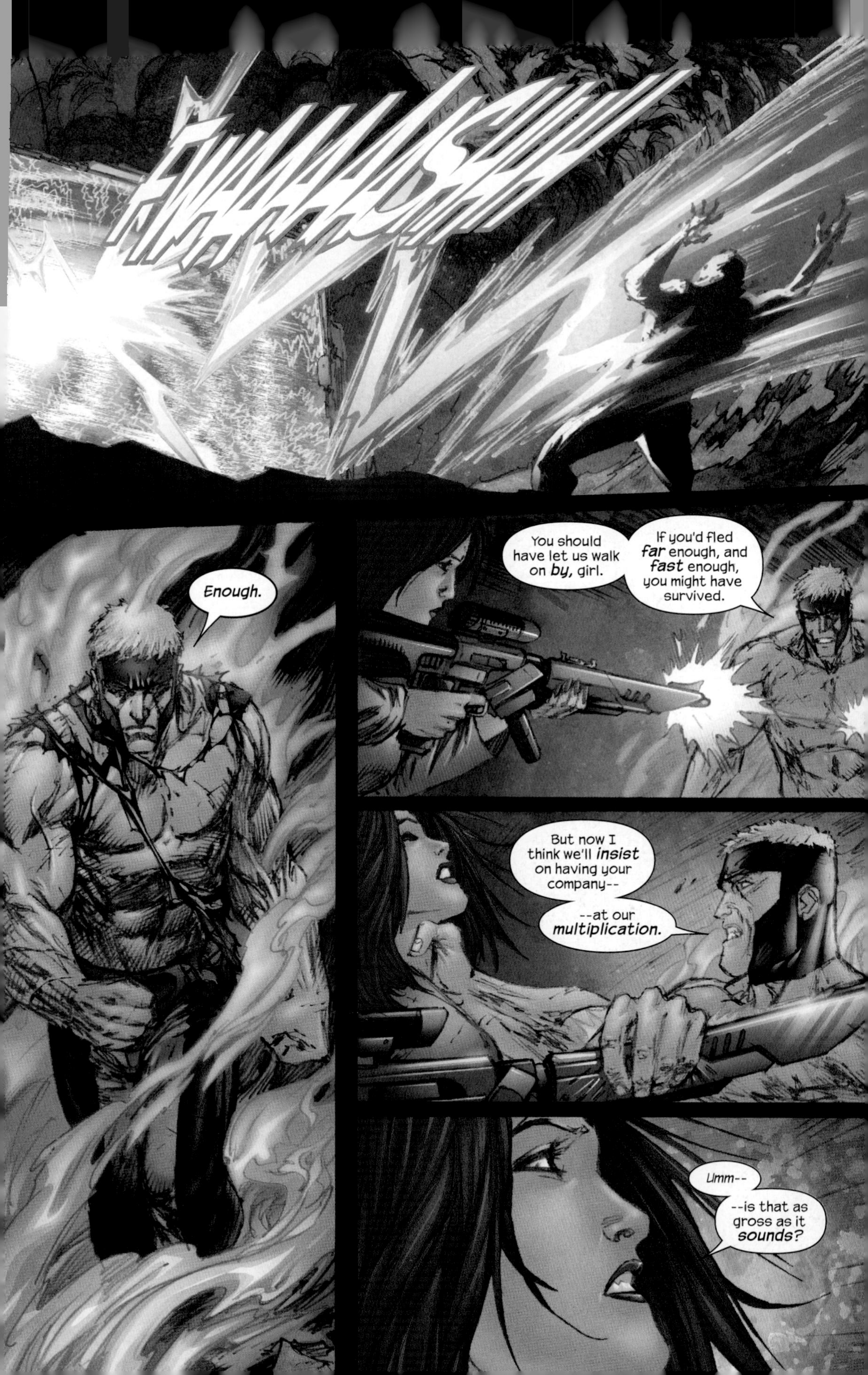
FWAAASHH
Enough.
You should have let us walk on by, girl.
If you'd fled far enough, and fast enough, you might have survived.
But now I think we'll insist on having your company--
--at our multiplication.
Umm--
--is that as gross as it sounds?

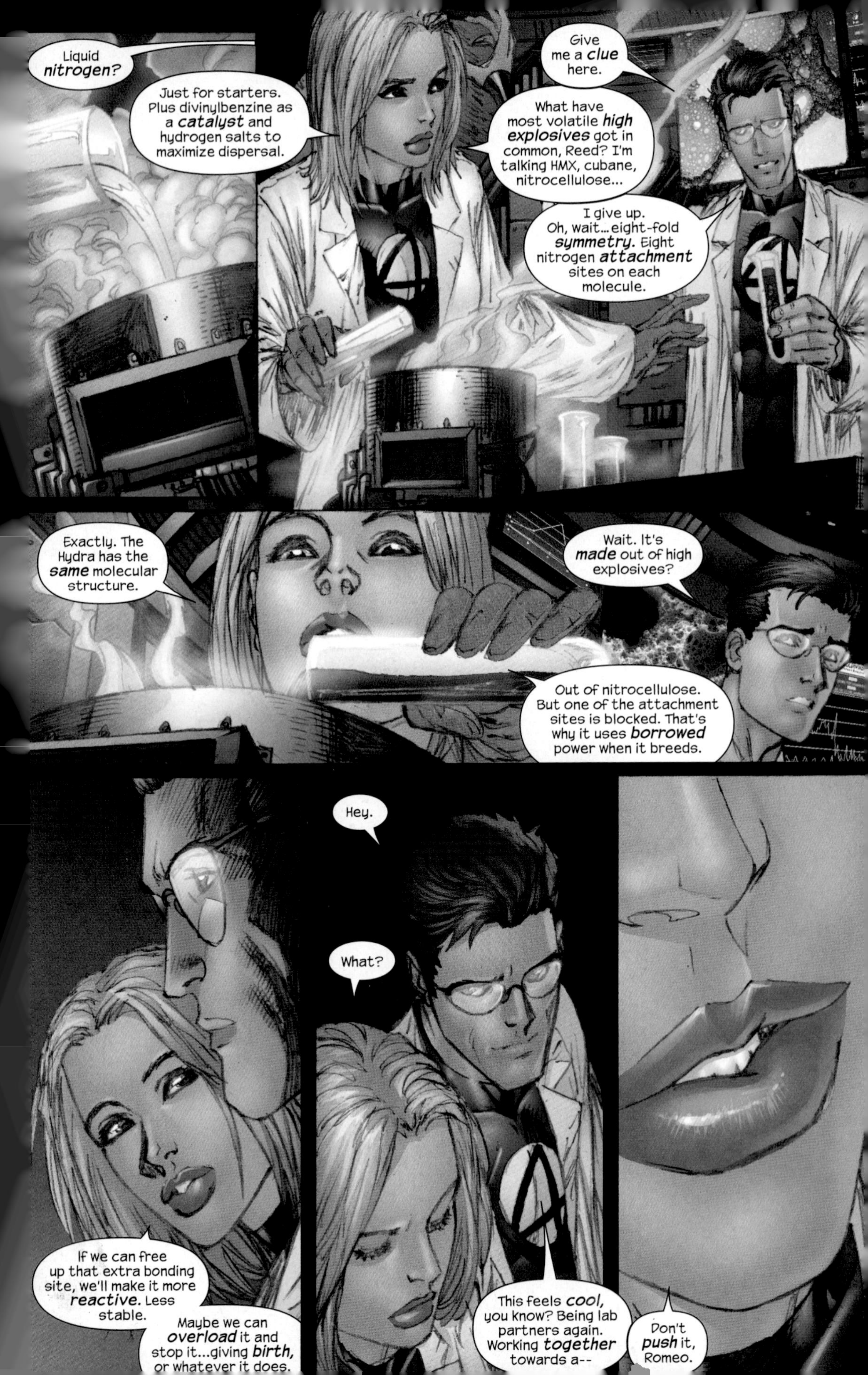

Liquid nitrogen?
Just for starters. Plus divinylbenzine as a catalyst and hydrogen salts to maximize dispersal.
Give me a clue here.
What have most volatile high explosives got in common, Reed? I'm talking HMX, cubane, nitrocellulose...
I give up. Oh, wait... eight-fold symmetry. Eight nitrogen attachment sites on each molecule.
Exactly. The Hydra has the same molecular structure.
Wait. It's made out of high explosives?
Out of nitrocellulose. But one of the attachment sites is blocked. That's why it uses borrowed power when it breeds.
If we can free up that extra bonding site, we'll make it more reactive. Less stable.
Maybe we can overload it and stop it...giving birth, or whatever it does.
Hey.
What?
This feels cool, you know? Being lab partners again. Working together towards a--
Don't push it, Romeo.

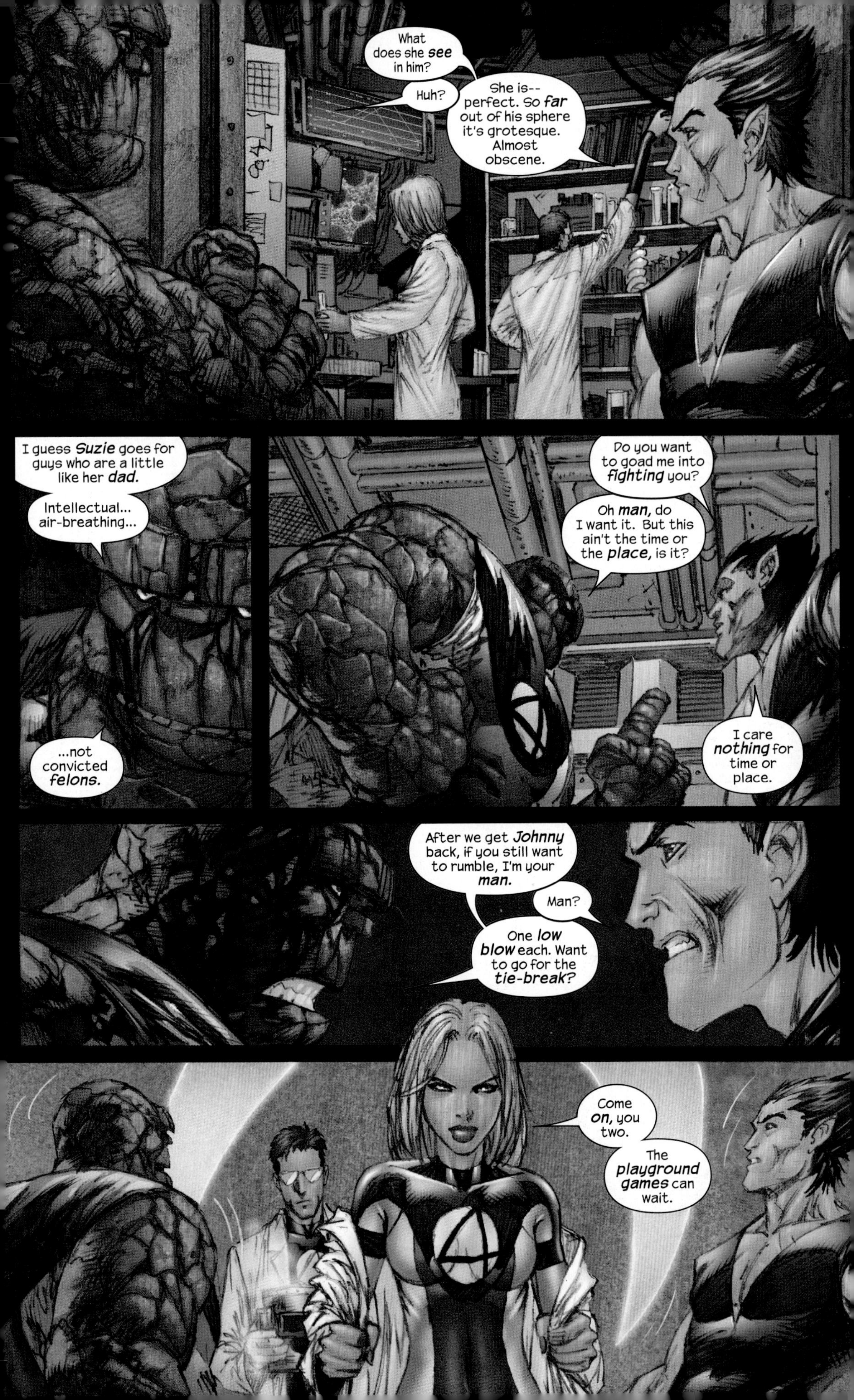
What does she see in him?
Huh?
She is-- perfect. So far out of his sphere it's grotesque. Almost obscene.
I guess Suzie goes for guys who are a little like her dad.
Intellectual... air-breathing...
...not convicted felons.
Do you want to goad me into fighting you?
Oh man, do I want it. But this ain't the time or the place, is it?
I care nothing for time or place.
After we get Johnny back, if you still want to rumble, I'm your man.
Man?
One low blow each. Want to go for the tie-break?
Come on, you two.
The playground games can wait.

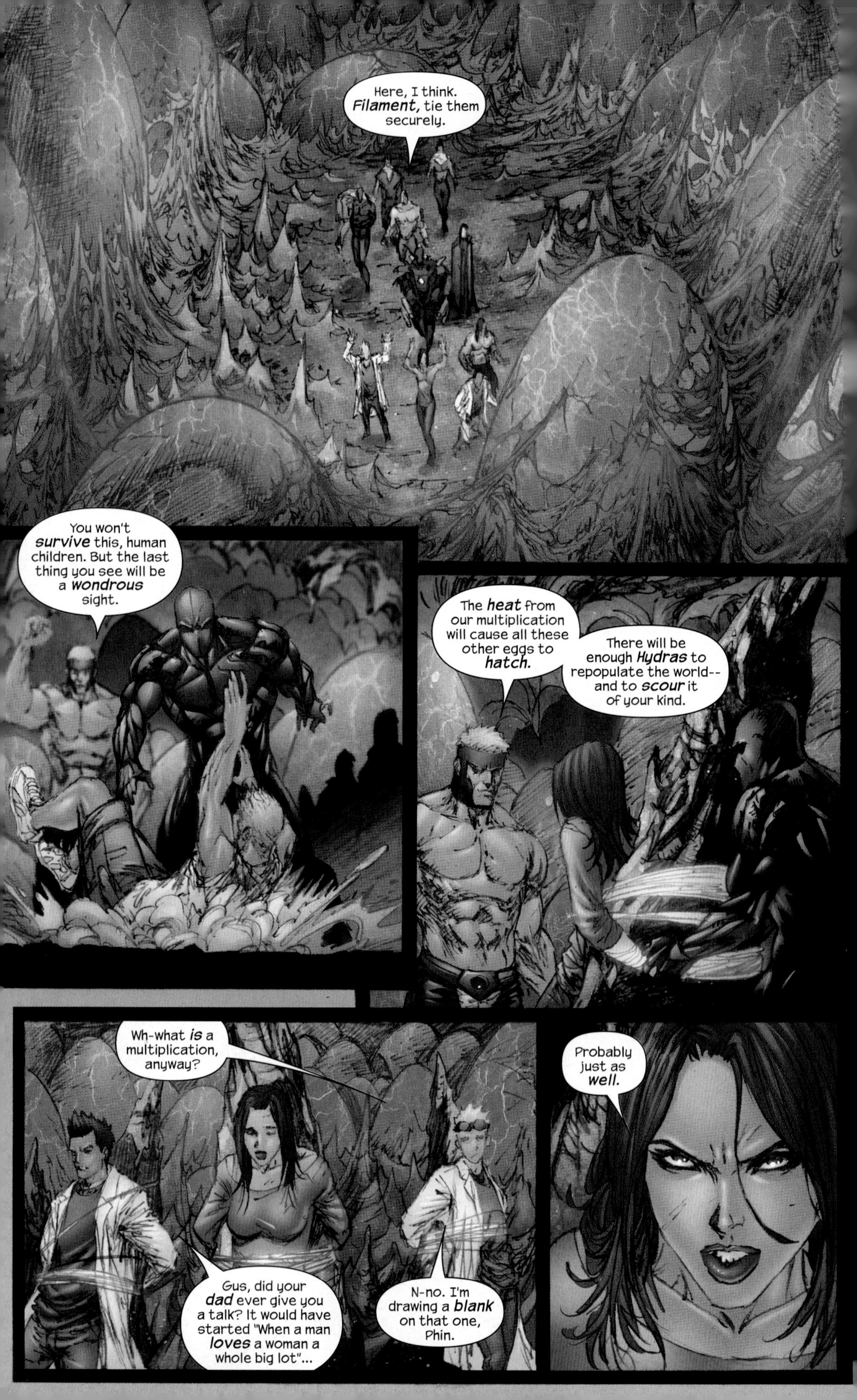
Here, I think. *Filament,* tie them securely.
You won't *survive* this, human children. But the last thing you see will be a *wondrous* sight.
The *heat* from our multiplication will cause all these other eggs to *hatch.*
There will be enough *Hydras* to repopulate the world-- and to *scour* it of your kind.
Wh-what *is* a multiplication, anyway?
Gus, did your *dad* ever give you a talk? It would have started "When a man *loves* a woman a whole big lot"...
N-no. I'm drawing a *blank* on that one, Phin.
Probably just as *well.*

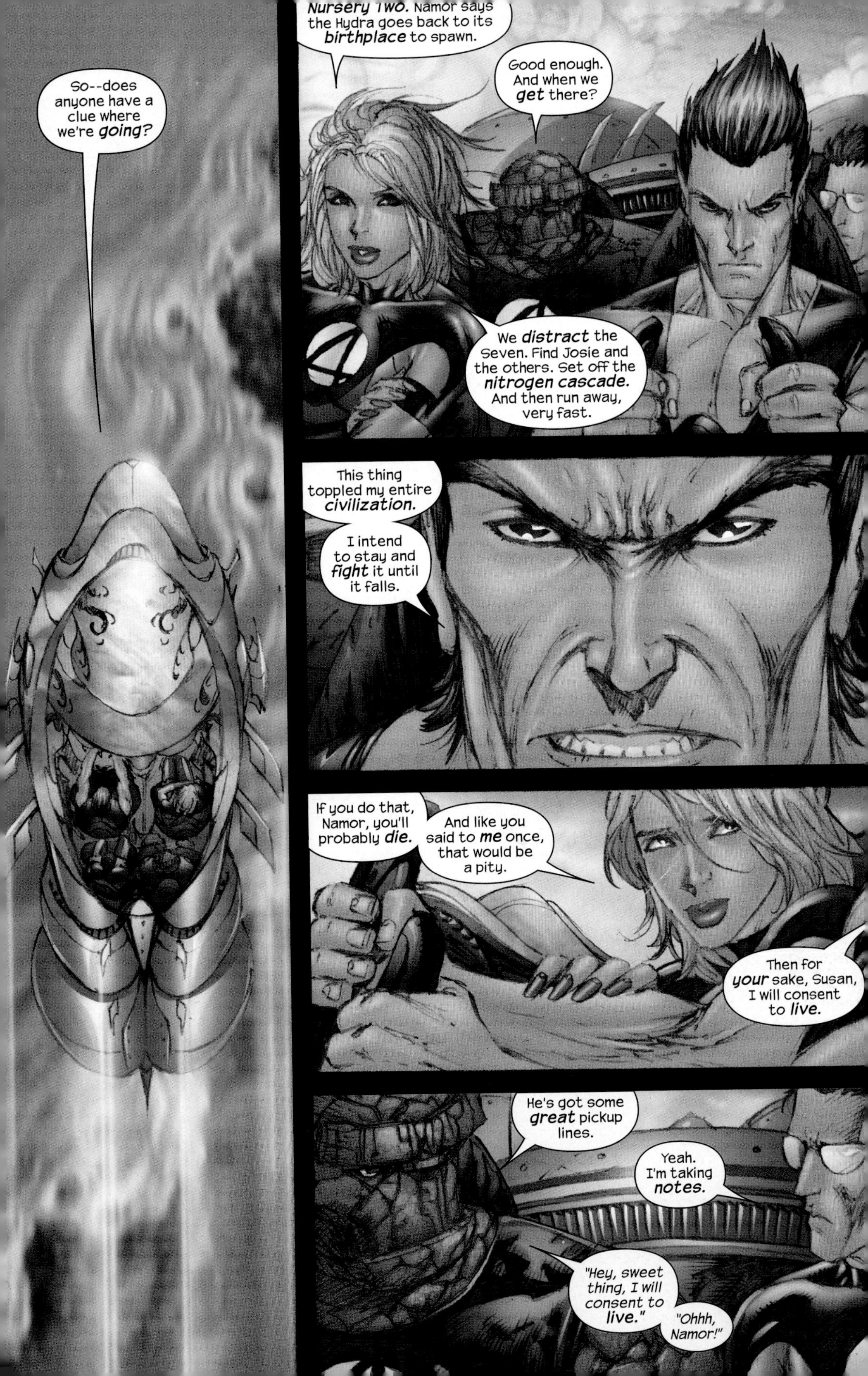
So--does anyone have a clue where we're going?
Nursery Two. Namor says the Hydra goes back to its birthplace to spawn.
Good enough. And when we get there?
We distract the Seven. Find Josie and the others. Set off the nitrogen cascade. And then run away, very fast.
This thing toppled my entire civilization.
I intend to stay and fight it until it falls.
If you do that, Namor, you'll probably die.
And like you said to me once, that would be a pity.
Then for your sake, Susan, I will consent to live.
He's got some great pickup lines.
Yeah. I'm taking notes.
"Hey, sweet thing, I will consent to live."
"Ohhh, Namor!"

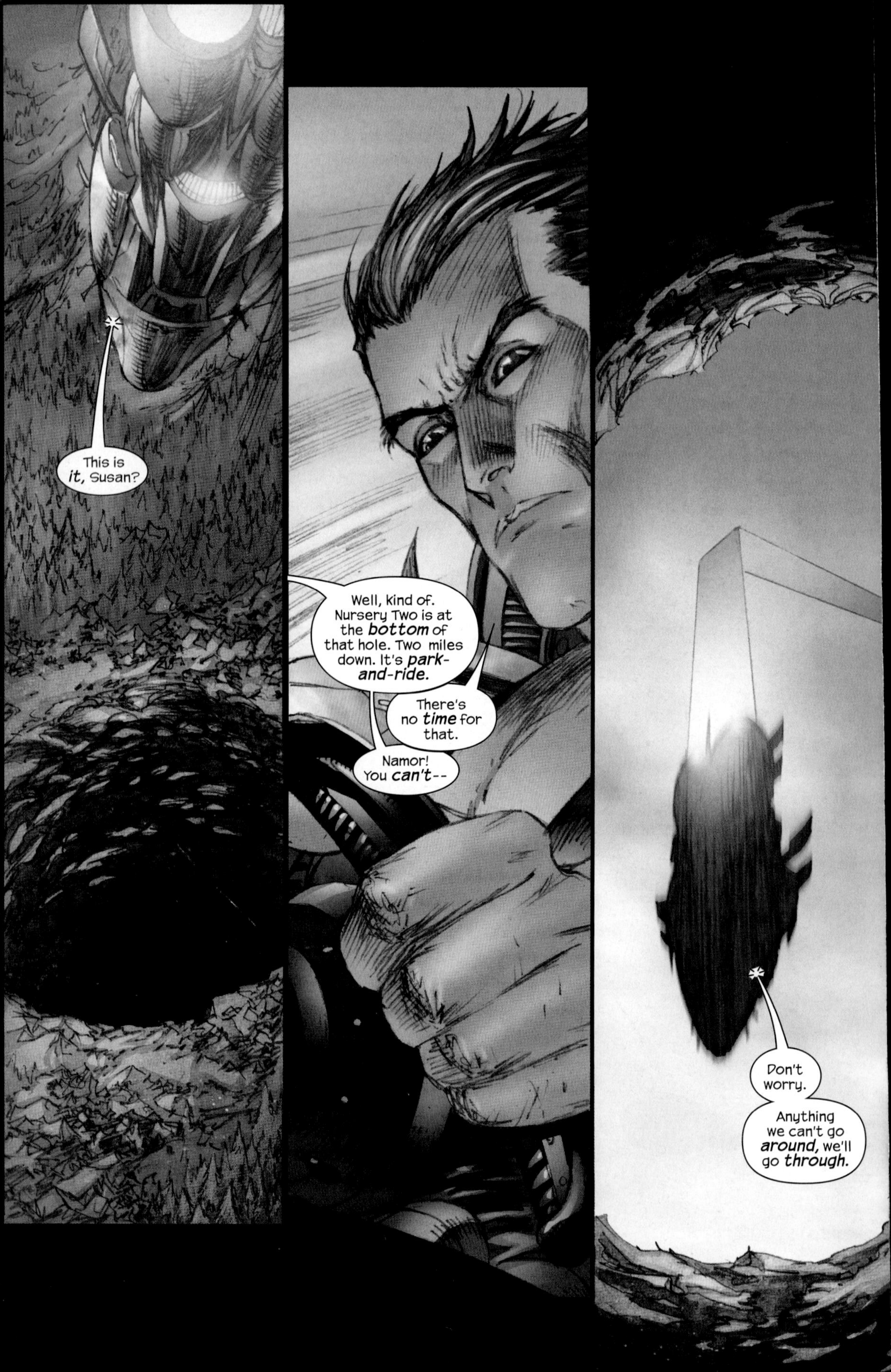
This is *it,* Susan?
Well, kind of. Nursery Two is at the *bottom* of that hole. Two miles down. It's *park-and-ride.*
There's no *time* for that.
Namor! You *can't*--
Don't worry.
Anything we can't go *around,* we'll go *through.*

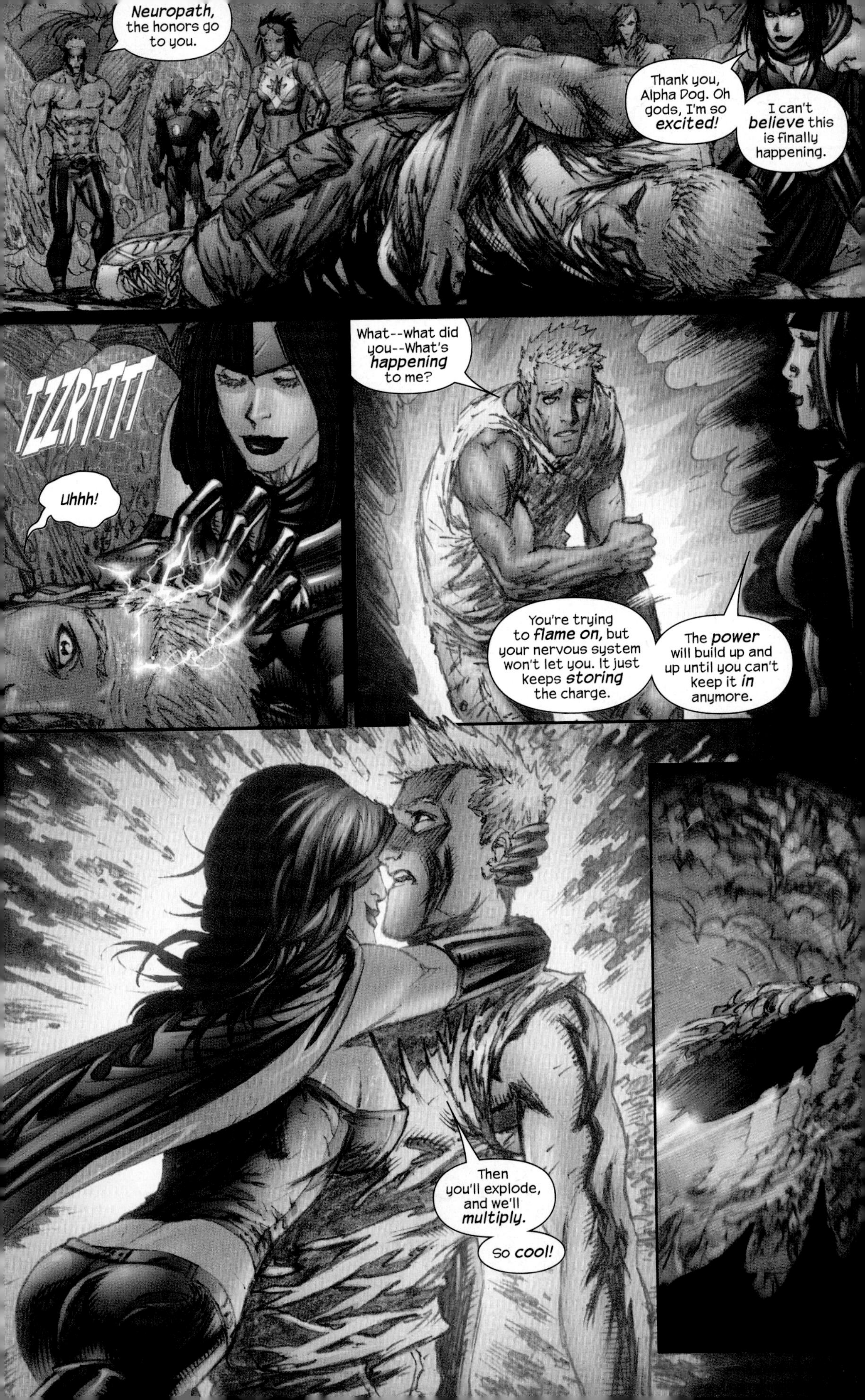
Neuropath, the honors go to you.
Thank you, Alpha Dog. Oh gods, I'm so excited!
I can't believe this is finally happening.
TZZRTTTT
Uhhh!
What--what did you--What's happening to me?
You're trying to flame on, but your nervous system won't let you. It just keeps storing the charge.
The power will build up and up until you can't keep it in anymore.
Then you'll explode, and we'll multiply.
So cool!

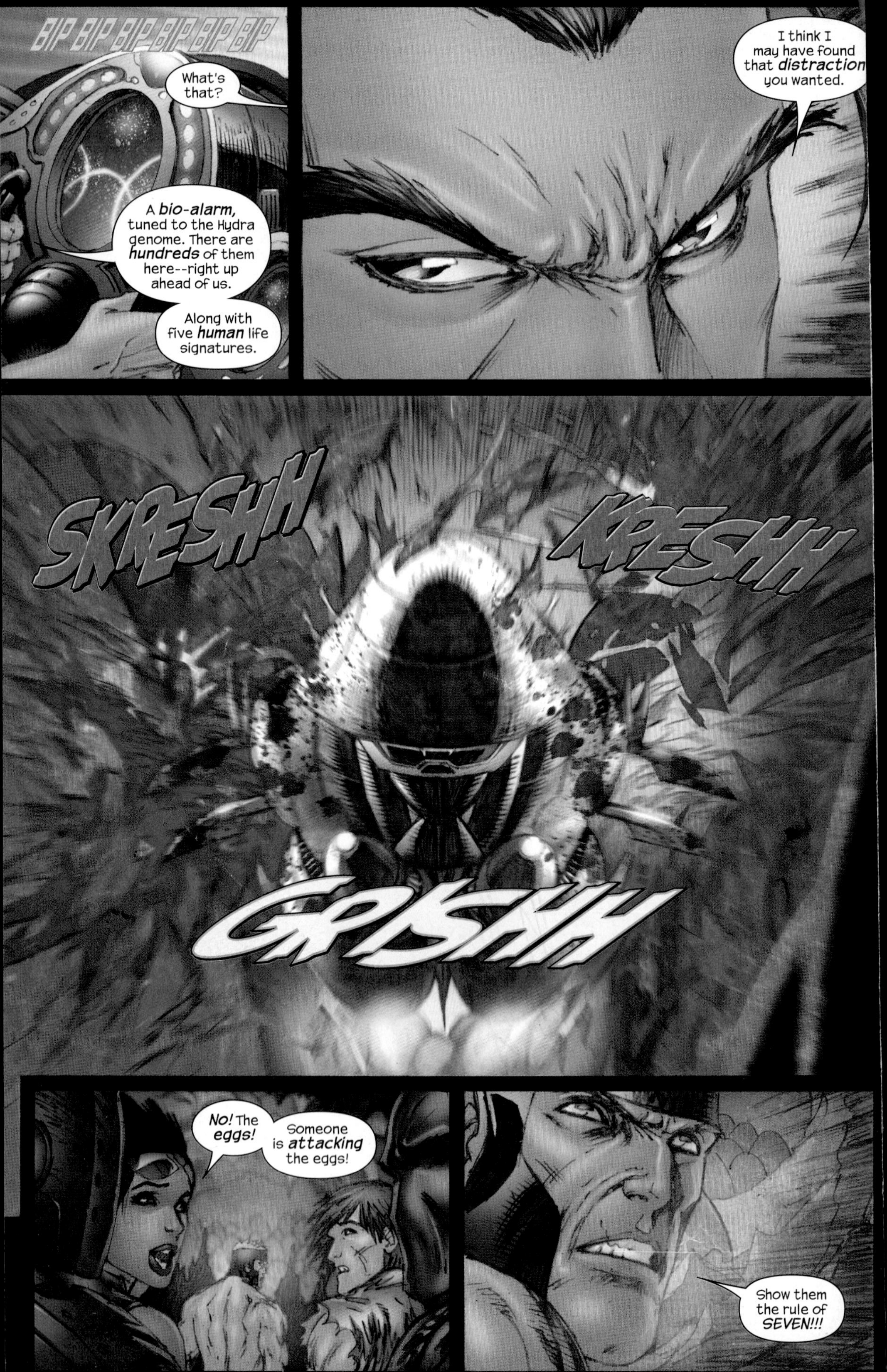

BIP BIP BIP BIP BIP BIP
What's that?
A *bio-alarm,* tuned to the Hydra genome. There are *hundreds* of them here--right up ahead of us.
Along with five *human* life signatures.
I think I may have found that *distraction* you wanted.
SKRESHH
KRESHH
GRISHH
No! The *eggs!*
Someone is *attacking* the eggs!
Show them the rule of *SEVEN!!!*

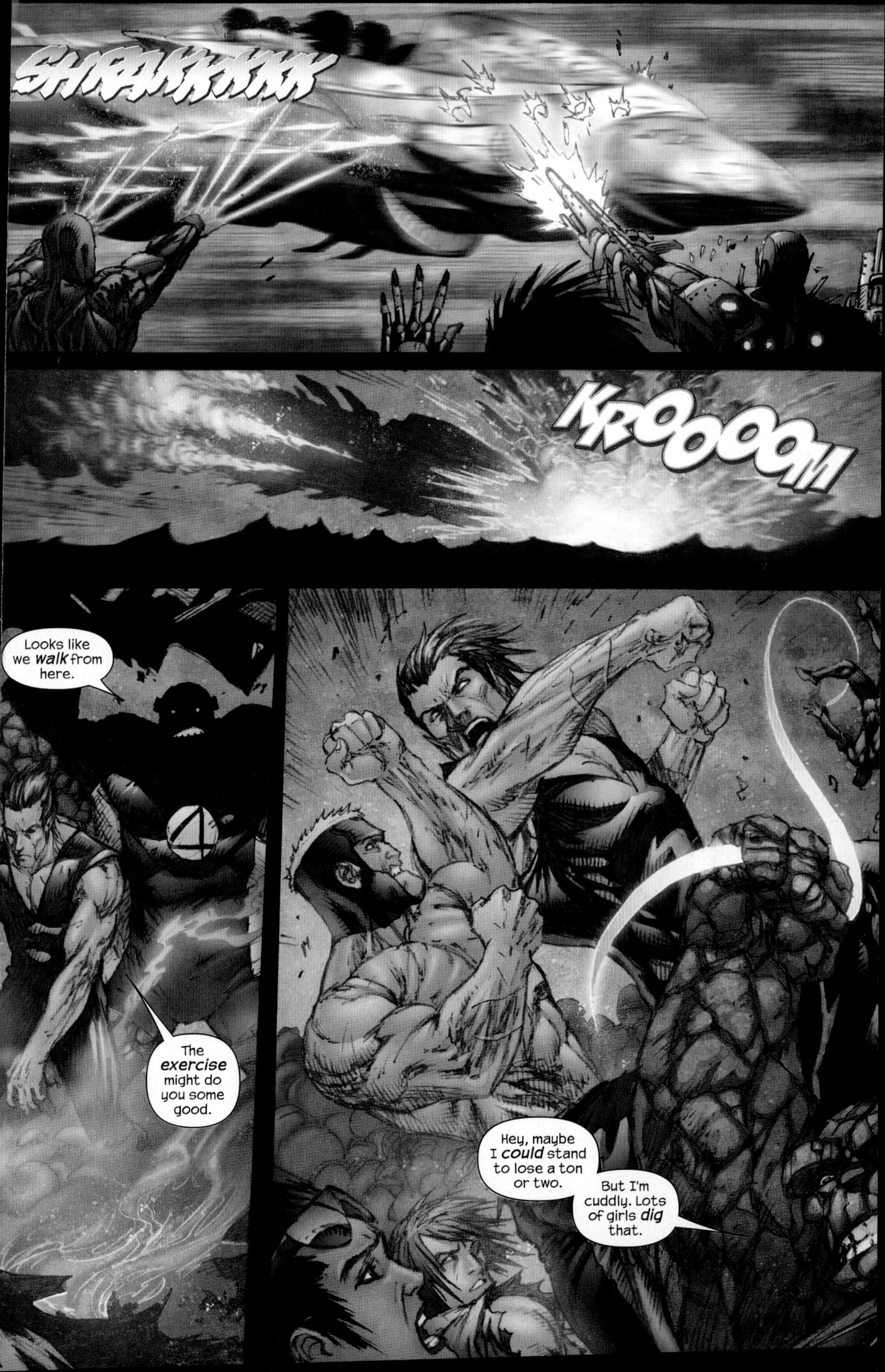
SHRAKKKKK
KROOOOOM
Looks like we *walk* from here.
The *exercise* might do you some good.
Hey, maybe I *could* stand to lose a ton or two.
But I'm cuddly. Lots of girls *dig* that.

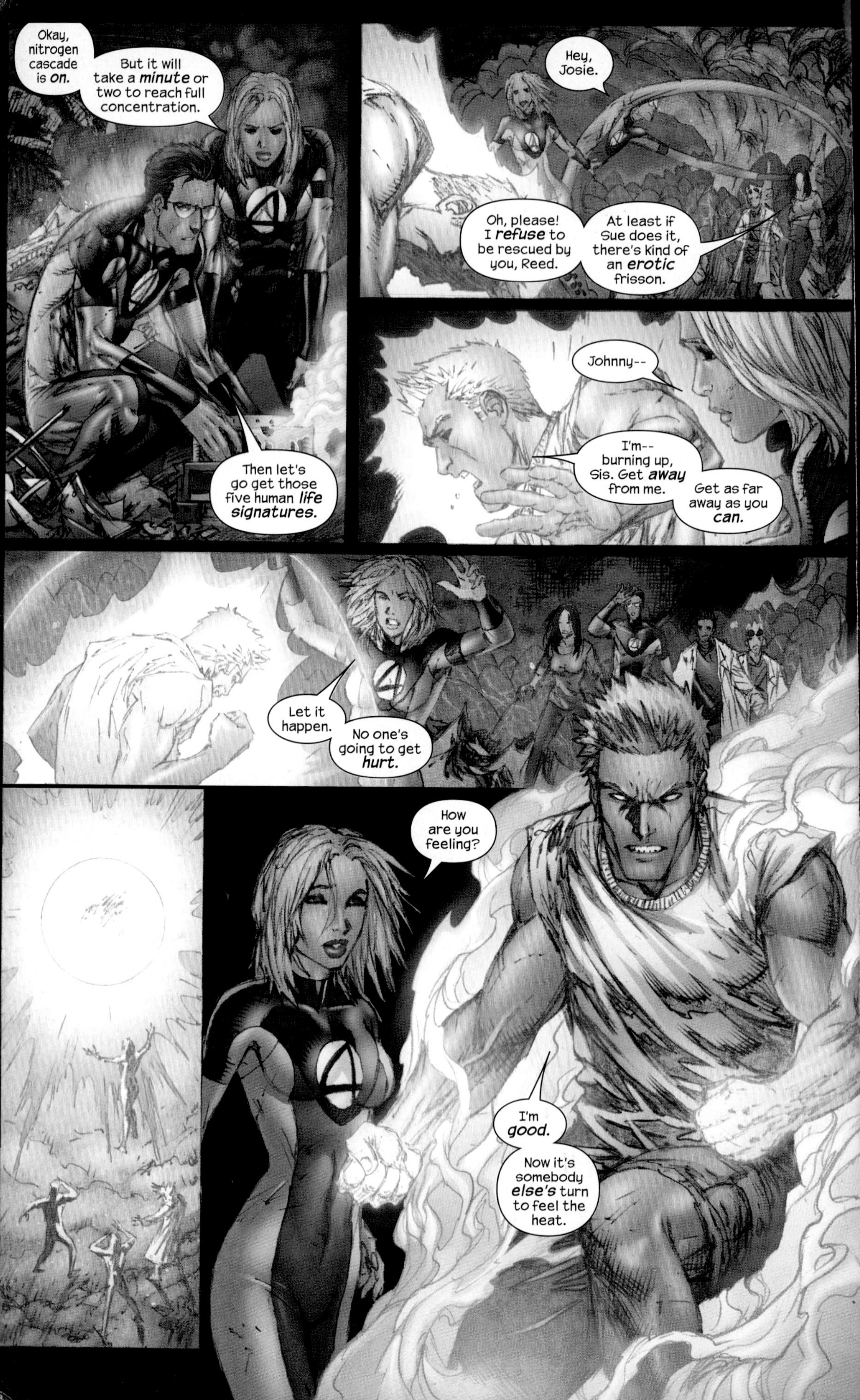
Okay, nitrogen cascade is *on.*
But it will take a *minute* or two to reach full concentration.
Then let's go get those five human *life signatures.*
Hey, Josie.
Oh, please! I *refuse* to be rescued by you, Reed.
At least if Sue does it, there's kind of an *erotic* frisson.
Johnny--
I'm-- burning up, Sis. Get *away* from me.
Get as far away as you *can.*
Let it happen.
No one's going to get *hurt.*
How are you feeling?
I'm *good.*
Now it's somebody *else's* turn to feel the heat.

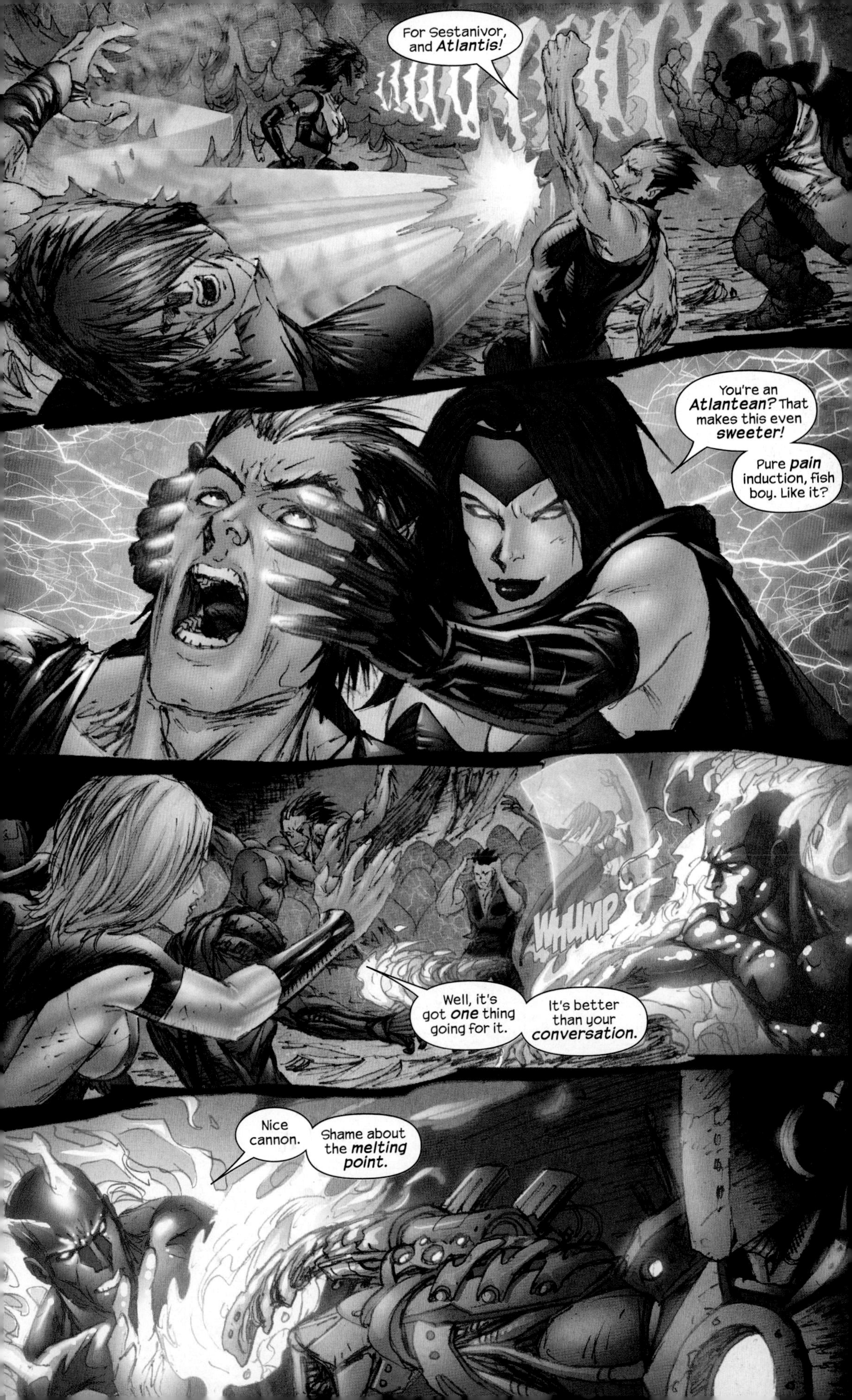
For Sestanivor, and Atlantis!
You're an Atlantean? That makes this even sweeter!
Pure pain induction, fish boy. Like it?
WHUMP
Well, it's got one thing going for it.
It's better than your conversation.
Nice cannon.
Shame about the melting point.

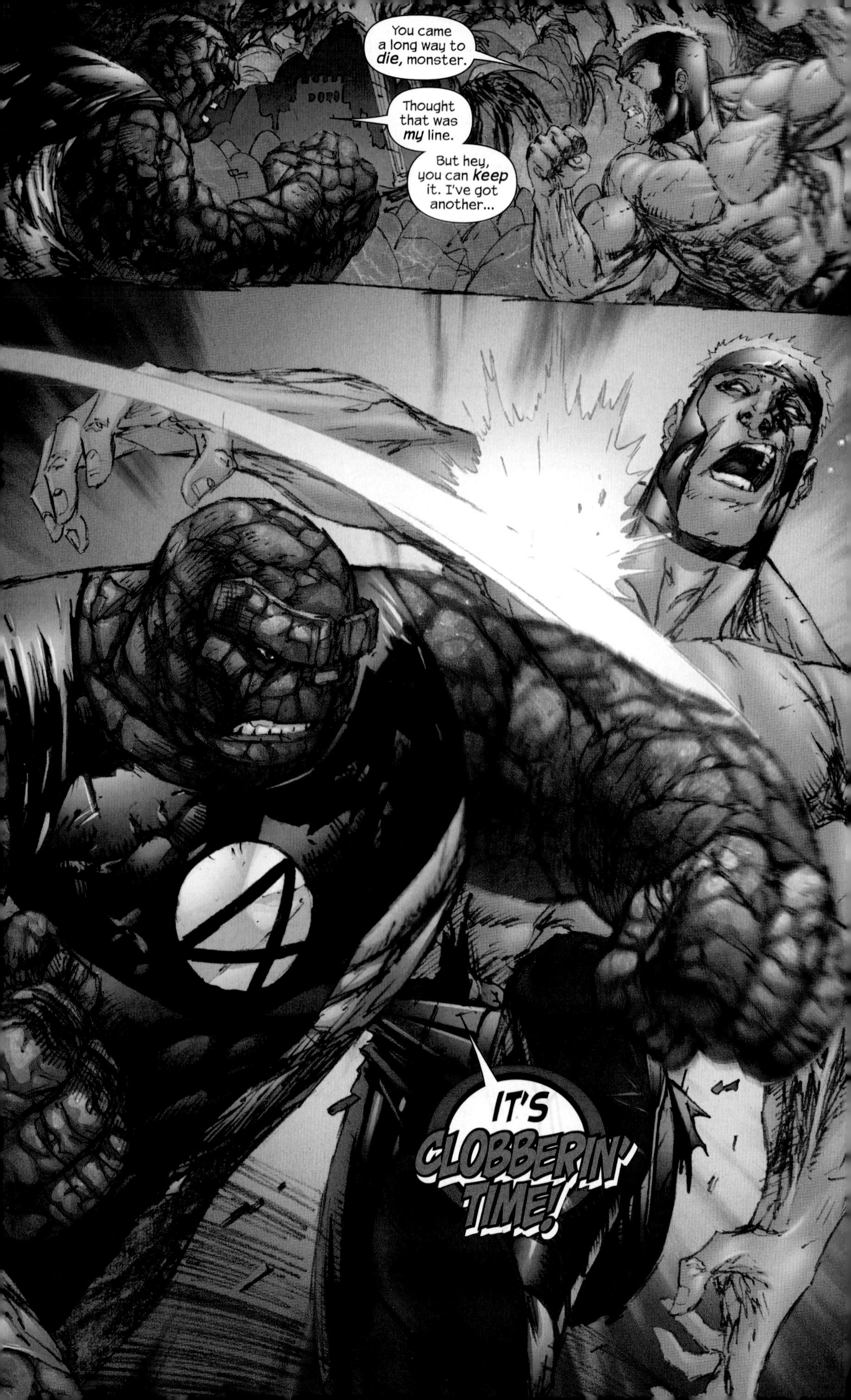

You came a long way to *die,* monster.
Thought that was *my* line.
But hey, you can *keep* it. I've got another...
IT'S CLOBBERIN' TIME!

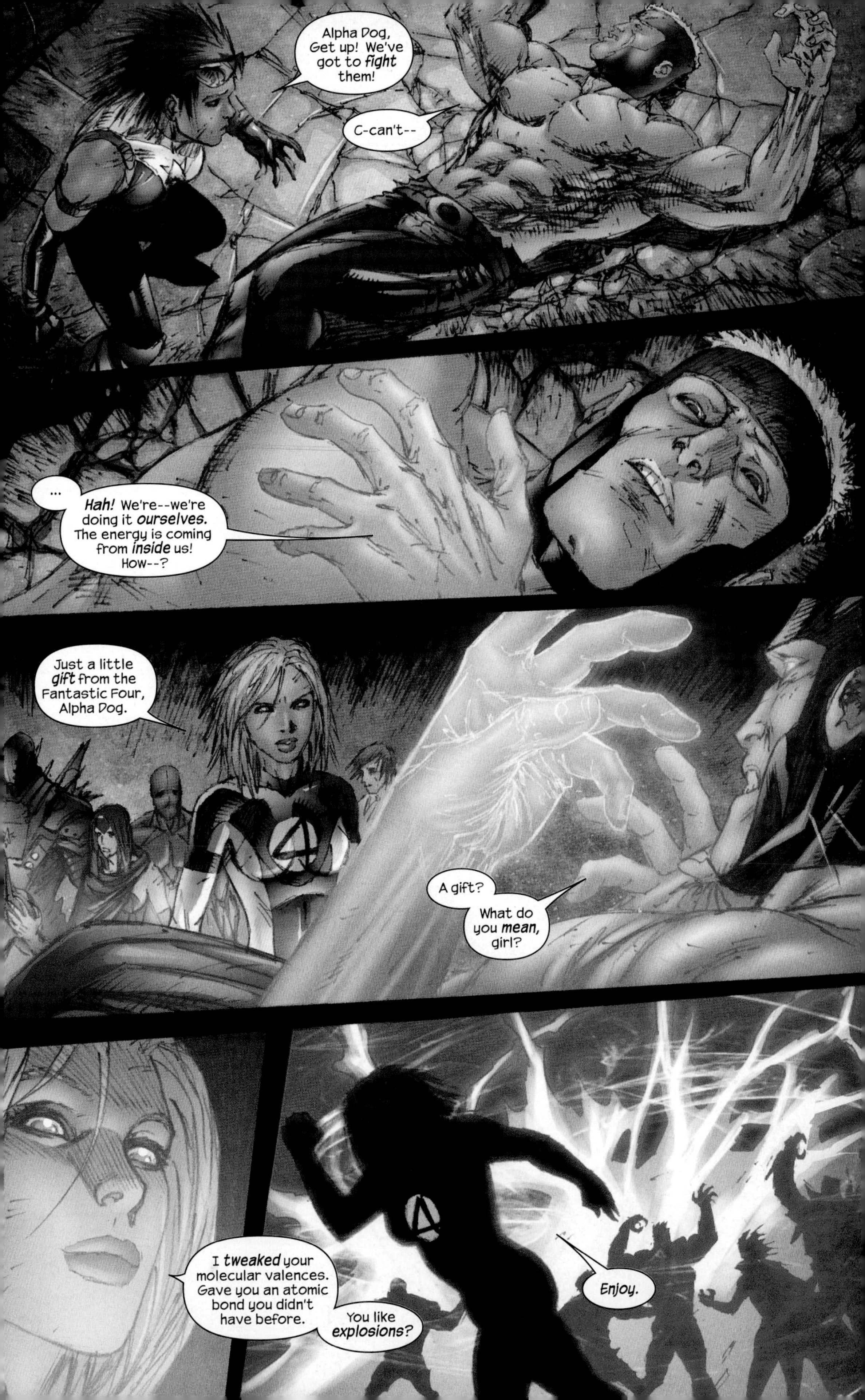
Alpha Dog, Get up! We've got to fight them!
C-can't--
...
Hah! We're--we're doing it ourselves. The energy is coming from inside us! How--?
Just a little gift from the Fantastic Four, Alpha Dog.
A gift?
What do you mean, girl?
I tweaked your molecular valences. Gave you an atomic bond you didn't have before.
You like explosions?
Enjoy.

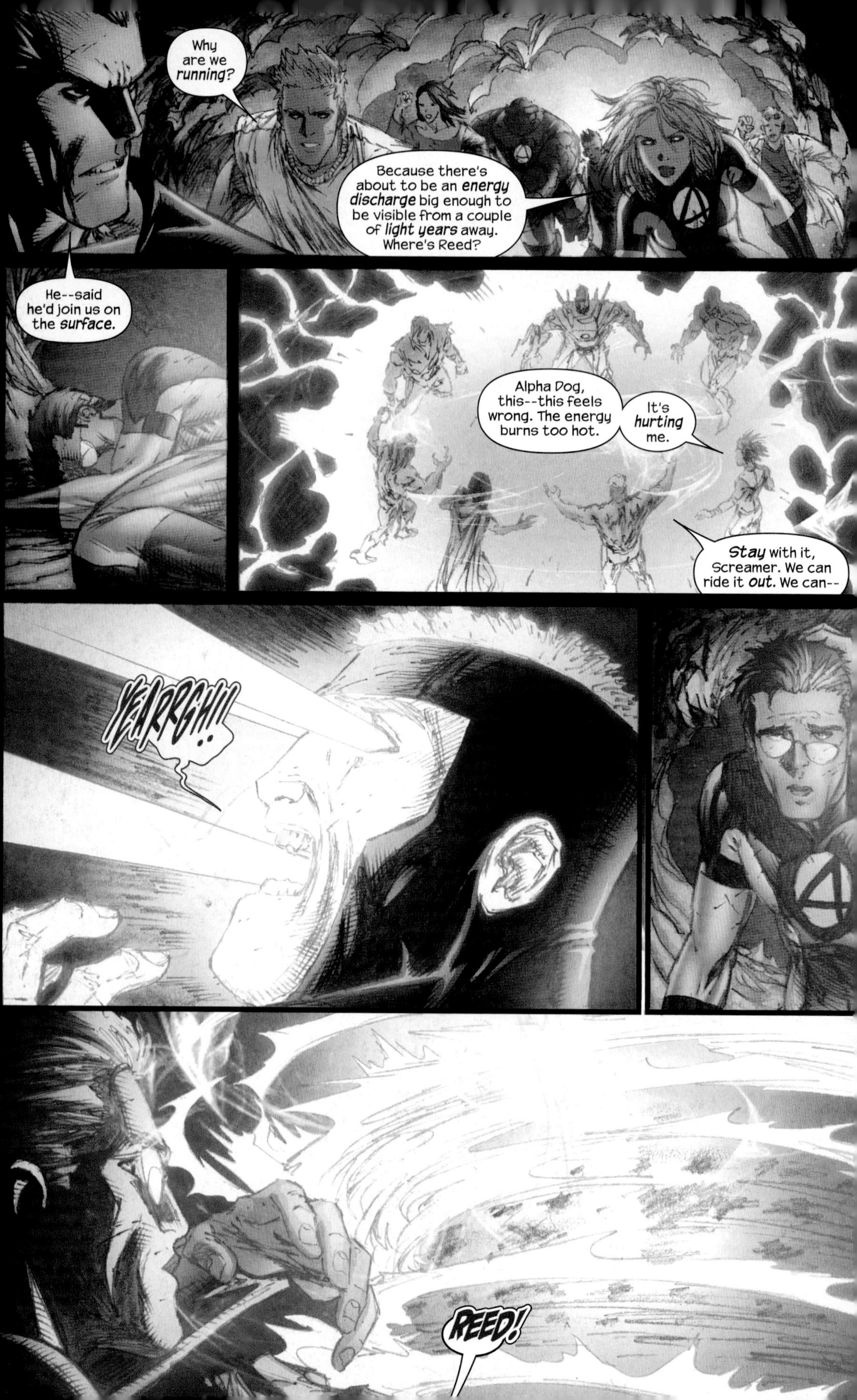

Why are we *running*?
Because there's about to be an *energy discharge* big enough to be visible from a couple of *light years* away. Where's Reed?
He--said he'd join us on the *surface.*
Alpha Dog, this--this feels wrong. The energy burns too hot.
It's *hurting* me.
Stay with it, Screamer. We can ride it *out.* We can--
YEARRGH!!
REED!

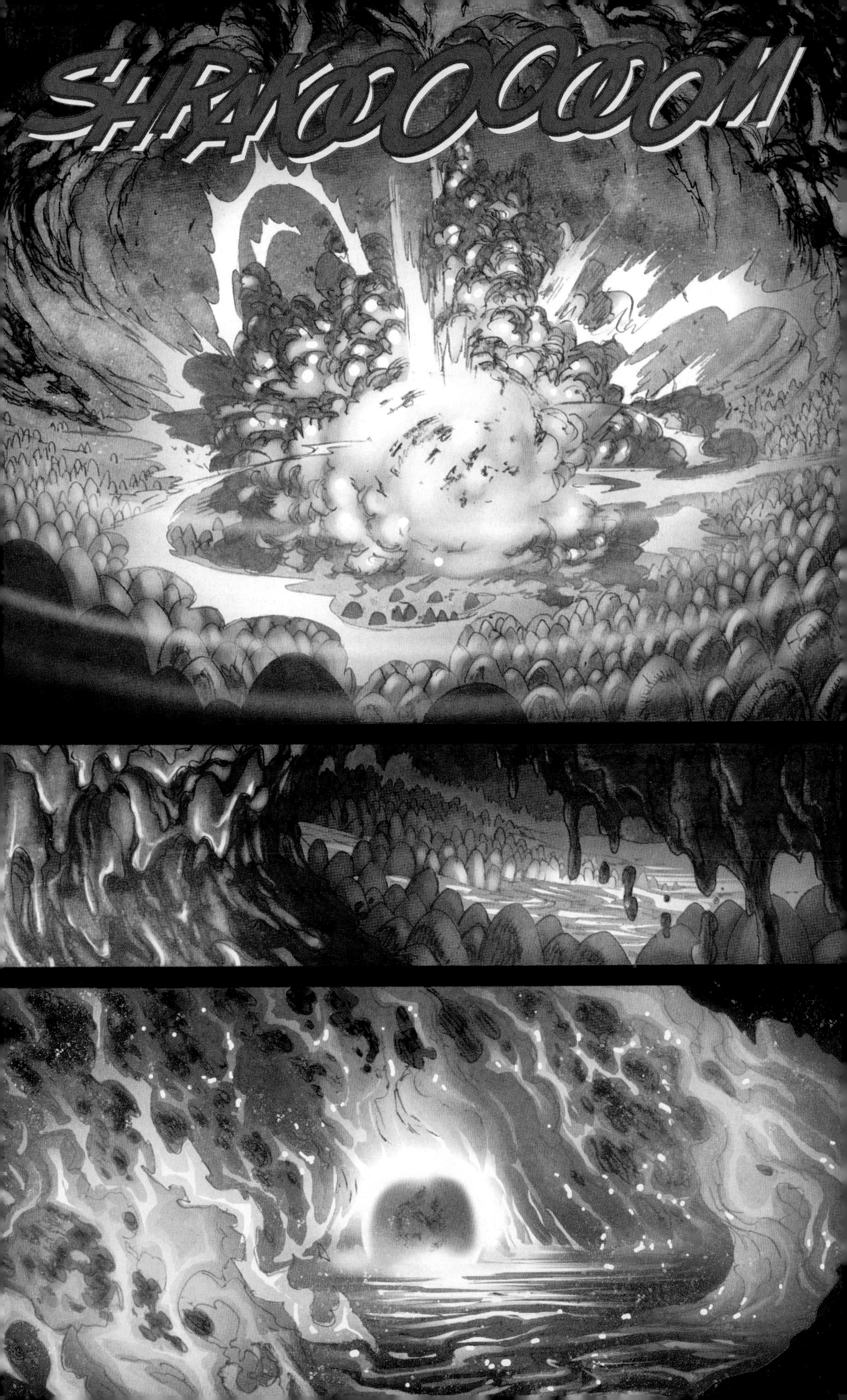
SHRAKOOOOOOM

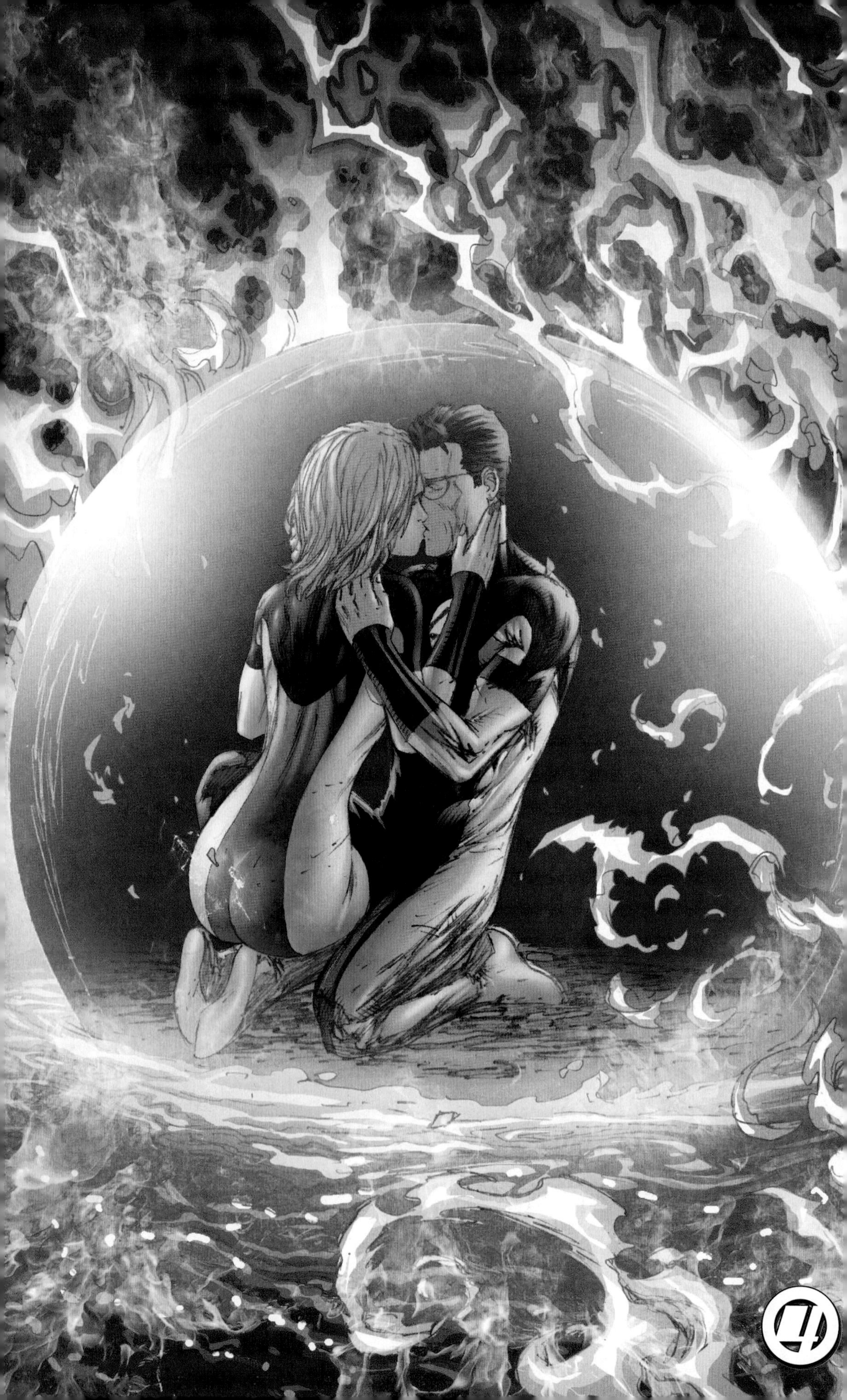

ULTIMATE X-MEN # 54
Script by Mike Carey

PAGE 1
Splash. We're in one of the titanic, city-sized caverns that the Mole Man excavated, and that we last saw in UFF Annual #2. The ruins of an ancient city lie sprawled around, and sitting right there in the middle of them is a colossal egg – about thirty feet in diameter at its broadest point. Actually, it's not an egg at all, any more: it's the cracked shell of an egg, the occupant having already broken out and headed off for pastures new. Two human figures, dwarfed by the size of the egg, stand beneath it and stare up at it: they are Sue Storm, the Invisible Girl, and Strange Josie, one of the Nursery Two kids also last seen in UFF Annual#2.
1 FLOATING TEXT: One vertical mile beneath Pinhead Buttes, Oregon.
2 FLOATING TEXT: Nursery Two.
3 SUE: Wow.
4 JOSIE: Yeah, exactly. Wow. That's why I thought you should see it, Suzie-girl.
5 JOSIE: Although since we split off from the Baxter think-tank, this feels like fraternising with the enemy.

PAGE 2

PANEL 1
Into two-shot. Sue has now knelt down and examines the broken edge of the shell thoughtfully, tracing the line of it with her fingers. Josie stands behind her, looking down on her with a cheeky grin on her face.
1 SUE: I thought your enemy was the phallocentric military-industrial complex, Josie.
2 JOSIE: Sure. That's why we bailed on you – you've all got S.H.I.E.L.D. stamped on your butts.
3 SUE: So did anyone see what came out of this thing?

PANEL 2
Tight on Josie. She looks off to the side, making a sour face.
4 JOSIE: Nope. When we found it, I rigged up a refrigeration unit. But the boys unplugged it for their giant TV.
5 JOSIE: Next day I come down here and - - y'know - - this bird has flown.

PANEL 3
Out to two-shot. Sue is now scraping a tissue sample from the goop still clinging to the egg-shell. In her free hand she has a re-sealable plastic bag. Josie still watches Sue work, but with her head tilted slightly and a look of over-elaborate innocence: this is now a chat-up.
6 SUE: Big bird.
7 JOSIE: Obviously.
8 JOSIE: So how are things between you and the round-headed kid?

PANEL 4
Tight on Sue. She carefully transfers the tissue sample to the baggie, intent on her work.
9 SUE: They're - - okay, I guess. We were apart for a while.
10 SUE: Now we're taking things slowly.

PANEL 5
Out to two-shot. Sue has stood again and the two girls face each other, Josie staring frankly at Sue, Sue looking at the baggie that she's raised to head height to examine.
11 JOSIE: You'd have so much more fun as a lesbian.
12 SUE: Well I'll take a leaflet if you've got one.
13 SUE: Listen, I'm gonna get this tissue sample over to the Baxter. If I find out what it belonged to, I'll call you.

PAGE 3

PANEL 1
Another part of the cavern. Sue and Josie walk towards us, but they're in deep background. In the foreground,

we have a two-shot on two more of the Nursery Two kids working with feverish enthusiasm on some kind of bread-board project. They are Phineas Mason and Gus Axelrod – visual ref in UFF Annual #2. Phineas is clearly in charge, working on a console that's both high-tech and crudely patched together. Gus tends a huge, chugging generator of a strange design.
1 PHINEAS: More current, Gus!
2 GUS: H - - how much more?
3 PHINEAS: All of it! Every last pica-watt!
4 GUS: Coming r -- right up, Phin.

PANEL 2

Pull back and reveal. The boys are working on a pet project – a TV screen so huge it would sprawl across two or three cross-town blocks of Manhattan: it comes alive now, criss-cross patterns of static chasing each other across its surface. The tiny figure of Phineas punches the air in triumph.
5 SFX: KRZZZTTT
6 PHINEAS: Yes!!! That's it! That's it!
7 PHINEAS: Lock those settings! Lock them right there!

PANEL 3

Tight on the screen. An image forms on it – not a very good or clear one at first. It's a network news bulletin of a conventional kind, with an attractive female presenter and an inset box bearing a still image and a caption naming the news item. The still image shows an aerial view of a small town. The caption reads **SALEM'S SEVEN**. The presenter smiles indulgently, as though this is the joke item at the end of the broadcast.
8 PRESENTER: - - reports that our state capital, Salem, has become the home to Oregon's first ever super hero team.
0 CAPTION (across silver bar): SALEM'S SEVEN

PANEL 4

Staying tight on the screen. It shows an airborne rescue being carried out by two of the Salem's Seven team, whose names and identities we'll learn later. Mike, full details are on p22, so I won't repeat them here – you can choose any two of the Seven for this shot, but they're basically just carrying civilians across a flooded street.
9 PRESENTER VO: The team, known locally as Salem's Seven, have already saved two lives.
10 PRESENTER VO: And also made themselves useful when a burst water main inundated downtown's Frederick Street area.

PANEL 5

Two-shot on Sue and Josie – high angle, looking down on them as they stare up at the screen.
11 SUE: Something to do with you guys?
12 JOSIE: No way. We mind our own business. And Salem's got, like, three people and a dog.
13 JOSIE: They need super heroes like the Pope needs Viagra.

PAGE 4

PANEL 1

Pull back a long way, for a ground level shot that's still centred on the two girls. Tyler, we're seeing them now through the eyes of the hydra, which we presume is invisible to them at this point. I'd like to reflect this either by adding in a sort of distortion to the panel art, as though we're seeing it reflected in a convex mirror, or by doing something to the area at the edge of the panel to suggest that we're seeing through some non-human eye – like a circular overlay of some kind.
1 SUE: Well, I'll be in touch, okay?
2 JOSIE: About the lesbianism?
3 SUE: About the tissue samples. Nice seeing you, Josie.
4 JOSIE: Likewise.

PANEL 2

Tight on Sue, seen from behind. The hydra is following her, unobserved, and we're still looking out through its eyes – as we will for the rest of this page.
5 HYDRA CAP: You? Possibly.

6 HYDRA CAP: <u>Possibly</u> you.
7 HYDRA CAP: But I don't <u>think</u> so.

PANEL 3
Out wide, high angle. Sue lifts herself into the air on a column of invisible force, rising towards us.
8 HYDRA CAP: Something you've <u>touched</u>, then. Something you're <u>close</u> to.
9 SUE: Surface.
10 HYDRA CAP: Close enough so that you still <u>smell</u> of it.

PANEL 4
Low angle shot looking up at Sue as the platform rises, taking her up towards the cavern ceiling high above.
11 HYDRA CAP: I'll <u>miss</u> this place. I really will.
12 HYDRA CAP: But we have to <u>learn</u>. We have to <u>grow</u>.

PANEL 5
On the surface. Out wide, high angle. Sue walks towards the waiting Fantasti-Car.
13 HYDRA CAP: We have to be so many <u>more</u>.

PAGE 5

PANEL 1
Inside the Fantasti-car. Sue flicks switches, prepares to launch. Reed's face is on the intercom screen and they talk as Sue busies herself.
1 REED: Hey.
2 SUE: Hey.
3 REED: So what'd they want to <u>see</u> you about?
4 SUE: Something <u>biological</u>.

PANEL 2
Cut to the other end of the conversation. Reed is sitting in his lab, talking into the monitor that shows Sue's face. Both of his arms are fully extended, though, stretching way out of shot. He looks unhappy, pained.
5 FLOATING TEXT: Baxter Building
6 FLOATING TEXT: New York City
7 REED: Oh God. Josie came on to you again.
8 SUE: It's not <u>my</u> fault I'm irresistible.
9 SUE: Anything cool going on where <u>you</u> are?

PANEL 3
Out wide, so that we can now see what Reed's arms are doing. He's conducting two different experiments in two different parts of the room, calibrating equipment with one hand, pouring chemicals with the other.
10 REED: Not much. I've got a couple of <u>experiments</u> running.
11 REED: I <u>miss</u> you.
12 SUE: I know. What about Johnny and Ben?

PANEL 4
Close-up on Reed's face. He looks off, slightly distracted.
13 REED: Haven't seen them in an <u>hour</u> or so, now that you mention it.
14 REED: I guess they're playing <u>video games</u> or something.

PANEL 5
Cut back to an external shot of the Fantasti-Car high in the air, flying across mountainous terrain.
15 SUE [on intercom]: Well I'm coming in <u>sub-orbital</u>, so I should be with you in about an hour.
16 SUE [on intercom]: Tell them I said hi. And - - y'know - -

PANEL 1
Cut to a huge, empty, cavernous room in the Baxter Building. The Thing lumbers towards us, carrying a block of sleek, shiny black metal that's about ten feet high by five feet wide by a foot thick.
1 SUE CAP: " - - don't let them <u>wreck</u> the joint."
2 BEN: Okay. How about <u>this</u>?

PANEL 2
Out wider, to bring Johnny into shot as Ben sets the massive block down without apparent effort. Johnny looks at it critically.
3 JOHNNY: Yeah, that looks <u>perfect</u>. Where'd you find it?
4 BEN: Store room G. Reed's got about five <u>hundred</u> of 'em.
5 BEN: I guess he uses 'em for <u>bookmarks</u> or something. What are the <u>rules</u> again?

PANEL 3
Rotate POV. Johnny points towards a weird little set-up a few feet beyond the block. There's a retort stand with a glass flask full of water clamped to it – in the water, a small egg floating. Beyond that is another retort stand from which a single matchstick protrudes vertically upwards.
6 JOHNNY: I've got to burn right through the <u>center</u> of the steel slab, boil the egg - -
7 BEN: <u>Soft-boil</u> the egg.
8 JOHNNY: - - and light the <u>match</u>. Inside of a minute.

PANEL 4
Tight on Johnny. He raises his right hand and flames on – the flames only extending to his forearm.
9 JOHNNY: And if I do it, you have to wear the <u>diving suit</u> all day.
10 JOHNNY: That's what we <u>said</u>, right?

PANEL 5
Out wide. Johnny cuts loose at the slab with a tightly-focused flame blast.
11 SFX: CHOOOOOOM
12 JOHNNY: Benjy-boy - -
13 JOHNNY: - - you'd better check those <u>oxygen</u> tanks.

PAGE 7

PANEL 1
Tight on the centre of the metal slab. The surface rucks and melts, the blinding white of Johnny's flame showing through.
1 SFX: SHOWWWWWWW

PANEL 2
Tight on the glass flask. The water starts to boil.
2 SFX: BLUG BLUG BLUG BLUG

PANEL 3
Tight on the match. It flares into life.
3 SFX: FRUFFFF

PANEL 4
Out wide. The huge steel slab – suddenly and without warning – crashes down through the floor of the room, which crumbles and shatters and gives way beneath it. Ben and Johnny are taken completely by surprise.
4 BEN: Wha - - ?!

PANEL 5
Low angle shot looking straight up through the ragged hole in the floor towards Ben and Johnny as they peer cautiously in.

5 JOHNNY: That couldn't have been us.
6 BEN: Absolutely <u>not</u>.
7 JOHNNY: But maybe we should split anyway.
8 BEN: I'm <u>gone</u>.

PAGE 8

PANEL 1
The hangar deck of the Baxter Building. The Fantasti-Car comes in for a perfectly controlled landing.

PANEL 2
Staying wide. Reed is waiting on the hangar deck, carrying a sign which reads STORM – as though he's a driver waiting to greet someone at an airport. Sue walks towards him, the baggie in her hand.

PANEL 3
Into two-shot. Se has already walked on past Reed, but he extends his upper body in a huge, wide loop and brings it back down again alongside her, so that his top half is keeping pace with her. Sue is calm and a little distant, not cutting him any slack.
1 REED: Welcome home.
2 SUE: Thanks.
3 REED: Can I give you a hand with your <u>stuff</u>?
4 SUE: This baggie <u>is</u> my stuff.

PANEL 4
Out wide. She walks on down a flight of steps. Reed doesn't bother with the stairs: legs stretched outrageously, he steps down onto the lower level ahead of her. He's still totally focused on her, attentive to a fault – but his kindnesses fall on deaf ears.
5 REED: Well maybe I can strew <u>palm leaves</u> in your path.
6 SUE: Did you <u>bring</u> any palm leaves?
7 REED: Or press the <u>elevator</u> button so you don't have to transfer your baggie to the other <u>hand</u>.
8 SUE: I'm <u>fine</u>, Reed. Thank you.

PANEL 5
High angle shot looking down on them. They've come to a massive hole in the floor, and we can see that there are corresponding holes in all the floors below them – a dizzying perspective.
9 SUE: Uh - - although, since you're here - -
10 SUE: - - I guess you can tell me how <u>this</u> happened.

PAGE 9

PANEL 1
And back into hydra-vision. The thing is still with them, unseen, and eavesdropping on their conversation. Again, this effect will continue for the rest of the page. We're in tight two-shot on Reed and Sue here. She's turned to face him, reacting in surprise to his words.
1 REED: Sure. Or else you could just make a wild <u>guess</u>.
2 SUE: Johnny and Ben? <u>Again</u>? Seriously?
3 HYDRA CAP: So what <u>is</u> closest to you, child?

PANEL 2
Tight on Reed. He tries to pull the conversation back on course, his expression serious.
4 HYDRA CAP: Him?
5 REED: I was hoping we could talk about - - well, about <u>us</u>.
6 REED: About where we're <u>going</u>. And whether you're going to give me another <u>chance</u>.
7 HYDRA CAP: Perhaps - -

PANEL 3

Out to two-shot. Sue looks away, Reed talks to her earnestly.
8 HYDRA CAP: Perhaps in a <u>sense</u>.
9 REED: I already <u>explained</u> what happened.
10 SUE: And I <u>believe</u> you, Reed.
11 HYDRA CAP: We'll <u>see</u>.

PANEL 4

Out wide. Sue walks away from Reed. He watches her go, unhappy. Our view of this is skewed, because the hydra is already turning away from them, looking towards an open doorway off to one side of the panel.
12 SUE: I just don't know how it leaves me <u>feeling</u>.
13 HYDRA CAP: There are a <u>thousand</u> scents here.
14 HYDRA CAP: A thousand <u>skeins</u> of thought and power.

PANEL 5

High angle shot looking down a steep stairwell as the hydra, still invisible, descends.
15 HYDRA CAP: One of them will <u>free</u> me.

<u>PAGE 10</u>

PANEL 1

The foyer of the Baxter Building. This is where the huge steel block finished up after its fall, and it's still embedded in the marble floor with crash barriers hastily erected around it. People ignore it as they go about their business. Two guards sit at a security/reception desk, also ignoring it. A woman – Agatha Harkness – walks towards them, but we're too far away to see her clearly as yet. Full description is in panel 3 below.

PANEL 2

Looking from behind Agatha towards the two guards, Ted and Sorsky, as she walks towards them. Sorsky stares at her in frank admiration. Ted is better at hiding it, but also can't tear his eyes away.
1 SORSKY: Oh man. Suddenly - - <u>sunshine!</u>
2 TED: Reel your <u>tongue</u> in, Sorsky. Try to be <u>professional</u> for once in your damn life.
3 TED: And I'm calling <u>dibs</u>.

PANEL 3

Agatha stops in front of the desk and holds out her ID for the guards to inspect. Ted isn't even looking at it, because, well, Agatha is there to look at and she's a lot more interesting. Mike, go to town here. First and foremost, Agatha has to look like a serious professional woman, stylish and well-presented to a fault. Underneath that, though, she's also the most gorgeous woman who ever lived – totally and unfeasibly beautiful and so sexy that every man undresses her with his eyes as soon as he sees her. My own feeling is that she should wear glasses, because we can use them for dramatic business, but they're not essential.
4 TED: Good morning, ma'am. What brings <u>you</u> to the Baxter Building today?
5 AGATHA: I'm here to see <u>Doctor Storm</u>.
6 AGATHA: Please. Take your eyes off my <u>breasts</u> and look at the ID.
0 BADGE: (across the top) COL. AGATHA HARKNESS
(across the bottom) ALPHA CLEARANCE

PANEL 4

Tight on Agatha's ID. It bears her name, AGATHA HARKNESS, the SHIELD logo, her acting rank (Colonel) and the words ALPHA CLEARANCE.
0 BADGE: (across the top) COL. AGATHA HARKNESS
(across the bottom) ALPHA CLEARANCE

PANEL 5

Out wide. Agatha walks on past the desk towards the elevators. Ted and Sorsky stare after her, shaken.
7 TED: Uhh - - if you'd like to wait in the <u>lounge</u>, ma'am - - Professor - - <u>Colonel</u> - -
8 TED: I'll <u>page</u> him and he'll come right down.
9 AGATHA: Thanks, but don't. I'd rather take him as I <u>find</u> him.

PAGE 11

PANEL 1
Cut away to a room elsewhere in the building. Tight on Doctor Storm, in stern, lecturing mode. He has two small squares of steel, one in each hand.
1 STORM: In my right hand, ordinary tool-grade steel, with a melting point of 1,375 degrees Celsius.
2 STORM: In my right, crystal-lattice vanadium. Melting point four thousand degrees. Now here's my question.

PANEL 2
Out wide. Letting his anger show, Doctor Storm holds the two squares of steel up close to the faces of Ben and Johnny, who are sitting in his office in the course of being chewed out.
3 STORM: When you pour enough heat into this to melt a hole through it - -
4 STORM: - - what happens to ceiling joists that are made out of this?

PANEL 3
Two-shot on Ben and Johnny. Glum and chastened, Ben tries for the straight answer. Johnny shrugs, resentment bubbling under his discomfort.
5 BEN: Umm - - I'm gonna go out on a limb here and say "nothing good."
6 JOHNNY: Jeez, dad, you've made your point.
7 JOHNNY: It's not like someone got killed or anything.

PANEL 4
Tight on Doctor Storm. He starts to lose it, exasperated by this flip answer.
8 STORM: Johnny, your powers are an awesome responsibility! Don't you understand that?
9 STORM: They're not a toy for you to play with!

PANEL 5
Two-shot. Johnny is on his feet and he and his father stare aggressively into each other's faces.
10 JOHNNY: It was an honest mistake, and I said I was sorry.
11 STORM: It was an avoidable mistake.
12 STORM: My God, son, if you can't use the brains you were born with - -

PANEL 6
Close-up on Agatha's hand as she knocks on the – already open – door.
13 SFX: RAP RAP RAP

PAGE 12

PANEL 1
Big pin-up shot on Agatha, standing framed in the doorway. She clearly doesn't approve of what she's seeing.
1 AGATHA: I'm Professor Harkness.
2 AGATHA: Is this - - typical of your management style, Doctor Storm?

PANEL 2
Out wide. Doctor Storm confronts Agatha, while Johnny and Ben stare at her with definite interest.
3 STORM: Professor - - ?
4 AGATHA: Harkness. Agatha. I assume you were expecting me.
5 STORM: No, I can honestly say I wasn't.

PANEL 3
Tight on Agatha. She frowns.
6 AGATHA: Then go and read your emails, Doctor. Specifically, those from the Triskelion.
7 AGATHA: I'm a social psychologist. I'm here to review your program and report back to S.H.I.E.L.D.

PANEL 4

Out wide. Agatha walks on past Doctor Storm, forcing him to turn to keep her in sight. She's looking at Ben and Johnny.

8 STORM: Report on <u>what</u>?

9 AGATHA: Fitness for <u>purpose</u>.

10 AGATHA: My goal is to <u>optimize</u> this facility to meet the needs of its young assets.

PANEL 5

Tight on Agatha and the boys. She looks at them with shrewd interest, and they stare back at her, awed.

11 AGATHA: I'm sure you'll agree - -

12 AGATHA: - - it's time they were taken in <u>hand</u>.

PAGE 13

PANEL 1

Tight on a computer monitor. We're seeing part of an email, the visible text running something like this:-

0 FROM: ANITA HILL
TO: FRANKLIN STORM
RE: PSYCHOLOGICAL EVALUATION
I REQUEST YOUR FULL CO-OPERATION
FESSOR AGATHA HARKNESS IN HER INVESTI
IMPERATIVE TO THE SMOOTH RUNNING OF

PANEL 2

Out wide. We're in Doctor Storm's office, and he's alone there with Agatha – him seated at the desk, her standing behind him. She watches him with arms folded as he glares at his computer monitor.

1 STORM: Damn.

2 AGATHA: I <u>told</u> you, Doctor. I have the broadest possible remit.

3 STORM: To the point of <u>absurdity</u>.

4 AGATHA: That's a point of <u>view</u>, certainly.

PANEL 3

Into two-shot. Agatha walks further into the room, but not towards Doctor Storm. In fact she's crossing to a filing cabinet. He follows her with his eyes, angry and indignant. She raises a hand to stop him speaking.

5 AGATHA: But the <u>history</u> of this program is one of squandered potential and wasted <u>opportunity</u>.

6 STORM: <u>Wasted</u>??? We've achieved <u>astonishing</u> things.

7 AGATHA: Working with astonishing <u>resources</u>.

PANEL 4

Rotate POV. Agatha rifles the filing cabinet. Doctor Storm throws out his arms in exasperation.

8 STORM: Some of whom are my own <u>children</u>. My contribution to this project - -

9 AGATHA: Is deeply <u>personal</u>, yes.

10 AGATHA: And of a kind that <u>precludes</u> any real objectivity.

PANEL 5

Tight on Agatha. She turns to stare coldly at Doctor Storm, a sheaf of files in her hands. The top one reads REED RICHARDS.

11 AGATHA: But you'll be allowed to <u>stay</u> in your post pending my report.

12 AGATHA: May I use this office? I <u>really</u> need to make a start.

PAGE 14

PANEL 1

Time lapse. Tight on Reed. He's sitting in a chair in Doctor Storm's office, being interviewed by Agatha. Whatever question she threw at him, he seems a little surprised by it.

1 REED: What are my <u>goals</u>?

2 REED: Do you mean <u>scientifically</u> - - or <u>personally</u>?

PANEL 2
Out wide. Agatha sits across from Reed, no desk between them. She has his file on her lap and is taking notes in it. She stares at him in a hard, challenging way. He looks back, civil but slightly unnerved by her attention.
3 AGATHA: Do you find there's a <u>tension</u> between the two, then?
4 REED: No. Not at <u>all</u>.
5 REED: Well, not unless there's - - if things aren't - -

PANEL 3
Tight on Agatha. She consults the file, thoughtful and stern.
6 AGATHA: Yes. And things <u>haven't</u> been. Have they?
7 AGATHA: You and Susan went too <u>deep</u> too <u>fast</u>, and now you're getting the <u>bends</u> as you try to come back up.

PANEL 4
Out wide. Reed glares at Agatha. She lowers the file to stare back at him, unabashed and unimpressed.
8 REED: That's a pretty ridiculous metaphor. And I seriously <u>doubt</u> it's based on anything in that file.
9 AGATHA: But it doesn't really matter <u>what</u> my sources are, does it, Reed?
10 AGATHA: The fact is that you've made some serious <u>mistakes</u> lately.

PANEL 5
Close-up on Agatha's face. Her eyes narrow as she drops the bombshell.
11 AGATHA: And mistakes <u>cost</u> us. In money. In public <u>opinion</u>.
12 AGATHA: Make any more - - and the <u>axe</u> falls.

PAGE 15
I'm thinking of a regular grid here, Mike – four tiers, two panels on each. All the shots are either head-and-shoulder shots or close-ups.

PANEL 1
Head and shoulders shot on Ben. He shrugs.
1 BEN: No, I'm not really part of the <u>think tank</u>, as such.
2 BEN: I mean, I'm <u>built</u> like a tank, but thinking's not my - -

PANEL 2
Head and shoulders shot on Sue. She looks coldly polite, hand raised in a "no thank you" gesture, palm out.
3 SUE: I'm <u>fine</u>, thanks.
4 SUE: Nothing to <u>discuss</u>.

PANEL 3
Head and shoulders shot on Ben. He's surprised. He points to his own chest.
5 BEN: Surplus to <u>what</u>? No, I wouldn't say that at all.
6 BEN: I'm kind of - - like - - <u>logistical</u> support. Yeah.

PANEL 4
Head and shoulders shot on Sue. She folds her arms grimly.
7 SUE: Well I'd say that's <u>my</u> business, wouldn't you?
8 SUE: Unless S.H.I.E.L.D. is opening up a <u>dating</u> agency now.

PANEL 5
Close-up on Ben's face. He frowns.
9 BEN: In a - -
10 BEN: - - hitting things until they fall <u>down</u> capacity.

PANEL 6
Close-up on Sue's face. She gasps in astonishment and outrage.

11 SUE: My God!
12 SUE: You want to go ahead and ask me what color <u>panties</u> I've got on, while you're at it?

PANEL 7
Close-up on Ben's face – blankly dismayed.
13 BEN: Over-compensating?
14 BEN: Like - - for <u>what</u>?

PANEL 8
Close-up on Sue's face. She scowls venomously.
15 SUE: Get out of my <u>face</u>, lady.
16 SUE: I <u>mean</u> it.

<u>**PAGE 16**</u>

PANEL 1
The corridor outside the office. Wide, but centred on Sue as she walks away from the office. Behind her, Agatha leans out to call Johnny, who's waiting on a chair outside. Johnny stares off after Sue, made anxious by the look on Sue's face. It's not one of anger, but it's scary by virtue of its very impassivity – it's obvious that she's keeping herself under control by means of huge, invisible effort.
1 AGATHA: Johnny.
2 AGATHA: I'm <u>ready</u> for you now.

PANEL 2
Sue's lab. Tight on Sue as she stands just inside the door, staring at her formidable array of test tubes, micro-scopes, centrifuges and all the other paraphernalia she uses in her research. Her head is bowed and her hands are clenched. She's starting to come to a boil…

PANEL 3
Out wide. She hauls off, and she does it as only the Invisible Girl can. Without us seeing any force field mani-festation, she sweeps her hand up in a sudden, violent gesture and trashes the entire room. Test tubes shatter, equipment topples or goes flying through the air, even metal retort stands and filing cabinets are dented. Sue growls, baring her teeth.
3 SUE: GNNNRRRRRRRR!

PANEL 4
Staying wide. Sue picks up a toppled piece of equipment, already moving on from her moment of cathartic rage. Reed has appeared in the doorway behind her and looks at her solicitously.
4 REED: Harkness is crazier than a box of <u>frogs</u>. Are you okay?
5 SUE: Nothing I can't <u>handle</u>.
6 REED: You mean by <u>wrecking</u> the joint?

PANEL 5
Tight on Sue. She raises the baggie with the tissue sample in and stares at it. Our POV is through it towards her.
7 SUE: No.
8 SUE: By burying myself in my <u>work</u>.

<u>**PAGE 17**</u>

PANEL 1
Back to Agatha and Johnny. Tight on Agatha. She consults her file, but her expression as she does so is warm and friendly and reassuring.
1 AGATHA: You start <u>fires</u>.

PANEL 2
Out to two-shot. Agatha stands rather than sitting opposite Johnny, looking down on him – but there's nothing

adversarial here: she's as flattering and friendly in her attentions as she could possibly be – just this side of flirting. Johnny is nervous, not sure what to expect here. The open door is in shot behind them.
2 JOHNNY: Well, yeah. But not in a psycho-with-a-can-of-<u>gasoline</u> kind of way.
3 AGATHA: I know.
4 AGATHA: But it must take extraordinary strength of <u>will</u> to control a
power like that.

PANEL 3
Rotate POV. Agatha closes the door – a meaningful gesture. Johnny watches her, surprised but curious.
5 JOHNNY: Oh yeah. It really <u>does</u>.
6 AGATHA: I imagine it could feel like a <u>burden</u>, sometimes.
7 JOHNNY: <u>Hah!</u> For someone <u>else</u>, maybe. I'm on top of it.

PANEL 4
Tight on Agatha. She tucks her glasses into her shirt pocket, subconsciously stripping for action.
8 AGATHA: Still. Massage and <u>relaxation</u> therapies will help you cope.
9 AGATHA: I'd like to teach you a few basic <u>techniques</u>.

PANEL 5
Two-shot. Agatha kneads Johnny's shoulders. It's kind of not what he expected, but he's liking it.
10 AGATHA: Is this <u>helping</u>?
11 JOHNNY: Yeah, it - - Wow. Yeah.
12 AGATHA: You still don't <u>seem</u> very relaxed.

PANEL 6
Close-up on Agatha's face. She looks thoughtful and detached and not at all like Anne Bancroft as Mrs. Robinson.
13 AGATHA: Perhaps if you stripped to the <u>waist</u>.

<u>PAGE 18</u>

PANEL 1
Back to Sue. She's at work and completely focused on what she's doing – which right now is spreading a swab from the tissue sample onto a microscope slide. In the background is a radio – actually an iPod docking station with radio functionality – which we need to establish now because we'll be using it on the next page.
1 RADIO MUSIC: Hi-de-hi-de-hi-de-hi, ho-de-ho-de-ho-de-ho…

PANEL 2
Close-up On Sue's hand as she puts the slide under the business end of a big electron microscope.
2 SUE: Pinhead Buttes sample <u>one</u>.
3 SUE: Primary <u>observation</u> notes.

PANEL 3
Tight on Sue – head and shoulders only. She looks through the viewfinder, tightening the focus as she does so.
4 SUE: Genetically this thing is more like a <u>lizard</u> than a bird. But the
cellular structure is flat-out crazy.
5 SUE: No, <u>scratch</u> "flat-out crazy." Insert "<u>anomalous.</u>"

PANEL 4
The view through the eyepiece of the microscope. The cells of the hydra are merging and separating as Sue describes, running into one another like a colony of amoebas.
6 SUE: The cells <u>merge</u> as well as split. It's like - - we've got fusion and <u>fission</u> going on at the same time.
7 SUE: I can't even <u>imagine</u> what that would look like at the phenotype level.

PANEL 5
Tight on Sue. She rubs another swab onto a petri dish – and the hydra is watching her do it, because we once again get the distortion effect that shows that we're looking through its eyes.

8 SUE: But I'm hoping to find <u>out</u> - -

9 SUE: - - when I <u>grow</u> one of my very own.

PAGE 19

PANEL 1

Out wide. Sue turns as she suddenly registers what's coming out of the radio – not music now but a news bulletin. She frowns, instantly alert.

1 RADIO: - - leaving gaping <u>holes</u> in the building's structure.

2 SUE: Uh-oh.

3 RADIO: Eye-witnesses were unable to describe the <u>source</u> of the strange energy blasts, but they've left this 50th street behemoth close to <u>collapse</u> and threatening - -

PANEL 2

The corridor outside the lab. Sue comes out at a run, and encounters the other three members of the FF also running from various directions. Johnny is conspicuously struggling into the top half of his costume.

4 SUE: Reed - -

5 REED: I heard it. It's right around the corner. We could practically <u>walk</u> it.

6 BEN: In Midtown on a <u>Friday</u>? Dream big.

PANEL 3

Tight on the Fantasti-Car as it takes off.

PANEL 4

Aerial view of Manhattan, with the Fantasti-Car foregrounded as it hurtles in towards the stricken building – Johnny flying alongside it, under his own steam. It's a very tall, very beautiful high-rise of modern construction, and it's been swiss-cheesed: some total disintegration beam has cut into and through it like a biopsy knife, leaving behind perfectly circular tunnels through its interior that intersect the building at various angles. What's left is starting to crumble, lacking the structural integrity to keep it together. People scream from some of the higher windows and wave as they see rescue coming. Down on the ground – maybe visible in this shot, more likely not – a police barrier has been erected and emergency vehicles (including several fire engines with their ladders fully extended) are standing by. A crowd of rubber-neckers stands behind the barrier, watching the drama unfold.

7 REED: There it is. My God, what could <u>do</u> that?

8 JOHNNY: Does it <u>matter</u>?

9 JOHNNY: Come on, let's do the <u>hero</u> thing!

PAGE 20

PANEL 1

In tight on the Fantasti-Car. A beam of energy from ground level hits it and envelopes it, making it tilt and list. Johnny backs air, reacting in shock and alarm.

1 SFX: FZZRAKKKKK

2 JOHNNY: What the - - ?!

PANEL 2

Inside the Fantasti-Car. Reed wrestles with the controls. Sue and Ben lurch and sprawl as the floor bucks under them.

3 REED: Some kind of <u>force</u> beam.

4 REED: We're being pulled down to <u>ground</u> level! I can't - -

PANEL 3

Out wide, low angle. The Fantasti-Car ploughs down out of the sky into the pavement, its trajectory taking it across the frontage of the damaged building so that it leaves a furrow of shattered stone behind it.

5 SFX: SKERRUNCHHHHH

PAGE 21

PANEL 1
Out wide. Johnny streaks down out of the sky towards the wrecked Fantasti-Car, full of panic fear at the thought that Sue might be dead.
1 JOHNNY: Holy crap! Sue!
2 JOHNNY: Sue!

PANEL 2
Tight on the Fantasti-Car. The door flies free of the mangled fuselage like a missile as Ben punches or smacks it from the inside. Johnny has to swerve to avoid being hit.
3 SFX: SFLANNNNNNG

PANEL 3
Tight on Ben as he steps out of the wrecked Fantasti-Car, Reed under one arm and Sue over his shoulder. He's in a truly foul mood.
4 BEN: Okay.
5 BEN: Whoever pulled that little stunt is gonna be needing a full body transplant.

PANEL 4
Looking towards Ben and Johnny as the silhouettes of two of the Seven appear in the foreground. Ben and Johnny both turn, surprised, at the sound of this newcomer's voice.
6 ALPHA DOG: Are we meant to be impressed, monster?
7 ALPHA DOG: You can't threaten us.

PAGE 22
Splash. Out wide for a big money shot of the Seven, who stand confronting the FF inside the police barrier. They're clearly ready to fight – standing in battle stances or with their powers already on display. And they are as follows:
Alpha Dog: the group leader, with powers that include super strength and invulnerability. His body is super-dense and he leaves footprints in solid concrete.
Synchron: alters probability in such a way that when he fights you he's simultaneously in several super-posed positions – hitting you with a great many possible attacks at the same time. He looks like someone filmed using one of those dodgy slo-mo effects so that they trail ghost images of themselves – except that the ghosts are all solid, even though they overlap.
Filament: cutting and slicing powers, involving the creation of hyper-dimensional threads which cut through all matter.
The Penultimate: a cyborg with lots of robotic body enhancements and high-tech weaponry. It was the Penultimate, as we'll later discover, who did the damage to the building and created this disaster.
GhostWare: can make either himself or any other person or object temporarily immaterial, "phased" – like Kitty Pryde on crack.
Primal Screamer: sonic powers.
Neuropath: powers relating to pain and pleasure induction.
No preference as to sex or race, Mike, except let's get a wide spread. Some of them can fly and some can't, so one or two or even three of them can be standing or hovering in the air. I can do more detailed descriptions if you want them, but I thought you might just want to play around. In terms of costumes, go for sexy and kind of wild. It would do no harm if there were subtle hints that they're actually from an ancient time, so the Penultimate's robot parts might be embossed like armour, one of the girls might have Grecian ringlets in her hair, or whatever – but none of that is obligatory. More importantly, it would be cool if there was some visual emblem or theme that links them all, so that despite the differences they're advertising that they're part of one unit.
1 ALPHA DOG: We are the Seven.
2 ALPHA DOG: And this crisis belongs to us.
3 FLOATING TEXT: To Be Continued!

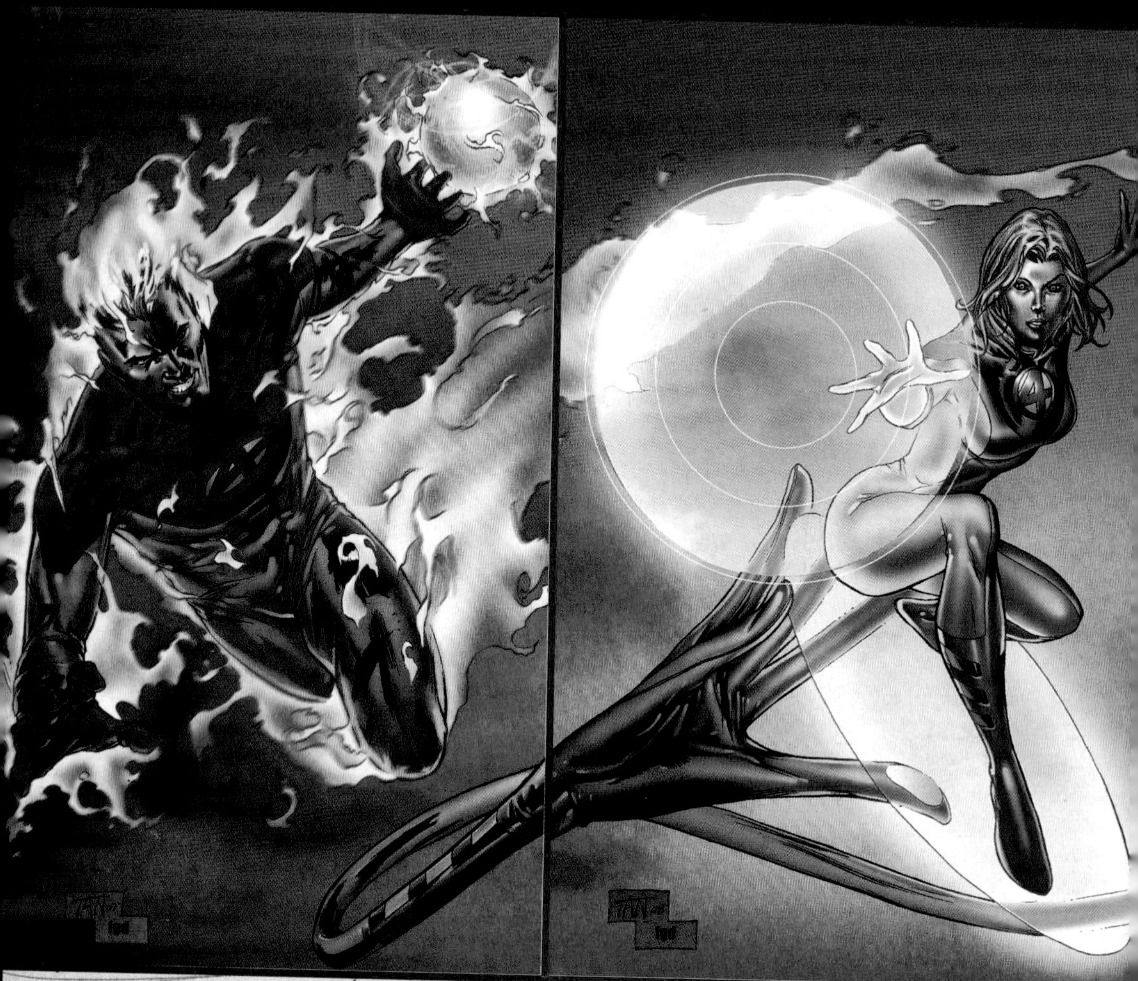

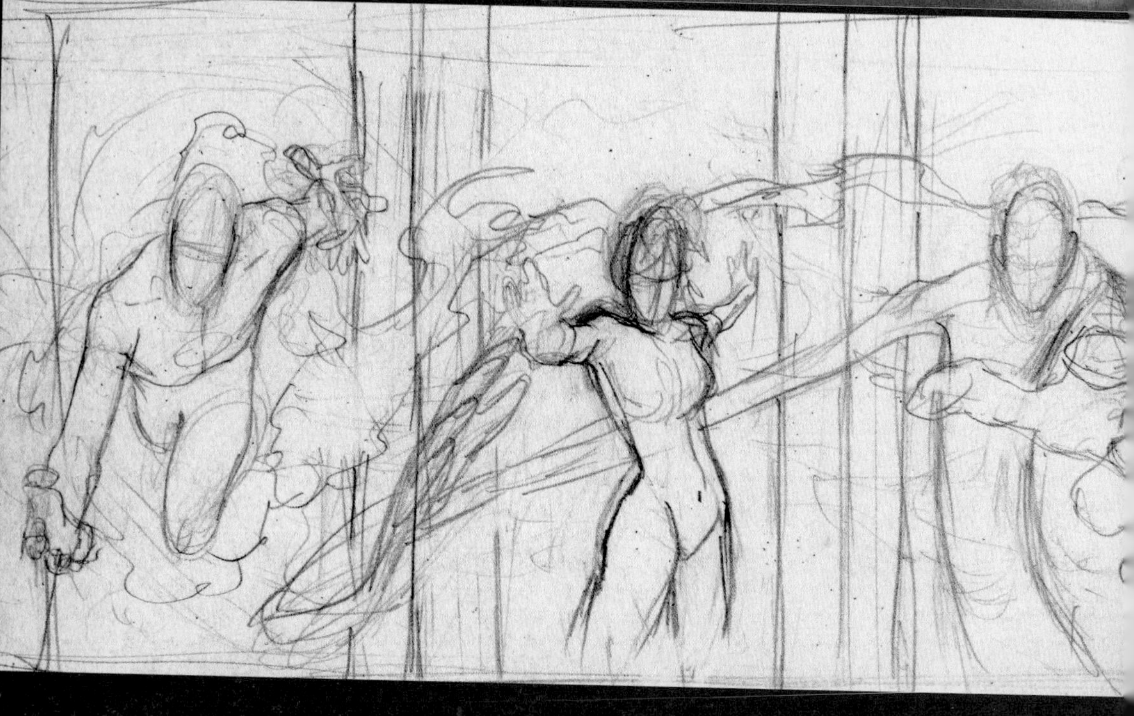

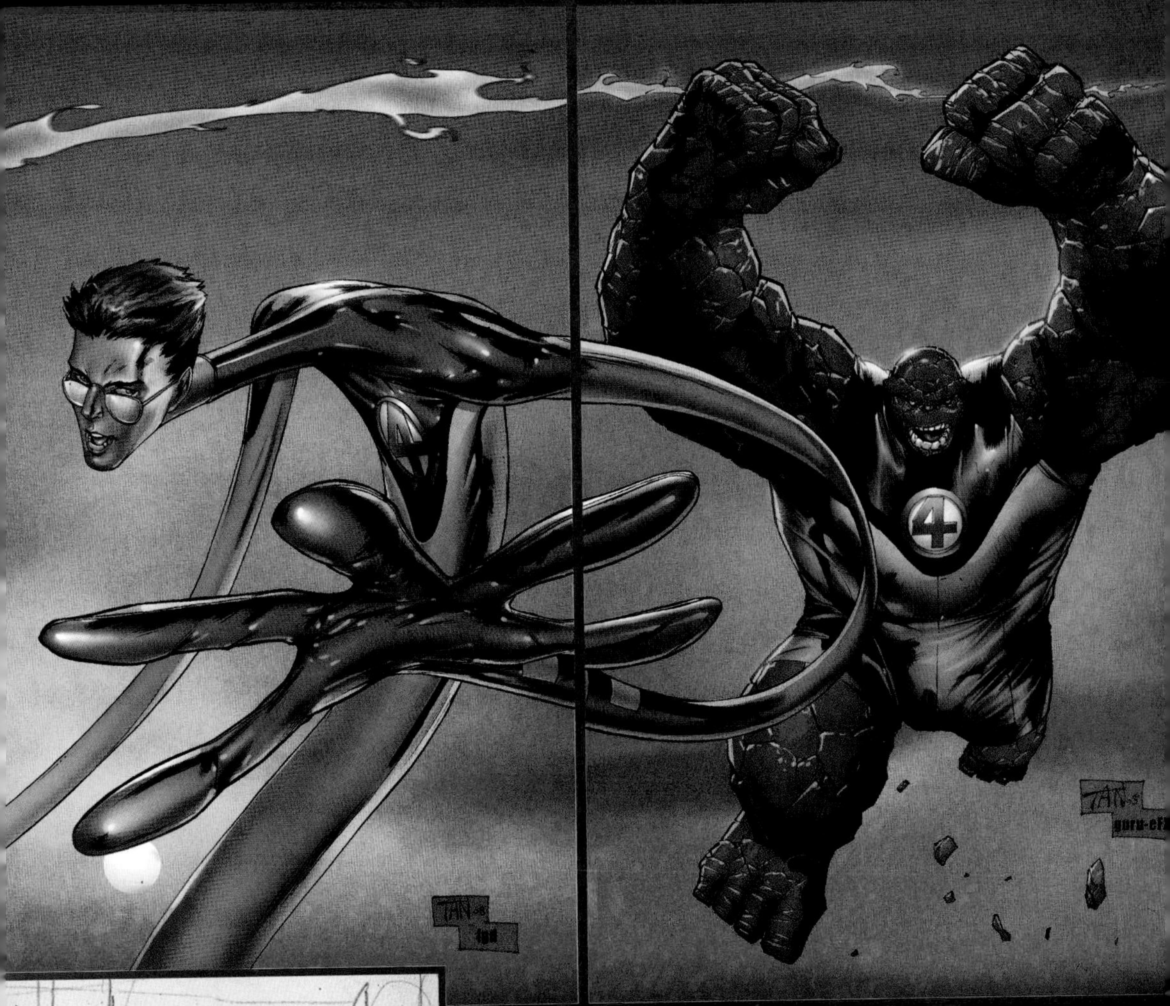

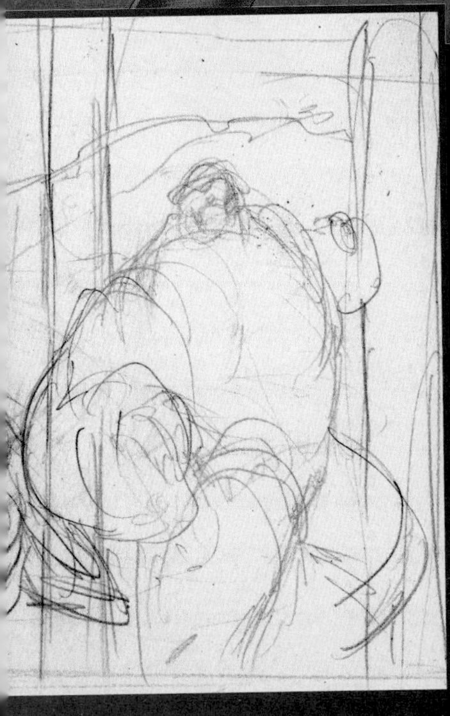

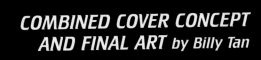

COMBINED COVER CONCEPT AND FINAL ART by Billy Tan

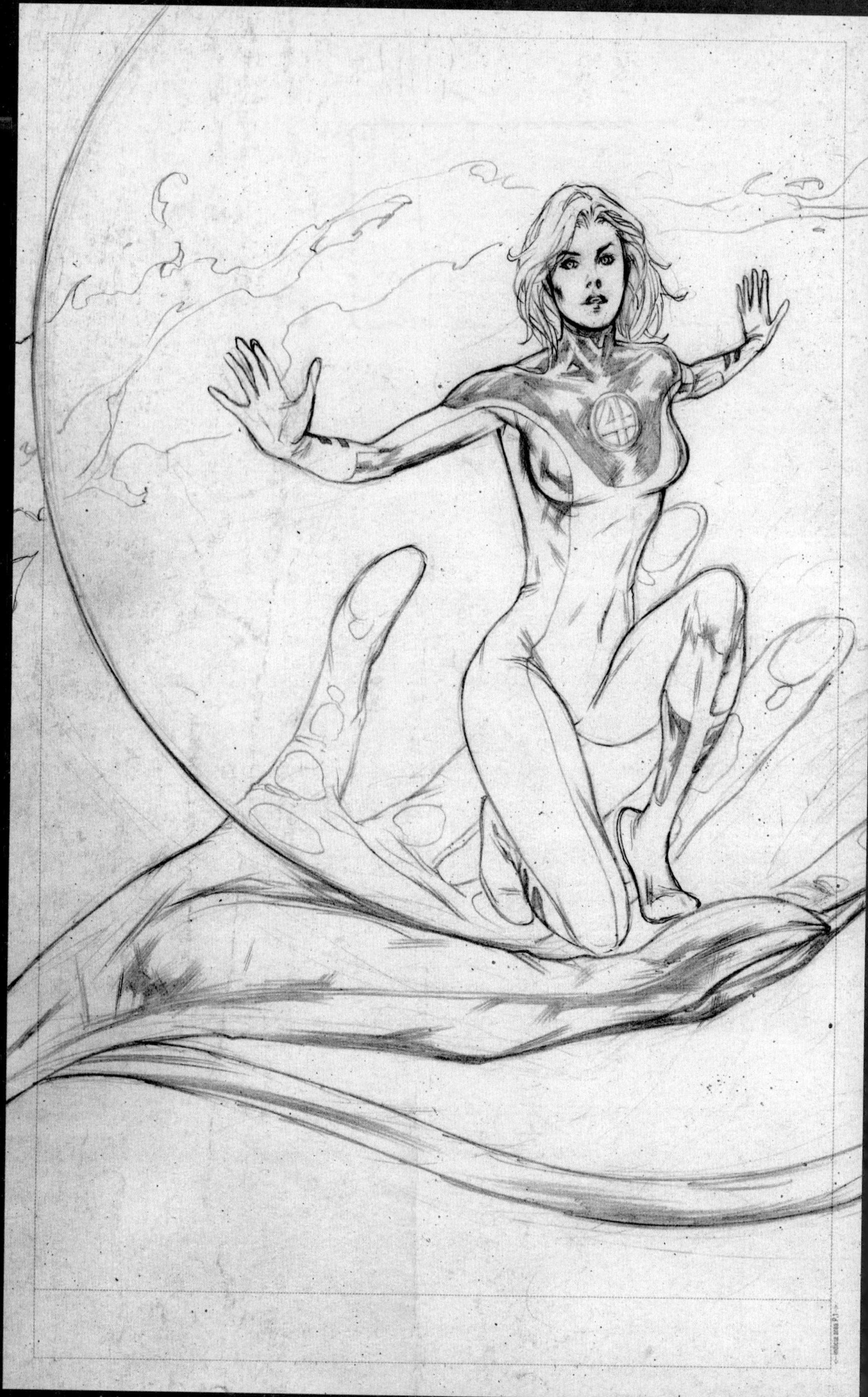

ISSUE #55 UNUSED COVER PENCILS by Billy Ta